Food Studies

ALSO AVAILABLE FROM BLOOMSBURY

Food: The Key Concepts, Warren Belasco

Food Studies: An Introduction to Research Methods, Jeff Miller and
Jonathan Deutsch

The Food History Reader, Ken Albala

The Handbook of Food Research, edited by Anne Murcott, Warren Belasco
and Peter Jackson

Food Studies

A Hands-On Guide

WILLA ZHEN

BLOOMSBURY ACADEMIC
LONDON • NEW YORK • OXFORD • NEW DELHI • SYDNEY

BLOOMSBURY ACADEMIC
Bloomsbury Publishing Plc
50 Bedford Square, London, WC1B 3DP, UK
1385 Broadway, New York, NY 10018, USA
29 Earlsfort Terrace, Dublin 2, Ireland

BLOOMSBURY, BLOOMSBURY ACADEMIC and the Diana logo
are trademarks of Bloomsbury Publishing Plc

First published in Great Britain 2019
Reprinted 2019 (twice), 2020, 2021 (three times)

Cover design: Liron Gilenberg
Cover image © vecteezy.com

A catalogue record for this book is available from the British Library.

Library of Congress Cataloging-in-Publication Data
Names: Zhen, Willa, author.
Title: Food studies : a hands-on guide / Willa Zhen.
Description: First edition. | New York : Bloomsbury Academic, [2019] |
Includes bibliographical references.
Identifiers: LCCN 2018056285| ISBN 9781474298674 (hardback) | ISBN
9781474298711 (pbk.) | ISBN 9781474298698 (ePDF) | ISBN 9781474298704
(ePUB)
Subjects: LCSH: Food–Study and teaching. | Food habits–Study and teaching.
| Food–Study and teaching–Activity programs. | Food habits–Study and
teaching–Activity programs.
Classification: LCC GT2860 .Z47 2019 | DDC 394.1/2071–dc23 LC record available at
https://lccn.loc.gov/2018056285

ISBN: HB: 978-1-4742-9867-4
PB: 978-1-4742-9871-1
ePDF: 978-1-4742-9869-8
eBook: 978-1-4742-9870-4

Typeset by Newgen KnowledgeWords Pvt. Ltd., Chennai, India
Printed and bound in Great Britain

To find out more about our authors and books visit
www.bloomsbury.com and sign up for our newsletters.

Contents

Figures

Acknowledgments

This book would not have been possible without the encouragement and support I have been given along the way. First and foremost, thank you to my students. They continually inspire me to do better and to find new creative ways of reaching them in the classroom. Among the many students I've had the pleasure of teaching, I am especially grateful to Fen Fenton, Liam Kamp, Matt Roscoe, Peter Berger, Tom Wu, Emily Panichello, and Mary Geyer for their insights.

My colleagues and friends at the Culinary Institute of America have cheered me on throughout this project. Thank you to Beth Forrest, Deirdre Murphy, and Bill Guilfoyle for seeing the potential in my ideas and for encouraging me to put pen to paper. I am also indebted to the support of my dean, Denise Bauer, and the support of the School of Liberal Arts and Food Studies at the Culinary Institute of America during the writing and editing process. Raven Fonfa and Nicole Semenchuk have generously supported my class activities in the library and the archives.

Outside of my institution, I am grateful for the time and energy that Jonathan Deutsch, John Lang, Ken Albala, and the anonymous peer reviewers invested in reading and commenting on early stages of this manuscript. Leo Pang, Scott Alves Barton, Amy Reddinger, Airin Martinez, and Kelly Donati graciously took the time to read and give feedback on different chapters of the manuscript. Fabio Parasecoli and Lucy Long kindly took the time to advise me on navigating the publishing process.

I owe a round of thanks to Bloomsbury, especially Miriam Cantwell and Lucy Carroll, who have been a pleasure to work with. Kalyani and the team at Newgen patiently proofread and put this manuscript into production. And special thanks to Jennifer Schmidt, formerly of Bloomsbury, who commissioned this text. Thank you for first seeing the potential in this project—and now it is a book!

Lastly, I am grateful to Dan, Bob, and Zelda for their good cheer, care, and love.

Introducing Food Studies

Introduction

It was not too long ago that at dinner parties and other social events, people would ask me why I study food. After telling them about my work, I'd get a polite, knowing nod and half-smile suggesting I am both naïve and a bit dim. Fast-forward to today, the question that is asked instead is how I study food. Faces light up when people hear about my work, and there are good questions directed my way about the work I do and the ways in which I teach my students. This shift in attitudes may be attributed to a variety of changes in public opinions about food. We are ostensibly living in a "foodie" culture and food media is pervasive—in traditional print media, on television and streaming services, and in social media. Food-themed documentaries like *Chef's Table* and food-based travel shows have wide audiences, as do books on food for the popular audience. There are entire networks on television devoted to food programming. Not to mention the rise of internet celebrities whose careers revolve around food—bloggers, YouTube stars, and so on. A colleague who teaches restaurant marketing has observed that restaurants are to millennials (a term describing people born between 1981 and 1998) and older gen Zs (a term describing the cohort born right after the millennials) what nightclubs were for baby boomers (those born between 1946 and 1964).[1] Whereas baby boomers (the parents of millennials and older members of gen Z) used to line up to get into the hottest, most legendary nightclubs like Studio 54, showing off their status and cultural capital (or "coolness") by rattling off the collection of places where they came, saw, and danced the night away, today their children seemingly brag about what and where they have eaten.

Nowadays, food is a significant form of cultural capital, or the knowledge, behaviors, and skills that people possess that shows off their cultural competence and standing in a society. Knowing about food is a way of marking that you are "cool" and knowledgeable about social trends. It signifies that you belong in a particular social group. As writer William Deresiewicz points out, "Food, for young people now, is creativity, commerce, politics, health, almost religion" (Deresiewicz 2012). Young people rattle off the names of celebrity chefs, debate the worth of Michelin stars, James Beard Awards, and San Pellegrino Top 50 rankings, and gain status among peers through the currency of "likes" and "retweets" and "shares" on social media. Some ambitious millennials and older gen Zs have even gone on to open their own pop-up restaurants, such as Flynn McGarry, who *New York Times* praised as "The Chef at 15" (see Chocano 2014), and Jonah Reider, a Columbia University student who opened a pop-up restaurant called Pith in his dorm room and was profiled in *New Yorker* (see Allen 2015). Others aspire to be celebrity chefs and dream of a life owning their own food establishment. This "culinary capital" shows off who we are (and who we wish to become) (Naccarato and Lebesco 2013). We could say that we have reached a new critical mass of popular interest in food.

In academic environments, food has long been a subject of inquiry and is not a new phenomenon per se. For instance, in my own academic discipline of anthropology, the founding father of American anthropology, Franz Boas (1858–1942), meticulously documented the harvest and treatment of salmon among the Kwakiutl Native Americans in the Pacific Northwest (Boas 1921). (He did not document recipes, which raises another series of questions for another day.) If we look to other disciplines such as history, geography, economics, political science, and sociology, we will also find that food holds a place as a subject of inquiry and topic of discussion often going back to the earliest days each discipline. Yet the formal articulation of Food Studies courses and programs in college and university settings dates back mostly to the last thirty years. What I mean by this is that professional conferences, professional associations, academic journals, degree-granting programs, and serious food-focused scholarship have been built up only in the last thirty years. Miller and Deutsch observe that "given its importance, one would think that Food Studies would have a prominent place in the academy, in mass media, and even in primary and secondary education" (Miller and Deutsch 2009: 7). Warren Belasco (2008: 6–8) suggests that these biases against studying food may be attributed to the dualistic tradition in Western philosophy that prioritizes the mind over the body, the association of food as a women's subject (and therefore less worthy of study), and efforts by the food industry to "obscure and mystify the links between the farm and the dinner table" (Belasco 2008: 4). Additionally, food is also fun (Rozin 1999)—therefore suggesting it is inherently less serious or worthwhile for study. Marion Nestle, one of the founders of New York University's Food Studies Program, reflects that there was a time when "nearly everyone considered food far too common and quotidian to be taken seriously as a field of study" (Nestle 2010: 160). Thankfully, this is less and less the case as food has become a major part of the educational experience (see Cosgrove 2015).

Food has come front and center in education, starting from very elementary levels of education to the most advanced. Schools and universities have added in campus gardens and incorporated sustainability programs. Campuses are increasingly making efforts to cut down waste by eliminating disposable plastic bottles on campus in favor of reusable cups and mugs. Some dining programs have removed plastic lunch trays to discourage overeating and to avoid food waste. Other institutions have built sophisticated recycling and composting facilities. Campus dining rooms have made efforts to buy from local, sustainable purveyors and switched fair trade products. Schools have also developed their dining programs to have tastier, healthier options. Campuses are being landscaped with edible gardens, and showcase them in their promotional materials. Some elementary schools even teach lunch as a subject. And increasingly, educational institutions are also addressing food inequality in their communities. Several American college and university campuses are now operating food pantries for students, staff, and faculty in need in response to the high cost of room and board fees and increasing sensitivity of debt among students, and the now-prevalent practice of hiring contingent and adjunct faculty who sometimes earn below a living wage for their labor. These actions taken by schools, colleges, and universities show that food and Food Studies are part of mainstream education.

Professional organizations like the Association for the Study of Food and Society, the Canadian Association for Food Studies, and others have cemented themselves as solid organizations dedicated to furthering intellectual inquiry into the study of food, signaling that the discipline has "matured" (Edge, Engelhardt, and Ownby 2013: 13). Professional organizations establish, promote, and regulate specialized knowledge and, through their membership, maintain this knowledge. These types of developments have made it easier for today's student to study food and to pursue Food Studies careers. This all suggests that one's decision to study food is not being questioned in the same way as it once was in the recent past. We are fortunate now to have to justify less and less why it is an admirable, important, and, dare I say, responsible task to study food.

Now we are at the forefront of the next stage, thinking about new meaningful and thoughtful ways to delve into this inquiry. It is in this spirit, and recognition of the pioneering work of the many colleagues and scholars before me, that this book is written. This text is different from other Food Studies resources in that it recognizes that Food Studies is at times devoid of, well, food. This problem came to me during my own education, as I pursued ethnographic fieldwork among cooks and in cooking schools in China. My purpose was to understand how cooks became cooks—and to do so, I decided to roll up my sleeves and do it alongside the people I was studying. As I trained in three cooking schools, I kept wondering why my work was considered so novel and strange among colleagues. I was often asked, "Why would you want to learn to cook? Wouldn't hanging out with the cooks be enough?" My answer to this was a resounding "no," as I contended that it would be difficult, if not impossible, to understand the pressures of cooking without standing behind the stove myself. As I began my teaching career, I began to think about this issue even more—why the teaching of Food Studies has often had very little to do with food itself. That is to say, the sensory, material, and experiential aspects of food are often left out of the conversation when discussing food. Some scholars have suggested that this unease with the hands-on aspects of food may be attributed to long-standing biases in Western thought (Belasco 2008: 2–4, 5–8; Miller and Deutsch 2009: 6–7). That may certainly account for a fraction of the reasons. But it does not quite capture the whole picture. Miller and Deutsch point out that Food Studies research tends to cluster into three themes: research methods with Food Studies examples, research that uses food to enhance methods, or research that employs methods unique to Food Studies, such as sensory testing for studying taste preferences (Miller and Deutsch 2009: 8–9). We could go on as to many reasons why Food Studies lacks food.

But instead of being weighed down by why Food Studies have been devoid of the materialities of food, some scholars have used this gap as a call to arms, a justification for why Food Studies should roll up their sleeves and dig in. Philosopher Lisa Heldke reminds us that we need "liberal artisans" in the twenty-first century, a play on educator John Dewey's belief that society needs well-rounded individuals who can both "think" and "do" (Dewey 15 1981: 280). Heldke urges readers to think of foodmaking as a "thoughtful practice" (1992: 203). She suggests that "foodmaking, rather than drawing us to mark a sharp distinction between mental and manual labor, or between theoretical and practical work, tends to invite us to see itself as a 'mentally manual' activity, a 'theoretically practical' activity" (Heldke 1992: 203).

Recent sociopolitical events have furthered the impetus among some scholars to participate and get our hands dirty. Fabio Parasecoli, writing on "Food Studies in Trump's United States" for the *Huffington Post* adds that "it becomes crucial to pair the insights and the analysis that are central to Food Studies with hands-on projects and initiatives for change and social innovation" (Parasecoli 2016). He suggests that it is through this combination of thinking and doing that will allow the next generation of "liberal artisans" to "not only find satisfactory careers, but also to have positive and creative impact on the environments in which they find themselves operating" (Parasecoli 2016).

As Berg, Nestle, and Bentley (2003) reminds us, Food Studies is not only an academic discipline but also a means to change society. Warren Belasco adds that Food Studies is "inherently subversive," as studying food involves crossing traditional disciplinary lines and asking "inconvenient questions" (2008: 6). To begin thinking about and asking good questions about food, we must consider the different ways in which we can approach food and Food Studies.

Thinking about food: Setting up the *mise en place*

Mise-en-place is the religion of all good line cooks. Do *not* fuck with a line cook's "meez"—meaning his setup, his carefully arranged supplies of sea salt, rough-cracked pepper, softened butter, cooking oil, wine, backups, and so on. As a cook, your station, and its condition, its state of readiness, is an extension of your nervous system—and it is profoundly upsetting if another cook or, God forbid, a *waiter* disturbs your precisely and carefully laid-out system. The universe is in order when your station is set up the way you like it: you know where to find everything with your eyes closed, everything you need during the course of the shift is at the ready at arm's reach, your defense are deployed.

(Bourdain 2000: 65)

Mise en place is a French term meaning "everything in its place." In culinary work, it refers to the setup and organization one must take care of before cooking or food service. Culinary work involves a lot of organization and planning, much of which takes place long before any stoves get turned on. *Mise en place* is important to chefs because it is a systematic approach to preparing for food service. This approach involves planning, reflection, and foresight. Cooks and chefs must think ahead and anticipate issues like the number of diners booked in for the night. The number that will likely walk in through the door. The number of no-shows for reservations. Thinking about how best to utilize the food that will soon spoil, before it does. And the countless other issues that arise within the course of normal restaurant operations. This is part of *mise en place*. Cooks and chefs also have their particular setup of how they like to arrange their seasonings, spices, and tools in their work stations. Servers might have a certain way of arranging their service station—where they put their silverware, napkins, bar mops and cleaning cloths, and the like.

I borrow from this term to consider what mental preparations the aspiring Food Studies scholar must need to know to study and practice Food Studies. We begin our journey into Food Studies by considering: What do you know about food so far? How have you set up your mental *mise en place*? What do you know about food? How did you learn this information? How might that change as you expand your understandings of food and the field of Food Studies? Furthermore, what have you been told about food? How might you challenge your preexisting ideas about food and to stop thinking like a foodie but more like a critically engaged food scholar?

Celebrity chef Ferran Adrià (1962–), one of the most well-regarded and innovative chefs at the turn of the twenty-first century, put it succinctly: "If you think about it well, you create well" (Ouzounian 2014). In an increasingly complex society, where food is front and center of many socioeconomic and geopolitical issues, the more prepared we are, trained in problem-solving and critical thinking, the better position we will be in to deal with these challenges. In a twist on Adrià's words, this textbook takes on the idea that you should create while you think. This book is not meant to be the end-all to Food Studies texts. Far from it. In fact, it is humbly meant to introduce the reader to some topical thematic issues in Food Studies today. The activities and themes are meant to encourage exploration and discussion in a multisensory fashion, to launch into further inquiry and work. This book sets out to organize your Food Studies *mise en place*.

We will examine the many dimensions of Food Studies, using key themes to explain how Food Studies is interdisciplinary, multidisciplinary, sensory, and also experiential. Built in to each chapter are case studies and hands-on activities to help understand key concepts in Food Studies. Each chapter also offers suggestions for further reading and exploration. Through this approach, the expectation is that you will become aware that there are many approaches to the study of food, and that humans continue to negotiate their relationships to and with food and the meaning of food in their lives. Ultimately, I want students to learn not only about Food Studies, but also about practicing Food Studies and experiencing food. To begin this journey, I have one simple request. Hold back your assumptions and challenge what you think you know about food; think beyond the plate.

Instructor's note

This textbook is meant to be a tool to support experienced and novice instructors alike. The purpose is to help encourage instructors incorporating hands-on experiential activities into their instruction. "Active learning," "experiential learning," and "peer learning" sound like popular academic buzzwords. Certainly, the trend has been toward incorporating more student-centric instruction. Research has shown that active learning can lead to improved learning outcomes and better material retention. Yet, I've heard other instructors grow reticent at incorporating hands-on activities for fear of it turning into all style with little substance. Others worry about the prep time it takes to organize these activities. Instructors with large class sizes worry about space and the number of students as an impediment. And so forth.

But if we were to think about it in terms of its definition, active learning is simply "anything course-related that all students in a class session are called upon to do other than simply watching, listening, and taking notes" (Felder, Celanese, and Brent 2009: 2). When framed in that way, active learning can be a low-stakes endeavor. Giving students just a few minutes to consider the material in a different way can be an effective teaching strategy. Adopting hands-on activities does not mean sacrificing. It means supplementing and enhancing. Activities can be adopted or modified as necessary and, if you feel comfortable, go and create your own. The idea is to give students the opportunity to approach an issue or problem from a different angle.

Each chapter includes several hands-on activities for use, and discussion/reflection questions. These class activities have been tested and tweaked in my classrooms and in those of my colleagues, who teach in a variety of educational environments around the world, ranging from culinary colleges to research universities. They have been tried in a variety of disciplines engaged in the study of food. These activities can be done without a kitchen, or can be modified as homework. The chapters also include food for thought—contemporary issues worth highlighting that show a concept in action that can serve as a launching point for further discussion. Essay prompts are also incorporated into the book to be modified into assignments or assessments. Lastly, this book is also meant to be used in conjunction with other texts and resources: Food Studies textbooks, ethnographies and monographs, case studies, news articles, websites, and videos. Each chapter includes a list of further resources. This book is written for the student reader, but also contains instructor's notes throughout to provide pointers and hints to navigate this unique approach to Food Studies.

Discussion questions

1. What led you to take a class on Food Studies? What attracted you to this subject?

2. Describe the food issues that concern you. Explain why they are of concern.

3. What might you hope to learn about food through this course?

I.1 Activity: Food Studies scavenger hunt

Students new to the field of Food Studies often have not considered how interdisciplinary, multidisciplinary, and broad-ranging the field can be. Students can also overlook the fact that Food Studies concerns impact them on campus. To help students gain perspective, send them on a campus-wide scavenger hunt in small groups. Each group should be responsible for searching different items. Students must document that they found the item by taking a photo with their phones. After completing the scavenger hunt, students should return to the classroom to discuss how food issues are also campus issues. The items will vary depending on the campus, but below is generic set of items suitable for most campuses.

- Junk food sold in the campus grocery store/mini-market
- Food left uneaten in the student dining hall
- Recyclable items thrown in the regular garbage can
- Vending machine selling processed foods and sugary drinks
- Dining hall serving an "ethnic" dish
- Student club advertising free food to attract members

Discussion questions

1. How successful were you in completing the scavenger hunt? Did you expect to complete this activity? Why or why not?
2. Why do you think these scavenger hunt prompts were chosen? How might they connect to broader Food Studies issues and themes?
3. How might you add to this list of scavenger hunt items? What Food Studies–related issues have you noticed on campus?

I.2 Activity: Defining your food knowledge

Where does your food knowledge come from? Ponder over your knowledge of food, considering where it comes from, how it is transmitted and preserved, and how this body of knowledge has been constructed.

- How did you learn to prepare food?
- How did you learn to consume food?
- What constitutes a healthy diet?
- How do you acquire your food (e.g., supermarket, farmer's market, campus dining hall)?
- Where does your food come from? How do you know this information?
- What role did your caregivers/family play in your food knowledge?

- What role did your broader community (e.g., school, clubs, social organizations) play in forming your food knowledge?
- How might your food knowledge evolve upon taking this course?

Instructor's note

This can be adapted into an essay assignment to be completed as homework.

Further resources

Food Studies organizations

Agriculture, Food, & Human Values Society (AFHVS) is an international organization engaged in the cross-disciplinary study of food, agriculture, and health. https://afhvs.wildapricot.org.

Association for the Study of Food and Society (ASFS) is the world's largest association devoted to promoting the interdisciplinary study of food and society. www.food-culture.org.

Canadian Association for Food Studies promotes critical, interdisciplinary scholarship on Food Studies in Canada. http://cafs.landfood.ubc.ca/en.

Documentaries

Cafeteria Man (2011) is a documentary on chef Tony Geraci's efforts to create food reform in Baltimore's school system.

Chef's Table (2015–) is a documentary series on some of the world's most renowned chefs. Each episode features the story of an individual chef.

Eat: The Story of Food (2014) is a multi-part television series produced by National Geographic on the history and culture of food.

El Bulli: Cooking in Progress (2010) is a documentary on celebrity chef Ferran Adrià's creative process as he and his team develop menus and dishes for his famed El Bulli restaurant in Spain.

Note

1   See http://www.pewresearch.org/fact-tank/2016/08/29/this-may-be-the-last-presidential-election-dominated-by-boomers-and-prior-generations/ft_16-08-26_generationsdefined_2016_silentgreatest/.

Further resources

Albala, Ken (2013). *Food: A Cultural Culinary History* [DVD]. Chantilly: The Great
   Courses.
Belasco, Warren (2008). *Food: The Key Concepts*. Oxford: Berg.
Estabrook, Barry 2012. *Tomatoland: How Modern Industrial Agriculture
   Destroyed Our Most Alluring Fruit*. Kansas City, Missouri: Andrews McMeel
   Publishing.
Miller, Jeff, and Jonathan Deutsch (2009). *Food Studies: An Introduction to
   Research Methods*. Oxford: Berg.

1

From Foodie to Food Studies

Introduction

Food is one of the most meaningful and personal topics to study because everyone knows something about food. Alongside shelter and procreation, food is one of the essential requirements to sustain life. Psychologist Abraham Maslow calls food one of the basic physiological needs that all humans have. Even though we must eat (to date, no human has yet learned to photosynthesize and live off sunlight, water, and air), we do not all eat in the same ways or for the same reasons. Humans have immense variation in what they eat, based on availability, geography, biological needs, ecological concerns, social and cultural factors, as well as individual taste preferences. What we also see is that the idea of edible versus inedible has evolved over time and different groups of people have very distinctly different ideas of what is acceptable as food or not. From babies to grandparents, we all need to eat to survive and we all have our responses to different types of food. We all have our own ideas and opinions about what is the best way to grow food, cook it, eat it, and share it. This is why food is an endlessly fascinating subject. There are an infinite array of topics and issues within its broad remit.

Many of you might consider yourselves interested in food, maybe even food-obsessed. That is, perhaps, one of the reasons why you were attracted to a book on food. Some of you might enjoy cooking or gardening. Perhaps you watch food shows and follow certain celebrity chefs. Others of you might even write about food by blogging or posting on social media. Perhaps you even follow Michelin rankings and the San Pellegrino World's 50 Best Restaurants list. A few of you might even call yourselves "foodies." In fact, many people nowadays consider themselves "foodies" (or "food nerds" or "food-obsessed" or "gastronauts" or other similar terms).

Being a "foodie" seems like the norm among college students today. Yet the term "foodie" came into popular usage only sometime during the 1980s. Several people stake a claim on ownership for coining the term, including former *New York Times* critic Gael Greene and British food writers Paul Levy and Ann Barr. They published *The Official Foodie Handbook (Be Modern— Worship Food)* in 1984, laying down parameters of good taste for the upwardly mobile and hungry. By their assertion, a foodie is simply "a person who is very very very interested in food" and who "consider[s] food to be an art, on a level with painting or drama" (Barr and Levy 1984: 6). Foodies, as they note, are everywhere, often hidden in plain sight. Foodies "look like anybody else" (Barr and Levy 1984: 6). More recently, sociologists Josée Johnston and Shyon Baumann (2010) have added that foodies are more than people who love food. They contend that foodies describe themselves as "well-informed, discovery-minded, discerning consumers (and most often producers as well) who lead food-focused lives and present themselves to others as uncommonly passionate about food" (Johnston and Baumann 2010: 67).

In fact, foodies probably include "everyone else" nowadays. Market research seems to match our perceptions that young people today are into food. Advertising agency BBDO found that half of millennials they surveyed describe themselves as "foodies" (BBDO Atlanta 2013). If their survey speaks for the larger population, that would mean roughly forty million young people would identify with this label. We can assume that for the next generation, gen Z (born in 1999 to the present), the cohort now entering higher education, being into food is no longer a trend but simply a part of life.

So how did we become a food-obsessed culture? This can be attributed to changes in popular culture. For those born in the 1990s and early 2000s, being interested in food or being food obsessed has been the norm during their lifetimes. Many hallmarks of foodie culture—food television, instant access to food content and media, and the rise of media-friendly food personalities (who are distinctly different from celebrity chefs)—date back to the 1990s. Food Network was launched in 1993, making a whole slew of stars household names. Alton Brown's *Good Eats* show premiered in 1998, while Rachel Ray, before she became a talk show personality, first had a cooking show on Food Network in 2001. Anthony Bourdain, who seems ever so pervasive nowadays, first published his memoir *Kitchen Confidential* in 2000, a no-holds-barred tell-all of the seedy underside of the restaurant industry. This led to a series of food and travel shows, starting with *A Cook's Tour* (2000). He has been making television shows for nearly two decades.

Food programming is also prime time and ever-present. Celebrity chef Gordon Ramsay's show, *Hell's Kitchen*, airs at 8 p.m., a prime network hour. *Top Chef* and *Masterchef*, two other competitive cooking shows, also held prime slots during their runs. For those who stream their content instead of watching through traditional networks and cable, food programming is accessible at any time. Scroll through the series lists on Netflix, Amazon, and other streaming services and there are endless documentaries, series, and films about food.

The internet has also made food accessible and sharable in ways that it previously was not. Instagram, Twitter, Facebook, and Snapchat connect people throughout the planet to foods and new food trends instantaneously. Yelp and other user-driven review platforms make everybody a potential food critic. The old standard of waiting for a food writer to make their pronouncements about the best place to eat, and their careful awarding of stars based on standardized criteria, has given way to user-driven content updated by the millisecond. Blogs and other social media platforms allow everyone to become a food writer, publishing content on their terms in their own time. All of these factors have contributed toward a foodie culture, allowing consumers to feel like they are part of an ongoing dinner party every day of the year.

Perhaps you dislike being labeled as a "foodie" and reject this food-obsessed culture. Maybe you would like to distance yourself from this term. You would not be alone. In fact, many foodies avoid calling themselves as such even if they fit the cultural patterns and taste preferences of foodies. Even if you dislike the term, you may exhibit some foodie behavior and you may consider yourself someone who loves food more than the average person. After all, you have made the decision to read this book on Food Studies. Even if you push back against this label, there may still be elements of it you identify with. As a group, foodies also tend to value certain aspects of food. Johnston and Baumann identify that (1) local, organic, and seasonal food, (2) ethnic foods and exotic flavors, and (3) gourmet, specialty, and artisanal ingredients as being essential to foodie consumption habits and identity are especially important to foodies and today's food-obsessed culture (2010).

In spite of our food-obsessed culture, calling oneself a foodie is still something a bit garish, perhaps even vulgar to declare publicly in many social circles. This label is often rejected because it is "associated with snobbery and the faddish trend-setting of elites" (Johnston and Baumann 2010: 49). It is true that foodie culture has tended to privilege the gastronomic and gourmet aspects of food culture and smacks of elitism. This reticence toward foodieism is present in many societies. In contemporary England, "an intense interest in food is regarded by the majority as at best rather odd, and at worst somehow morally suspect—not quite proper, not quite right" (Fox 2014: 420). Dwight Furrow suggests that "good taste" is "widely perceived as an indicator that one lacked genuine American virtue" (Furrow 2016: 2).

American politicians have been slammed and criticized for what they will and will not eat, as a metaphor for whether they can truly represent America and its values. To illustrate, former US president Barack Obama has been famously called a "foodie president" for his embrace of good food (Johnson and Jacobs 2015), his dinner choices meticulously documented through social media. The food-loving crowd has given him and former first lady Michelle Obama props for embracing celebrity chefs, dining out at some of the hottest restaurants in America, encouraging mindful eating habits among the nation's children and families, and even putting an organic garden in the United States. The same practices that have earned the Obamas praise have also drawn criticism for being out of touch with working people, and elitist. During a campaign visit to rural Iowa in 2007 before his first presidency, Obama famously was captured asking, "Anybody gone into Whole Foods lately and see what they charge for arugula? I mean, they're charging *a lot of money* for this stuff" (original emphasis, Zeleny 2007). Arugula (also known as rocket), is a dark, bitter salad green, and Whole Foods is an upscale supermarket known for its natural and organic products and high prices. It is also jokingly referred to as "Whole Paycheck" in regard to its cost. Both arugula and Whole Foods are seen as markers of an elite, upper-middle-class lifestyle, especially in a state without a Whole Foods and where the people are more commonly known for being "corn-fed" and identified as "blue collar" or as America's workers.

Religion also offers some clues regarding American reticence to fully embrace food. Gluttony, after all, is one of the seven deadly sins in Christianity. The medieval theologian and philosopher Thomas Aquinas (1225–1274) even documented five ways to commit gluttony:

1. *Laute*—eating too expensively

2. *Studiose*—eating too daintily

3. *Nimis*—eating too much

4. *Praepropere*—eating too soon

5. *Ardenter*—eating too eagerly

Incidentally, *ardenter*—the sin of eating too eagerly—is considered the most serious of the five types. This is something that many foodies and food lovers could be accused of.

This unease with food is meaningful. In the Protestant tradition, too keen an interest in food may be constructed as sinful. The film *Babette's Feast* (1987) illustrates this belief. The film tells the story of two elderly and pious sisters in nineteenth-century Denmark. Daughters of a priest, they live an austere life and are served by Babette, a refugee from Paris who had escaped the French revolution. Babette wins the lottery one day and uses the entire proceeds to cook an extravagant French feast for the sisters and their friends. The guests, worried about the potentially sinful nature of the dinner, agree to dine without commentary on the food. It is revealed, through the story, that Babette was once a chef at a renowned restaurant in France. Throughout the film, a keen interest in food—and the enjoyment of it—invokes the sinful pleasures of the earthly world, of the flesh, which run counter to Christian teachings and edicts.

These views toward food as potentially sinful persist in Christian societies. Puritan values of simplicity, self-reliance, and asceticism shape some of our food views today. Food scholars have suggested that these Puritanical values have shaped American eating habits (Levenstein 1988, 1993; Stearns 2002). Regional fare in New England, in keeping with Protestant views toward functionality rather than pleasure, tends to be relatively bland and unspiced. This plain fare also borrowed from the food habits of the English settlers that colonized the land. This type of food also became the basis around which American nutritional science was designed. Nutritional science, which emerged in the nineteenth century, tended to focus on educating people on "what was good for them" rather than accommodating to "what they liked" (Levenstein 1980: 370), reverberating Christian teachings about the morality of simple eating. During the late nineteenth and early twentieth centuries, with the rise of industrialization and the start of industrial food processing, many new foods were introduced to the market. These items were based on nutritional science and selling the masses what was good for them, and sought to temper heated emotions through blandness. The thought was that the mind and body could be regulated through proper eating. This belief was driven mostly by faddism and some pseudoscience. Graham crackers and cornflakes are two foods that come to mind, the result of this nutritionism. An invention of Presbyterian minister Sylvester Graham, the graham cracker was thought to help reduce sinful desires and to stop masturbation. Cornflakes, now a breakfast staple, was developed by John Harvey Kellogg, a Seventh-day Adventist from the nineteenth century. Kellogg promoted his ideas throughout the United States, encouraging the consumption of bland natural foods and denouncing meat consumption, claiming it would lead to a deterioration of mental faculties and the arousing of animal passions. The wrong diet, he claimed, could cause any number of health problems ranging from depression, headache, fatigue, to mental illness, moral deterioration, and violence (Kellogg 1888).

There are, of course, foods that are sinfully good, so to speak. Consider food names that suggest excess or temptation. Devilled eggs, an egg dish made of hard boiled eggs cut in half and filled with mashed egg yolk and seasonings, or Devil's food cake, a type of rich chocolate cake, both invoke the sinful nature of rich foods. These names play with those tropes of food as sin. However, these dishes are meant to be indulgences rather than mainstays of the American table.

Warren Belasco counters this argument that our Puritanical heritage has held back our relationship to food by questioning, "Whose Puritan heritage?" reminding us that not everyone descended from the same Protestant tradition (Belasco and myself included) (Belasco 1999: 28). To his point he adds, "Considering the environmental impact of this country's unrelenting consumerist self-indulgence, perhaps we need more Puritanism, not less" (Belasco 1999: 28). In a similar vein, writer B. R. Myers proposes a "moral crusade against foodies," noting that "gluttony dressed up as foodie-ism is still gluttony" (Myers 2011).

Thus, it is only relatively recently that the enjoyment of food and the proclamation of calling oneself a "foodie" would even be considered a positive label, a badge of honor among certain social groups rather than a source of sin. In some cases, this labeling is being retroactively applied to historical figures, such as George Washington, Thomas Jefferson, and Benjamin Franklin, who author Dave DeWitt calls the "founding foodies" (DeWitt 2010) and who he credits for revolutionizing American cuisine during the early days of the nation. It is unlikely that the founding fathers would have called themselves foodies, but they exhibited many behaviors that, through a contemporary lens, would be considered in alignment with foodie habits and a keen interest in food, including growing their own food, brewing their own beer and distilling their own spirits, and serving the finest gourmet meals inspired by culinary trends in France and abroad. (It should be noted that many of these activities were propped up through slave labor, a fact that some foodies would perhaps like to overlook in this food-centric history of their American heroes.) As we have become more comfortable with celebrating the pleasures of food in the United States, it has also opened us up to think critically about the food we take in.

As described earlier, an interest in food used to suggest gluttony or concern only on the gourmet aspects of food. But contemporary foodies have sought to distance themselves from gourmets, who only want the so-called best food. Today, foodies are more omnivorous in their tastes and interests. In addition to being interested in ethnic foods and new flavors, increasingly, people also want to know about their food origins and consider the ethical and moral issues of food—including environmental sustainability, fair labor practices, and living wages for workers. Journalist Mark Bittman calls this "the new foodieism," proclaiming that "to care about food is now to care about the future of this country" (Bittman 2017). Foodies today are just as likely to take on social justice issues like fair wages and sustainable agriculture as they are likely to tackle discussions of the best *pad Thai* in town. Perhaps these are the issues that drove you to Food Studies.

Or you might reject the "foodie" label, eschewing the term and all of its cultural, social, and economic connotations. You may find the term to be elitist. Perhaps your interests are in the lesser seen and less glamorous parts of food. You may care about fair labor and food justice. You are concerned about where your food is from and about your health. Perhaps you worry about living wages for food workers, about environmental waste, or health and nutrition. These are what we may call the "hidden costs" of food, the impacts and the results of our decisions to produce and consume food in the way we do.

You are not atypical. Many of my former students became interested in food and cooking, and later food activism, because their childhood was defined by the lack of quality food. It was not the glamorous, Michelin-starred side of food that got them interested, but they wanted to learn to cook because it meant they would have something to eat. Some took up home economics or vocational "vo-tech" culinary classes in middle and high school because their parents and other caregivers weren't around to cook meals for them. Students of mine have written about childhoods where they were fed slop in school cafeterias and were inspired to do something about it. Others spoke about their experiences growing up in poverty and receiving food assistance, and how difficult it was to have nourishing meals while growing up terribly economically and food insecure.

Furthermore, the food industry has caught on to this shift in consumer attitudes. Alison Pearlman notes that a blend of "morality and materialism" (Pearlman 2013: 144) has been adopted by brands catering to foodies. Food marketing now extends its pitch beyond the quality of the food to highlight the conscientiousness of the product. Labels like local, sustainable, non-GMO, fair trade, cage-free, grass-fed, heirloom, heritage, and ancient are just as much of sell to consumers today.

It suffices to say that nowadays foodies are also interested in the morality of their eating choices: they eat what they preach. Mass market books like Michael Pollan's *The Omnivore's Dilemma* (2006), Eric Schlosser's *Fast Food Nation* (2001), Raj Patel's *Stuffed and Starved* (2008), Barry Estabrook's *Tomatoland* (2011) have even become required reading on many college and university freshman reading lists. Food documentaries like *Food, Inc.* (2008), *Forks Over Knives* (2011), *Super Size Me* (2004), *Cooked* (2016) also regularly appear as part of classroom and community discussions. This is a clear cultural shift to thinking about food in a broader sense.

While we seem to be concerned with food issues, there are also many contradictions in our foodie culture. While we've never had such a food-obsessed generation, many of the forty million millennial foodies do not always practice what they claim to preach. Of the 1,000 millennials surveyed by advertising firm BBDO, 60 percent eat fast food at least once a week (BBDO Atlanta 2013). Fast-food establishments have long been considered the antithesis of "good" food, in terms of labor practices, production and cooking techniques, health impacts, and cost. Yet, those who call themselves foodies regularly partake in this type of food. This may be, in part, because of millennials' financial status.

Millennials are one of the most financially insecure generations to come of age in recent times. As a whole, they have higher student loan debt, poverty and unemployment, and lower levels of wealth and personal income than previous generations at the same stage of their life cycle, despite being better educated (Pew Research Center 2014). As a culture, we claim to enjoy, value, and derive a level of unprecedented pleasure from food. Yet, we don't (or can't) always put our money where our mouths are.

These examples point to why food is complex and why when examining food there is often more than what meets the eye and the belly. Regardless of where your interests in food lie, what we can quickly ascertain is that there is always a story beyond the plate. For those of you who are interested in food, who might be lumped into the category of a "foodie," being interested in food is not the same as probing deeper and engaging with the issues that underlie ever-beautiful photos of homemade mac 'n cheese on Instagram or the stories behind every heirloom carrot at the farmers' market. We need to ask, What is going on beyond the plate?

My point here is that being a foodie or interested in food issues is not quite the same as going deeper into the field of Food Studies, although foodies can be a subject of study in the field of Food Studies (see Johnston and Baumann 2010; Vásquez and Chik 2015; Furrow 2016). Having a strong food obsession is also a good position to begin thinking more thoughtfully about the food system. This unease with food, given its associations with sin and gluttony, may also account for, at least in part, why Food Studies has been slow to establish in academic and broader public consciousness. Americans have begun to relax, and even embrace, food as something to enjoy, as well as something enjoyable to study. After all, food is "fundamental, fun, frightening, and far-reaching" (Rozin 1999).

Being a foodie or concerned about food issues is a good springboard toward Food Studies. What separates someone casually interested in food from a Food Studies scholar is the systematic way in which Food Studies looks at food. We are not simply interested in gourmet or the best-tasting food, what we might call the study of gastronomy. But we look at food more broadly, and try to question, investigate, and understand how food shapes our relationships: to other humans, to our society and culture, to the land, and other sites where we can have affiliation and draw meaning.

What is Food Studies?

Warren Belasco's seminal book, *Food: The Key Concepts*, posed the question, "Why study food?" (2008: 1). Given the intense interest in food nowadays, it is seemingly more apropos to say "let's study food" and consider which aspect of food we want to engage with.

Food Studies is an academic discipline that studies the relationships between food and the human experience (Miller and Deutsch 2009: 3). Food Studies deals with a variety of topics, disciplines, theoretical approaches, and incorporates a variety of methodologies. While food has been written about since the invention of the written word, it has not been systematically studied and recoded until relatively recently. Food Studies started reaching critical mass during the 1990s, when academic departments and academic journals and conferences devoted to the subject became normalized. Food Studies is thought of as categorically separate from culinary arts and hospitality, as well as food science, nutrition, agricultural sciences, and other subjects that deal with the study of food itself. Although, increasingly, the lines are blurred as culinary arts programs, home economics classes, and hospitality programs are incorporating Food Studies courses and Food Studies principles in their teaching; nutrition courses take on the cultural aspects of health and wellness; and food scientists consider psychological responses to food; these and other traditional disciplinary boundaries are being crossed.

Because of its broadness, it can be difficult to define what Food Studies is. Even among Food Studies scholars, there is often discussion as to what constitutes Food Studies. Berg, Nestle, and Bentley remind us that "scholars investigating food topics have not yet reached complete agreement on what it should and should not include" (Berg, Nestle, and Bentley 2003: 16). To this, Miller and Deutsch add that Food Studies is "diverse as food itself" (Miller and Deutsch 2009: 8). To avoid being essentialist and reductive about definitions, it is easier instead to consider the broadness of Food Studies.

It is more helpful to understand what it includes rather than erect boundaries as to what it is not. Food Studies is loosely divided into two camps—those focused more on the production and distribution issues, what we might call *food systems*. A food system involves all activities, infrastructure, social institutions, and cultural beliefs within a social group across the stages of the production, processing, transport, and consumption of food. Increasingly, scholars have expanded the definition to consider what happens in the life "after" a product is consumed: where the waste goes and what is made of it (e.g., whether is recycled, composted, or sent to a landfill). How these individual components work together and how relationships between these components are formed are important to defining a food system. While the point of a food system is to "provide nutrition to keep us all alive" (Hesterman 2011: 4), yet food systems vary greatly in terms of their size, efficiency, and success, depending on the structure of each society and its needs. They also impact a society's social and environmental well-being. What people eat shapes the food system. Conversely, the food system also shapes what people eat.

Less commonly, food system is also used to refer to the means of food acquisition in a society. Sometimes this term is used as a synonym for subsistence system. Food acquisition systems will be covered later in Chapter 3.

Other scholars turn their attention toward consumption, in what is often termed *food culture*. Those who focus on food culture are often interested in understanding the foodways of an area or group of people. *Foodways* are "the study of what we eat, as well as how and why and under what circumstances we eat" (Edge 2007: 8). It considers "the beliefs and behaviour surrounding the production, distribution, and consumption of food" (Counihan 1999: 2). Foodways are focused on the consumption of food and how these food-related behaviors mark membership in a community, group, or society. Foodways consider how food events impact consumption habits, as well as the foods themselves. Foodways are "rich ground in which to explore the construction and presentation of identity, including issues of creativity, function or use, traditionality, competence, change and continuity" (Kaplan 1984: 11).

This term grows out of its connections with folklore and folkways. The first recorded use of the term dates to the Great Depression in the United States. Under the New Deal, a program of civic revitalization following economic decline during the 1930s, President Franklin D. Roosevelt authorized a series of programs intended to record the folklore and folkways of everyday Americans, particularly rural and underserved communities. This type of popular anthropology captured the eating habits and practices of everyday Americans. Later, the term foodways was only popularized during the 1960s through the work of folklorist Don Yoder, who used it to replace "folk cookery." Foodways are meaningful because they reflect complex, long-term interactions between humans, their nutritional needs, ecology, and historical changes. The circumstances by which we eat are never accidental, and reflect a long series of actions related to our need to meet our nutritional requirements.

Gastronomy is sometimes used as a synonym to describe Food Studies. This term takes from the ancient Greek words of *gastro* and *nomos*, meaning stomach and laws that define or "the laws of the stomach." Gastronomy is popularly described in dictionaries as "the art and science of good food." Put another way, gastronomy is about the rules of what we might consider good food. The term came into popular use through a poem by Joseph Berchoux on "Gastronomie" (La gastronomie ou L'homme des champs a table) (1801). The term gastronomy is often linked to Jean Anthelme Brillat-Savarin and his work on taste. His book *The Physiology of Taste* (*La Physiologie du Gout*) (Brillat-Savarin 2009) laid down the rules of taste in nineteenth-century France. Brillat-Savarin himself was a gourmand, known for pursuing the best ingredients, cooking, and meals. As a result, the term and the study of gastronomy is often defined as trying to understand what is "the best" or "good" food—the practice of identifying, choosing, and eating good food. *Larousse Gastronomique*, the French culinary bible, points out that "true gastronomes, while appreciating the most refined products of the culinary art, enjoy them in moderation; for their normal fare, they seek out the simplest dishes, which are, however, the most difficult to prepare to perfection" (Montagné 2001: 547). Naturally, gastronomy has tended to favor haute cuisine and elite practices, although this is no longer entirely the case. For instance, there are degree programs focused in gastronomy (such as at Boston University), which has considered more than just matters of good taste.

Although Food Studies is roughly split between food systems and food culture, Marion Nestle points out that these lines are becoming increasingly blurred and these divisions can be, at times, artificial (Nestle 2010). Increasingly, food scholarship has been trying to connect consumption and food systems. A solid example is Margaret Gray's *Labor and the Locavore: The Making of a Comprehensive Food Ethic* (2013), a recent volume that reveals the cracks in consumer knowledge about their consumption habits. Gray contends knowledge of food workers cannot be divorced from the broader food system.

As Food Studies has expanded as an academic discipline, the canopy of its umbrella has also expanded. At its start, Food Studies often housed in humanities and, occasionally, social science departments. Nowadays, Food Studies subjects are taught in all manners of institutions: culinary schools and colleges, medical schools, and even business schools. The field of Food Studies is inherently interdisciplinary and multidisciplinary. Scholars often rely on methods, approaches, and themes from other disciplines in order to study and analyze food. Food Studies is also multidisciplinary: history, communications, anthropology, geography, environmental studies, and other subjects sit next to one another in a way that is uncommon at most academic conferences. Books on food also run the gamut of approaches: historical, cultural, behavioral, biological, and socioeconomic. In addition, culinary, gastronomic, and medical approaches also add to the study of food. We should remember that "Food Studies researchers are not constrained by the methods and approaches of any one discipline, and they enjoy the freedom to study what they like in whatever way seems most appropriate" (Berg, Nestle, and Bentley 2003: 17). But this flexibility and freedom can also be misunderstood by those outside the field. "Because this flexibility may be perceived as unfamiliar or lacking in rigor no matter how excellent the quality of work, the academic study of food itself, as opposed to studying food within a traditional discipline, is established in only a few universities" (Berg, Nestle, and Bentley 2003: 17).

Regardless of your interests in Food Studies, what makes the study of food so enjoyable is that you already know something of it based on your experiences eating, drinking, and existing on this planet. What makes food worthy of study is that every single human, and the cultures and societies they are parts of, has had a slightly different experience of food. This volume takes the stance that Food Studies is both, and will engage with Food Studies from a range of disciplines and perspectives. The hands-on nature of this book also adds in the experiential or applied component of Food Studies, remembering to keep the food in Food Studies.

Food communicates

We begin our foray in to the field of Food Studies by thinking about what we know in terms of food. We start by considering food's ability to say things—to communicate information about ourselves, as individuals, and about our wider group affiliations, as well as our social and political beliefs. Communication is the process of sharing and transferring ideas, feelings, and information through verbal and nonverbal means. Spoken language, eye contact, body language, and written information are ways of sharing thoughts and knowledge. Successful communication involves much more than transferring information. The information needs to be understood—in the same ways—by both the transmitting and receiving parties in order for it to be considered a successful act of communication. This process can involve invoking emotions or speaking through themes that resonate with the recipient.

Scholars consider food a form of communication because it is a means by which we share information with each other. As pointed out by Roland Barthes, food is a

> system of communication, a body of images, a protocol of usages, situations, and behavior. Information about food must be gathered wherever it can be found: by direct observation in economy, in techniques, usages and advertising; and by indirect observation in the mental life of a given society. (Barthes 2008: 22–4)

In other words, food enables us to share and transfer ideas, feelings, and information through verbal and nonverbal means. Food helps express personal and group identities, as well as cementing social bonds. In a similar vein, anthropologists Claude Lévi-Strauss (1969) and Mary Douglas (1972) have added that food can be viewed as a type of language because food serves as a type of "code" that expresses patterns about social relations. The messages will reveal "different degrees of hierarchy, inclusion and exclusion, boundaries and transactions across the boundaries" (Douglas 1972: 61).

Annie Hauck-Lawson coined the term *food voice* to capture the ways in which food communicates. This term refers to the ways that food serves as a "dynamic, creative, symbolic, and highly individualized" channel of communication (Hauck-Lawson 1992: 6). Food expresses an individual's view of themselves and of their society and culture, revealing insights about community, economics, gender, and other aspects of identity. Food speaks and it has a lot to say. Food comes in a wide range of voices, "solo, ethnic, gender, old new, traditional, spiritual, harmonious, or discordant" (Hauck-Lawson 1992: 7). Deutsch and Murakhver (2012) illustrate the concept of food voice by describing different scenarios. They write, "If I invite you over for dinner and offer you oysters, champagne, and filet mignon, what is the food saying differently than if I offered you spaghetti and meatballs? And how would the food voice change if the spaghetti were homemade?" (Deutsch and Murakhver 2012: xii). Food tells others something about you.

Food can speak volumes when someone isn't allowed to raise their voice. In "Bad Sauce, Good Ethnography," Paul Stoller and Cheryl Olkes (1986) describe their encounter with Djebo, a Songhay woman living in Niger. Djebo is the wife of the youngest son of Adamu Jenitongo, one of the most knowledgeable healers in all of western Niger. Stoller and Olkes have come to meet with Adamu Jenitongo, and they are welcomed into his home. As the youngest female, Djebo is tasked with cooking dinner for Stoller and Olkes and prepares good food, especially fine sauces, as a show of hospitality, over the course of many days. Growing annoyed with this task, the quality of her sauces decline until she prepares a disgusting sauce that clearly projects what she isn't allowed to communicate through words.

Furthermore, food's ability to elicit reactions and conjure old memories makes it an especially successful instrument in communication. Consider the 2007 animated film *Ratatouille*. The protagonist, Remy, is a passionate food lover and aspiring cook. He also happens to be a rat. Over the course of the film, he befriends humans who enable his dream of cooking in a restaurant. Ultimately, he is faced with wooing a jaded food critic named Anton Ego. Remy's dish of ratatouille wows the critic, as it launches a bittersweet flashback to his youth dining at his mother's table. That a distant memory and nostalgic feelings can be conjured through food is something that we can all relate to.

Ratatouille's flashback scene is reminiscent of a famous passage from Marcel Proust's *Remembrance of Things Past* (Proust 1934). While on a visit to his mother's village home, the protagonist Swan has an encounter with a madeleine, a small French cake, that sends him on a nostalgic trip back in time. Upon dipping the cake in his mother's tea, he recalls boyhood memories of his aunt, her home with its smells and decorations, and the village as it once looked, long ago. Both of these anecdotes, one from popular cinema and one from literature, are examples of food memories. *Food memories* capture the connection between food and emotion.

Anthropologist David Sutton's research on Greeks living in the islands of Kalymnos provides insight to the importance of food as a connection to the past through food memories (Sutton 2001). Residents of the Kalymnos who have moved away remember fondly and nostalgically the tastes of home. Food becomes the physical, tangible way of interacting with feelings and past moments. Happy memories are described as "sweet as honey." Things that taste good are reminiscent of orange. Family members also go to great lengths to bring back feta, a white salty cheese that is a foundation of the diet, to their locales. The taste of feta from home is paramount to the stuff they can find in local supermarkets in their new locations.

Food memories can also lend a sense dignity in times of desperation. *In Memory's Kitchen: A Legacy from the Women of Terezin* (De Silva 1996) illustrates the power of food and memory. This book, based on a manuscript of seventy recipes, is a remarkable testament to the human character. They originate from the women of Theresienstadt concentration camp near the Czechoslovak town of Terezin. These recipes were written in the context of utmost desperation and hunger, and in defiance of the Nazi regime that imprisoned them. They capture these women's tastes and identities and their reflections of better, happier times of the past and also hopes for future dinners in a world beyond. It was the cookbook of remembering.

The emotional charge of food extends beyond the art forms of film and literature. Good poetry also transcends time and space, and captures an aspect of the human experience. Food is a particularly powerful and evocative subject for poets, as it is a topic to which all humans can relate. Consider the poetry of Matsuo Bashō (1644–1694), the most famous poet of Edo Japan. Stop and read aloud this haiku, a form of syllabic-based short poetry.

> in the morning dew
> spotted with mud, and how cool—
> melons on the soil[1]

What type of imagery does this poem generate? What situation is presented? How does it make you feel as a reader? Though written over 300 years ago, Bashō's poem resonates with readers today because you can envision yourself in that scene, admiring the sweetness of a melon patch on a cool morning.

Now muse upon the words of American poet William Carlos Williams (1883–1963) in "This Is Just to Say" (1938).

> I have eaten
> the plums
> that were in
> the icebox
>
> and which
> you were probably
> saving
> for breakfast
>
> Forgive me
> they were delicious
> so sweet
> and so cold

Ask yourself the same questions as before. What type of imagery does this poem conjure? What scenario is presented? What emotions does it raise?

Though composed in markedly divergent time periods and context, both poems resonate with readers today. Bashō's serene description of melons brings the reader to a gentle morning in the garden, while Williams's revelation about the plums can be read in different ways. Who hasn't enjoyed the sweet taste of forbidden fruit? Or conversely, experienced anger after discovering that your treats have been pilfered by another? The emotions elicited by Bashō and Williams are familiar and seemingly timeless. By connecting people through shared experiences, food is an effective vehicle for communication.

Food Studies, by its nature, is subversive and challenging. It asks, and sometimes demands, that we consider multiple perspectives and worldviews. To begin, we need to first understand what food is saying, how food communicates. Food has the power to communicate attitudes, values, beliefs, and customs—and to identify who you are, as well as who you are not. To borrow from that age-old line, "you are what you eat (or don't eat)." It has the ability to support prevailing ideas in a society or to subvert them. What does food say about who we are? What does the narrative suggest? How might things differ if we change the narrative?

1.1 Activity: Food and poetry

Food and poetry are a natural pairing as both elicit emotions, engage the senses, and help create a sense of shared understanding. Food also communicates. How might you communicate your emotions and experiences through poetry? In this exercise you will write a food-themed poem that engages the senses to consider how food, the senses, and emotions intersect.

Directions

1. Pick a food experience or memory from your own life that could also be universal—a moment that others could relate to or understand. Take inspiration from Bashō and Williams.
2. Take a sheet of paper and divide it into five columns. Name each column after one of the senses: sight, smell, touch, hearing, and taste.
3. Think about how you could describe that experience through the senses. For instance, the nutty-burnt smell of brewed coffee. The meltingly soft texture of a warm cookie just pulled out of the oven. The hiss fizz sound emanating from a can of soda.
4. Look through your list and think about how you could weave these descriptions together into a poem.
5. Compose your poem by writing at least one line per sense. Think of how the words, phrases, and descriptions can link together to elicit an emotional response.

Instructor's note

Encourage your students to share their poems with their classmates. Poetry is meant to be shared and enjoyed out loud. The poems can also be completed as homework and later shared in class.

The stories we tell (or don't)

Foods themselves carry stories—about their origins, cultivation, values, and properties. How these stories are told is meaningful, because they become the basis for establishing a food's identity and role in a society, and perhaps even the source of its value. Pu'er tea, a type of aged, prized tea grown in China's southwestern Yunnan Province, is the stuff of mythology. Collectors bid on prized vintages. Different producers' products carry different premiums. Connoisseurs talk about the taste of the tea, and how it reflects the interactions between man and nature. In a story about pu'er tea published by National Public Radio (NPR), Max Falkowitz, food magazine editor, writer, and publisher, offered these statements about the beverage. "Pu'er offers a narrative and emotional thread over the course of time and brewing the leaf again and again. You're not just drinking tea; you're participating in a story" (Neimark 2017).

What is interesting is that similar comments have made about cheese, wine, and any number of other products where ecology, environment, and human interaction intersect to produce a food product. What is prized about these food or beverages is not just the item itself per se, but what is fetishized, recalled, and passed on are the stories—the *narratives*.

Why would people care about how the tea is grown, the conditions under which it was aged, who produced it, and how the taste of the tea captures all of these aspects (and more)? Colleagues of mine at the Culinary Institute of America who specialize in wine and beverage service, who are trained sommeliers (individuals who are educated in and prepare wine for service), comment that selling wine is selling a story. We can draw a parallel between these stories and religious rituals. These stories help create a sense of social solidarity or "we-ness," a feeling of belonging within a group of people. Sociologist Emile Durkheim (1976) contends that religions help create this sense of "we-ness" through repeated rituals, storytelling, and reinforcing a narrative.

Similarly, in food, the repetition of rituals, the common storytelling, and reinforcement of a narrative help create the perception that there is something *special* or unique about a food product or a food experience. Consider the role of restaurant reviews in framing our expectations for an eating establishment and the food. Restaurant reviews rarely focus solely on the food—they describe the *experience*. Osteria Francescana, ranked the number one restaurant in the world in 2016 by the San Pellegrino World's 50 Best Restaurants list, is run by a chef named Massimo Bottura. In a *New York Times* profile of Bottura, written a few months after he had been awarded the distinction of being the best in the world, they described his food as such:

> Bottura's mind is like a butterfly net that swings to and fro in the hopes that a stray beauty will land in its mesh. Potential inspiration hovers everywhere. A dessert called "Oops! I Dropped the Lemon Tart" arose from a moment, years back, when Takahiko Kondo, one of Bottura's closest kitchen allies, accidentally smashed a sweet on the pastry counter. Bottura decided that it gave the dessert exactly what it had been needing. A dish called "An Eel Swimming Up the Po River" is somehow representative of a collision between an odd squabble in Italian history and Bob Dylan and Johnny Cash's duet on "Girl From the North Country." (Gordinier 2016)

This description—"mind is like a butterfly net," a dish that sounds like a squabble between legendary musicians and legends of history—brings the reader in and presents a certain vision of the chef and restaurant. If the reporter had adopted more mundane prose such as "his mind is nimble" and his dish is "full of argumentative contrasts," this is far less engaging and creates a different narrative.

In the food world, actors are increasingly taking control of their own narrative and controlling the way others see their work and efforts. Consider the number of social media accounts, websites, curated Instagram feeds that show you a particular vision of a food world. But some groups seek to challenge and disrupt the usual narrative. Take Conflict Kitchen. Conflict Kitchen challenges its diners to think about current events in a different way. Conflict Kitchen rewrites the narrative of current events and global affairs through food. It challenges diners to rethink what they know by first engaging with their stomachs.

1.2 Food for thought: Conflict Kitchen

Conflict Kitchen was located in Pittsburgh, Pennsylvania. It is, in its simplest terms, a take-out restaurant. But its social and educational mission is so much more. Founded in 2010, Conflict Kitchen uses food to communicate: to educate Pittsburghers about countries, cultures, and peoples most Americans know very little about but often hear about in the news and social media. The restaurant team, led by cofounders Jon Rubin and Dawn Weleski, and culinary director Robert Sayre, work with members from the ethnic community featured to develop menus, record their stories, and to craft a responsive menu. The foods and cultures of Afghanistan, Cuba, Iran, the Iroquois (the Haudenosaunee Confederacy), North Korea, Palestine, and Venezuela have been featured on its rotating menu, which changes several times a year based on geopolitical events. Conflict Kitchen also hosts public events, performances, discussions, and workshops to engage discussion and educate about geopolitical events. Even the food wrapping and packaging becomes a site of engagement—food wrappers are decorated with art reflective of the featured community on the menu and often contain informational material or stories from that community. See www.conflictkitchen.org for more information.

Writing (and rewriting) the food narrative

Stories, tales, and folklore are part of our ways of communication. Stories seek to inspire, transmit lessons about morality, safety, and ideology, and become part of how we see ourselves as individuals or as members of a society. We are told these stories and later repeat these tales.

What is useful to analyze about stories is not the story itself—the mundane facts, details, characters, times of day involved. What Food Studies scholars are interested in analyzing is the narrative, or how the story is told and why it is told in that manner. The story and resulting lessons will change depending on who is telling the story and what perspective the story is being told from.

Increasingly, the food world has embraced the use of storytelling and narrative to sell products, to convey a mood, or to resonate with their customers in advertising. Consider the rise of "artisanal" food in the early 2000s (see Leitch 2003; Meneley 2004; Wilk 2006; Trubek 2009; Paxson 2012; Cope 2014). Suzanne Cope (2014) suggests that this rise of artisanal food could be considered a rejection of industrialized, homogenized, mass-marketed food. Specially crafted pickles, cheese, chocolates, and spirits became the antidote to big food, especially in the wake of the 2008 financial crisis when consumers sought to reengage with smaller economies of scale. Consumers sought to spend their money at small businesses, supporting independent entrepreneurs instead of major corporations. Making these specially crafted items also served as an avenue for independent entrepreneurship and business during a recession, when jobs were low and unemployment was at a high. Pursuing a business in making artisanal products was especially driven by middle-class, educated twenty- and thirty-somethings living in or near urban centers as a way to exercise individual agency and control.

While artisanal foods are intended to refer to small-scale and small-batch products, suggesting a shortened food chain between producer and customer, the term has since been co-opted and used by major food companies as a marketing buzzword. McDonald's offers an artisan grilled chicken sandwich, which is a "grilled chicken breast sandwich made with 100% chicken breast filet that has no artificial preservatives, flavors or colors and perfectly marinated for juicy flavor. Layered with crisp leaf lettuce and tasty tomato, and topped with a vinaigrette dressing, all on our delectable artisan roll" (McDonald's 2017). Starbucks offers artisan breakfast sandwiches, while Panera promotes that its bread is made by bakers who "work each and every day, hand-shaping and scoring the dough to bring you freshly baked bread every morning and throughout the day" (Panera Bread 2017). These uses of the word "artisan" and "artisanal" are divorced from their small-batch, independent roots. But to consumers, they may invoke a level of quality that is not what is being provided to them.

Narrative also shines through when marketers try to connect with consumers by being cool. One of the most popular characters in advertising is "the most interesting man in the world," a character created to sell Dos Equis beer. The "most interesting man in the world" is a debonair man in his seventies. Commercials featuring this character show his exploits around the world as a younger man, which include winning the Olympics, freeing a bear from a trap, and winning a staring contest against his own reflection. The commercials include the line "I don't always drink beer, but when I do, I prefer Dos Equis."[2] This character has become the stuff of viral videos and internet memes, and has helped increase sales of the beer worldwide.

To conclude, this leads us to ask, what will be the next chapter in food? What are the stories that have been told? What has yet to be written? For students of Food Studies, this means thinking about what narratives within the large field of Food Studies you are connecting to. Or perhaps are seeking to change and rewrite the script.

1.3 Activity: Retelling the story

To consider the importance of narrative in storytelling and the representation of food, in this assignment you will consider the proverbial "other side." You will be rewriting a popular food slogan from a different perspective. This activity will allow you to consider how food communicates and how different actors in the food system would want to communicate different ideals and values.

Companies and Slogans

McDonald's—I'm Lovin' It
KFC—Finger Lickin' Good
Burger King—Have it Your Way
Hardee's—Where the Food's the Star
Taco Bell—Think Outside the Bun
Subway—Eat Fresh
Wendy's—It's Way Better Than Fast Food. It's Wendy's
Chili's—License to Grill
Applebee's—It's a Whole New Neighborhood
Papa John's—Better Ingredients, Better Pizza

Actors in the food chain

Restaurant worker
Restaurant manager
Company CEO
Customer—fixed income senior

Customer—high school student
Customer—busy single parent
Health inspector
Farmer/food producer

Directions

1. Choose a food slogan from the list above.
2. Rewrite the slogan from the perspective of a different actor.
3. Read out loud and share with the class.

Discussion questions

1. Who is the original slogan selling to? Who is their target audience? What values or ideals are featured in the original slogan? Whose perspective is being featured?
2. Describe the perspective you took on. Why did you choose to adopt this role? How would you characterize your actor?
3. How does the slogan shift when told by a different actor? What values and ideals were you attempted to communicate in the new slogan?

1.4 Activity: Analyzing community cookbooks

Community cookbooks are cherished recipe collections of a group. They are often humble, user-submitted recipes of family favorites. Community groups produce and share these items as a way to celebrate their identity and sometimes also to raise funds for the organization or a charity. Community cookbooks say a much about who a group is—through the types of recipes, the ingredients featured, and even the narratives cookbooks provide, as these documents often contain stories, information about the group's history and organizational mission, and even advertisements from local businesses. Studying community cookbooks allows scholars to analyze how food communicates values, identities, and ethics, in addition creating a cohesive identity through something tangible.

Directions

1. Gather a variety of community cookbooks. See the instructor's note below if you are facing difficulty in sourcing them.

2. Consider the creator of each cookbook. Then ponder over its intended audience.
3. What messages does each cookbook send? What is the dominant narrative, if there is one? What visual and textual clues does the cookbook send about the community?
4. Does your cookbook present the image of a unified community? Does it suggest that the community has been scattered?
5. Does the community even matter to your particular community cookbook?

Instructor's note

Local libraries, church groups, and civic groups often have collections of community cookbooks. Current and vintage community cookbooks can be purchased from local organizations or online. Thrift and second-hand stores, as well as public library sales, are good places to source these cookbooks.

Further resources

Bower, A. L. (1997). "Our Sisters' Recipes: Exploring 'Community' in a Community Cookbook." *The Journal of Popular Culture*, 31(3), pp. 137–151.
Cotter, C. (1997). "Claiming a Piece of the Pie: How the Language of Recipes Defines Community." *Recipes for Reading: Community Cookbooks, Stories, Histories*, pp. 51–71.
Longone, Janice Bluestein (1997). "'Tried receipts': An Overview of America's Charitable Cookbooks." In Anne L. Bower (ed.), *Recipes for Reading: Community Cookbooks, Stories, Histories*. Amherst: University of Massachusetts Press.

The Mennonite Community Cookbook is a compilation of mid-twentieth-century recipes from Mennonite communities across the United States and Canada. Mennonites belong to an Anabaptist Protestant sect of Christianity and are recognized as an ethno-religious group. In certain regions of the United States, they have developed distinct foodways and cultural habits. http://mennonitecommunitycookbook.com is the online home of this community cookbook.

The University of Southern Mississippi operates the online Mississippi Community Cookbook Project. This project aims to collect, digitize, and study Mississippi's culinary heritage. http://mscommunitycookbooks.usm.edu.

Summary

- Foodie culture is part of mainstream culture.
- While food is popular as a mainstream subject, Food Studies is not the same as being interested in food.
- Food Studies can be split into food culture and food systems.
- Food communicates; it tells stories.

Discussion questions

1. Describe your strongest food memory. Why has this remained with you? How has this impacted your life?

2. Reflect on the poems by William Carlos Williams and Matsuo Bashō. Can you think of another timeless, transcendental food experience? What feelings or emotions might your food experience communicate?

3. What stories have you heard about the food system? What might you want to investigate to better understand the food system?

Notes

1   This version of Bashō's haiku on melons was translated by Makoto Ueda. It was published in his *Basho and His Interpreters: Selected Hokku with Commentary*. Stanford: Stanford University Press, 1992.

2   Seth Stevenson, writing for *Slate*, explains the appeal of the "most interesting man in the world" (Stevenson 2009).

Further resources

Cramer, Janet M., Carlnita P. Greene, and Lynn M. Walters (eds.) (2011). *Food as Communication, Communication as Food*. New York: Peter Lang Publishing.

Feed Me a Story is a collective created by Theresa Loong and Laura Nova. Their work captures food stories and focuses at the intersections of oral history, food, and art. http://www.feedmeastory.com.

Foodies: The Culinary Jet Set (2014) is a film about ultra-elite foodies who live to eat at the world's most prestigious restaurants.

The Southern Foodways Alliance's Oral History Program documents the stories of the American South through the lens of food. https://www.southernfoodways.org/oral-history/.

Walker, Harlan (2001). *Food and Memory*. Devon, UK: Prospect Books

2

Defining Food: Meals, Morals, and Manners

What is food? This seems like a silly question, but it is raised here with serious intent. What do you consider food? How do you know that something is food as opposed to non-food? How might your understanding of food differ from others around you? How might your understanding of this term be impacted by environmental, ecological, geographic, economic, cultural, and political factors?

The simplest answer to the question "What is food?" is that "food" is anything that can be consumed for its nutritional content to sustain life. Prosper Montagné, editor of the famed *Larousse Gastronomique*, a canon on French food and gastronomy first published in 1938, points out that food is a "substance eaten to sustain life; as part of a well-balanced diet, it promotes growth and maintains health" (2001: 507). Often, the items consumed are done so to provide nutrients and calories, and serve as source of energy and potentially fuel growth.

Now if food were simply about calories and survival, then there would likely be little to no need for this textbook and courses on Food Studies. This book would perhaps, instead, be focused on nutrition, foraging, horticulture, the food supply chain, or other topics directed related to the "feeding" aspects of food. If food were merely about calories and survival, then why have humans expended such efforts over food? In fact, it might be more efficient, practical, and even cost-effective to ingest just powders and pills instead of spending time, labor, and effort in growing, producing, shopping, cooking, plating and presenting, serving, and eating food.

But as food scholars have astutely noted, food is so much more than fuel. Once we start looking at the particulars of food, we quickly determine that people care about what they eat. People care about how their food looks. They care about the way their food tastes. They assign value to different foods and beverages. These factors seem to suggest that food is seemingly more of an intellectual and social exercise, not merely a biological one. We don't feed, we *dine*. We care about what we ingest and place value on what we will and will not eat (and how we will produce, prepare, cook, and consume it). Thus, we realize that there is a huge range as to what humans consider food, and a lot of differentiation and value is placed on what we consider to be "good" as opposed to "bad" food.

Anthropologists have noted that humans define themselves on their propensity to eat—and not eat—certain foods. Legendary gastronome Jean Anthelme Brillat-Savarin's famous saying, "Tell me what you eat and I will tell you what you are," infers that class, status, religion, gender, geography, and environment are part of the plate as much as the foods that fill it. As Barbara Haber points out, you must "follow the food" if you want to understand how a society works (Haber 2005: 65). Thus, what one considers food varies depending on biological, socioeconomic, cultural, ecological, and environmental factors. Agricultural and food acquisition practices also impact what one considers food. That is why there is a huge range of what people eat, differing from place to place, culture to culture. Even within delineated society or culture, there are huge variances if we look at the habits of one person versus another.

To begin our inquiry into what is food, this chapter is organized around three principles. In this chapter, we will explore the symbolic value placed on food through the principles of meals, morals, and manners. If we look more closely at what people are eating, and have eaten throughout history, we find that food is often about more than acquiring nutrients and filling the belly. As the old saying goes, "Animals feed, while humans dine." That is to say, humans have ideas about what they will and will not eat, beliefs about the quality of the food, and practices related to how best to cook, serve, and eat food. Humans place immense symbolic value on what they ingest. For humans, food can be thought of as a combination of ideals and practices regarding meals, morals, and manners. Right food is as much scientific judgment as it is moral decision. As humans we "discipline our desires, our appetites and our pleasures" at the table (Coveney 2006: i). This leads us to ask how and why humans have put such effort into regulating their food consumption. These efforts suggest that food is not simply an act of biological feeding, but eating the so-called right food also weighs in scientific judgment and moral decisions.

Meals

For the overwhelming majority of the planet's creatures, the answer to what is food is straightforward. Most animals have limited diets and fall neatly into the category of either carnivore or herbivore. But for omnivores, the issue of food is a bit more complex. *Omnivores*, the "all-eating" creatures like humans, bonobos, pigs, can eat from a wide range of food sources. As "flexible" eaters, omnivores can devour both meat and plant foods, so long as they are not poisonous.

The ability to eat both meat and plant foods provides an evolutionary advantage for humans and other omnivores. Because we can eat so indiscriminately, humans are able to meet their nutritional needs more easily than specialist eaters who can eat only plants or flesh. Given the wider range of options available, humans were less vulnerable to environmental conditions and food stocks. Unlike specialist eaters, who are tied to a specific type of food, humans could more readily replace or supplement one food item with another if stocks were low, if disease wiped out a species, or if climate conditions made it difficult to acquire that food. Humans were able to adapt to a variety of new food sources and incorporate them into their diets, thus expanding the quality and range of their nutritional intake. As a result, humans were able to migrate and inhabit different parts of the planet, in part because of their ability to consume a wide range of foods and adapt their taste preferences to accommodate local availability.

Humans have the added advantage of being "superomnivores" (Allen 2012), as we have the widest access to the greatest number and type of foods. Of course, there is no one perfect food. Humans must eat a variety of foods in order to sustain life, to achieve a balance of the necessary vitamins and nutrients. Overreliance on one type of food can cause an imbalance, leading to malnutrition, poisoning, or perhaps even death.

Our omnivorousness has served us well, as it also helped fuel the growth of the human brain. Our brains are approximately four times the size of chimpanzees. Humans have relatively large brains, but size is not the determinant of function. Human brains are also capable of complex thought and planning—something that distinguishes us from chimpanzees and earlier hominins. For proper function, the human brain utilizes approximately 20 percent of an adult's caloric intake. Our brain size is the result of our diets. Some researchers speculate that early humans had varied and rich diets (see Sahlins 1988). They argue that the hunter-gatherer lifestyle allowed early humans to experience a range of foods and to develop a broad palate for different foods in order to survive. Our ability to eat a wide range of foodstuffs was furthered by the fact that we also developed many tools to process our food. We will return to tool use again in Chapter 5.

Although we might call ourselves omnivores, we clearly do not eat everything. Every single person on the planet has boundaries and preferences as to what they will and will not eat and these boundaries are often informed by the wider society around them. Thus, humans face what scholars have called "*the omnivore's dilemma*" (Rozin 1997; Pollan 2006; Armelagos 2010). In theory, humans can eat a wide range of foods, yet in practice they clearly choose not to. Part of this dilemma has been driven, at least until the relatively recent past, with the start of domestication around 10,000 years ago; prior to that, humans were entirely dependent on wild food sources. The ability to control our food supply through agriculture is one of the factors that has made us superomnivores, as we were able to enter into "synergistic or coevolutionarly relationship[s]" with other species (Allen 2012). Were able to actively and conscientiously select certain plants and animals, breed them to preferences and needs, and spread them throughout the world. No other creature has been capable of expressing such control over their food sources and surroundings.

Nowadays we are omnivores not just for survival, but by choice. Because humans are presented with such a wide range of choices, we put parameters on the possibilities. Consciously and subconsciously we group the food and drink we encounter into categories of "good" versus "bad." Broadly speaking, we have preferences, aversions, fears, and taboos.

Our preferences are shaped by cultural factors and biology, as well as taste preferences and availability and ease.

Some of these boundaries may be biological. Our senses and ability to perceive sweet, salty, bitter, sour, and *umami* (savory) serve biological purposes. These are the five basic tastes, which evolved to help our ancestors survive. Survival was a matter of taste. Taste and smell are linked to the involuntary nervous system and emotions. Humans developed preferences for specific tastes, which helped them to survive as a species. The taste for sweet is something common in many mammals. The preference for sweetness is linked to the need for energy. Humans and other mammals begin life by consuming mother's milk, which is a rich source of proteins and sugars (carbohydrates) in the form of lactose. Salt is necessary for nerve function. Sodium ions help spur nerve impulses in addition to supporting other cellular functions. Bitter signals the presence of toxins or poisons. Our ability to perceive sour is considered an adaptation to detect spoilage or unripe food. *Umami*, a Japanese term describing the taste of savoriness, signals the presence of protein.

2.1 Food for thought: Cravings—nature or nurture?

Scientists used to think that food cravings stemmed from biological needs—specifically, nutrient deficiency. The now-debunked specific hungers theory suggested that humans craved certain tastes and flavors to regulate homeostasis, to maintain sufficient and consistent concentrations of minerals in the body. For instance, a craving for salt suggests a sodium deficiency, while a craving for beefsteak might suggest a deficiency in iron or a strong craving for cheese might suggest a need for calcium. While animals need to regulate homeostasis, this does not appear to be the case for humans.

Human preferences for salt pose a challenge. Biologically, humans need salt to function and our tongues have the ability to perceive salt through our taste buds. Salty is one of the basic tastes. Humans crave salt and modern humans consume far more than they need. About 1.1 to 3.3 grams per day is plenty, yet Europeans and Americans eat many times that amount and sometimes suffer the consequences in the form of hypertension, heart disease, stroke, and other so-called lifestyle diseases. Yet there are human societies that have lived without meaningful added salt consumption, such as indigenous Australians and indigenous North American groups like the First Nations and the Inuit. Their salt intake was derived through animal proteins.

This complicates our understanding of taste: that the discussion is not simply nature or nurture, but sometimes a discussion of both.

Further resources

Mystery of the Senses: A NOVA Miniseries (1995), [TV Program] PBS.
Shepherd, G. (2011). *Neurogastronomy: How the Brain Creates Flavor and Why It Matters*. New York: Columbia University Press.
Spence, C. (2015). "Multisensory Flavour Perception." *Cell*, 16(1), pp. 24–35.
Stuckey, B. (2012). *Taste What You're Missing: The Passionate Eater's Guide to Why Good Food Tastes Good*. New York: Simon and Schuster.

Our likes and dislikes of certain foods may sometimes be attributed to biological differences. Cilantro (or coriander leaf) is a popular herb used in Mediterranean, Mexican, and Southeast Asian cuisines and draws strong reactions from eaters. This herb can taste soapy to some people, while others consider it to taste green, citrusy, and fresh. This difference in perception may be put down to genetic differences in smell receptors; those who dislike cilantro are likely missing receptors that allow them to smell the fresh, citrusy scents of cilantro. This impacts smell perception and decides whether or not one enjoys cilantro. Biology can also shape whether certain foods are safe. For instance, someone with a life-threatening allergy to peanuts would be unlikely to eat a peanut butter cookie or a Thai red curry peanut sauce, no matter how delicious it smells.

Preferences and avoidances cannot be put down to biology alone. It is also important to keep in mind that taste preferences and avoidances are highly social and are learned. That is to say, each and every person carries with them ideas about food that are informed by individual likes and dislikes as well as their broader culture, or society's ideas about food. One's version of "normal" is also dependent on the worldview they come from and what they were taught to consider acceptable as food. Take, for instance, the American preference for "fresh meat." Americans are one of the highest consumers of meat around the globe, consuming approximately 270.7 pounds per person each year. In fact, many cultures have a "special esteem for animal flesh" and use "meat to reinforce the social ties that bind campmates and kinfolk together" (Harris 1998: 27). The taste for meat has a biological basis, as humans crave protein.

What varies is the type of meat humans choose to consume and how. The most popular type and cut of meat in America remains boneless, skinless chicken breast, sold in Styrofoam trays wrapped in layers of plastic wrap. This meat is sold as "fresh," is kept in chilled refrigerated cabinets, and is divorced from its original animal source. There are no signs of bone, skin, feathers, or other evidence of animal life. The breasts in that package may also come from several different chickens, each from different farms many miles away from the supermarket where it is being sold. By contrast, in other societies, "fresh" may have a different meaning. In China, while supermarkets are part of the local foodscape, consumers generally avoid buying fresh food items there. Instead, many still prefer to visit wet markets. Good wet markets sell live chickens, which are held in cages or pens. To buy a chicken, one goes to the chicken vendor (each vendor often only sells one type of protein) and pick the chicken you desire. The vendor then slaughters the chicken on site (sometimes they do you the courtesy of going into a back room, if available). The butcher drains its blood, plucks the feathers, and even chops up the chicken into pieces, if requested. The chicken still feels warm when you pick it up in the plastic bag holding its flesh. This, to a discerning Chinese eater, is "fresh"—an animal killed just before consumption.[1]

Due to different governmental regulations and social ideals for food consumption and food safety, "fresh" chicken means two different things in China versus in the United States. To illustrate why group boundaries are also important, ask yourself this. Would you be able to purchase a freshly slaughtered on premise chicken from a supermarket in the United States? The answer is likely no. The closest example to this is buying a live lobster from a fish tank, although this practice is becoming less common as some animal rights activists have protested against it on the grounds of animal cruelty.

Thus, our ideas of what is "natural" or "normal" to eat is also highly informed by the society and the environment we grow up in. Breakfast, as American parents are told and children are expected to believe, is the most important meal of the day.[2] American breakfasts are often composed of foods that are only eaten at this meal time—cereal, pancakes, waffles, or, for more gourmet meals, dishes like eggs benedict. In other societies, what's served at breakfast may be very similar or even the same as what appears on the menu at another mealtime. Or breakfast may be a passing thought, a little something to break the fast but more substantial meals are served at midday. This is evidenced in the language used to describe different means. In French, *petit déjeuner* means the little breaking of the fast, or breakfast. Lunch, *déjeuner*, is the "breaking of the fast." Breakfast is of middling importance in France, perhaps a little bread and some coffee, at times accompanied with a little fruit or yogurt.

Americans also enjoy snack foods, a bite of something to eat between meals to stave off hunger. A normal snack for American kids after school may involve fried potato chips, sugary cookies, and other industrialized, processed foods. The practice of snacking is unfamiliar to many other cultures around the world. In France, for instance, eating between mealtimes is a relatively new invention, a habit adopted from the Americans. In fact, the French term for snacking is "*le snacking*," a Gallization of the English term "snacking."

Avoidances also involve the role of culture and environment in influencing dietary preferences and habits. Religious practices also impact dietary habits, including proscribing rules about that which is forbidden or taboo. Lev. 11:7–8 points out that pigs have divided hooves and do not chew the cud. An observant Jew who follows kosher dietary laws would be unlikely to partake of a pepperoni and cheese pizza. Pepperoni is made of pork, which is forbidden for consumption. Kosher dietary laws also prohibit the mixing of milk and meat, in this case represented through the presence of pepperoni and cheese. Likewise, an observant Muslim (a follower of Islam) would likely eschew pork. Observant Muslims follow *halal*, or that which is lawful, and avoid things considered *haram* (unlawful). The Qur'anic verse 5:5 deal with slaughter, pointing out the proper way to kill animals and dictating what is appropriate for consumption—what is *halal*.

2.2 Food for thought: Eat what bugs you

The United Nations Food and Agricultural Organization (FAO) stresses that eating insects is important to help our future food security. Though many accustomed to Western diets may balk at insects, they have been part of our diets since our hunter-gatherer days. Entomophagy continues to be regularly practiced in parts of Asia, Africa, and Latin America by roughly two billion people. Producing insects requires significantly less land, water, and resources, and also results in less environmental pollution in the farm of animal waste and greenhouse gases, than producing animal proteins. Scientists note that eating insects can provide a relatively inexpensive, nutritionally rich form of protein that is less stressful on the planet (see Food and Agriculture Organization 2013).

While bugs have been on the menu in places like Thailand, Mexico, and Zimbabwe for quite some time, they are also finding their way onto the American palate and not just as novelty items meant to titillate and scare. Protein powders made of ground-up insects are all the rage, appearing in nutritional shakes, cookies, chips, and even energy bars. Restaurants are also purposefully featuring bugs on a menu as tasty treats (Gordinier 2010). The growing popularity of bugs shows how taste preferences can change over time.

Further resources

Chapul Cricket Protein Bars www.chapul.com.
Exo Protein Bars www.exoprotein.com.
Dicke, Marcel (2010). Marcel Dicke: Why Not Eat Insects?
    [Video file]. Retrieved from https://www.ted.com/talks/
    marcel_dicke_why_not_eat_insects.

Since the earliest days of our species, humans have been in a constant battle against nature to control our access to and supply of food. Our evolution over the millennia has taken into account our responses to the environments around us. Our earliest existence as foragers (also known as hunter-gatherers) made us largely vulnerable to the world around. In lesser developed societies and in food insecure environments, the choice and range of foods available can be limited. Given the wide range of foods available to humans, we have also developed a series of rules, habits, and customs around food to regulate our eating habits. These have resulted in food classifications and rules, both formal and informal, guiding the way we cook. These rules are socially constructed. That is to say, these are not rooted in biology but on a society or

FIGURE 2.1 *Grilled starfish for sale at a street vendor in Beijing, China. Photo courtesy of the author.*

culture's ideas of palatability. Anthropologist Mary Douglas reminds us that "dirt" is simply "matter out of place" (Douglas 1966). That is to say, there are no universal laws or rules about what is "dirty" or "bad." But instead, humans socially construct the rules as they see fit based on their society's norms, customs, and cultural practices, as well as considerations of the ecology and surrounding environment (see Figure 2.1).

Evidence of these rules can be seen in *cuisine*. The term cuisine is has its roots in the Latin word *coquere*, meaning to cook, and *cocina*, the place for cooking—the kitchen. *Cocina* eventually morphed into *cucina* (Italian), *cocina* (Spanish), and *cuisine* (in French), *kuche* (in German), and *kukhnya* (Russian). In popular use, the word cuisine often is conflated with high-end, fancy, expensive, gourmet food. The definition in a standard English dictionary is also reductive, taking it to mean food cooked in a certain way or as a style or method of cooking representative of a place, country, or region. These are certainly aspects of cuisine, but in the field of Food Studies, the term cuisine takes on a broader definition.

Food scholars have debated over how to define the term cuisine. Warren Belasco provides one of the most commonly employed definitions. A cuisine has five components composed of a set of "basic foods" selected from broader environment of available edibles, "manipulative techniques" or a distinctive manner of preparing food, "flavor principles" or a distinctive way of seasoning dishes that also becomes representative of group identity, manners and etiquette regarding the acceptable behaviors surrounding consumption, and lastly, the food chain, an infrastructure of how food moves from the place of origin or production to the consumer (Belasco 2008: 20–3).

To the definition of cuisine, anthropologist Sidney Mintz adds another key element: community. He reminds us that

> what makes a cuisine is not a set of recipes aggregated in a book, or a series of particular foods associated with a particular setting, but something more. I think a cuisine requires a population that eats cuisine with sufficient frequency to consider themselves experts on it. They all believe, and *care* that they believe, they know what it consists of, how it is made, and how it should taste. In short, a genuine cuisine has common social roots, it is the food of a community—albeit often a very large community. (Mintz 1996: 94–96)

Mintz's key point is that cuisine is far more than dishes or cooking, but it is about people producing and reproducing this food because they have feelings and assign value to it. As Stephen Mennell points out, "Ways of cooking become woven into the mythology and the identity of nations, social classes and religious groups. People take sides, and exaggerate differences" (Mennell 1985: 3).

Cuisine is often associated with the world of the elite. High-end and fancy cooking is what food scholars call "haute cuisine" (see Goody 1982; Trubek 2000; Ferguson 2004). This type of cuisine is often heavily rule bound, codified in recipes and texts, and highly structured, and is often, although not always, the purview of professional cooks (see Figure 2.2). Culinary institutions like the Culinary Institute of America train students in haute cuisine methods. This type of cuisine is reflective of the tastes of an elite socioeconomic group, as well as those who are trained in its tastes to serve them.

Cuisine takes on different meanings and can become the flag, so to speak, of a people. National cuisines stand in for national identity and cultural homogeneity, both imagined and real. Cuisines have become more important with the formation of the modern nation state. To illustrate, Italian cuisine (along with Mexican and Chinese) is one of the most popular types of food in America. Yet what we consider to be Italian cuisine only began to emerge in the nineteenth century following the unification of Italy in 1871 (see Capatti and

Montanari 2003; Helstosky 2004). Previously the peninsula was composed of different kingdoms, each highly distinct from the other in terms of language, culture, and, of course, food. Arjun Appadurai notes that national cuisines are invented; that communities can be formed through the formation of a national cuisine (Appadurai 1988).

National dishes themselves represent values and may represent specific communities within a nation. Many nations pride themselves on having a national dish: Belgian waffles are strongly associated with the small European nation of Belgium and sushi with Japan. But national dishes can also change over time. Fish and chips, and more recently, Chicken Tikka Masala (CTM) has taken over as the "national dish" of England. CTM is a dish of roasted marinated chicken cooked in a spiced curry sauce. Its origins are debated, but it was likely invented by a British Bangladeshi cook in the United Kingdom. This shift from fish and chips to CTM is meaningful, reflecting migration,

FIGURE 2.2 *A duck press used to make the sauce for pressed duck* (Canard à la presse), *a complex dish representative of classical French haute cuisine. Photo courtesy of the author.*

multiculturalism, and new sensibilities of who the British think they are (and want to say they are).[3]

National cuisines are about identity (creating and reinforcing a community through food), as well as differentiation, a statement proclaiming "our" food is not like *their* food and thus we are not like them. Sometimes nations fight over who invented or owns a dish. For instance, the fight over the rights to *hummus*[4] via the "hummus wars," a series of competitions between Syria, Lebanon, Israel, and Palestine were never just gastronomic statements but were ways of expressing geopolitical dominance in a tense Middle East. These countries competed to produce the world's largest bowl of hummus and also bickered over who is the true inventor of the dish (see Ariel 2012; Avieli 2016).

Thus leads us to our second parameter regarding food: morals. Food is not neutral but instead carries ideological and symbolic weight. Tastes are acquired and appetites are civilized through morals and manners (Elias 1978; Mennell 1985).

2.3 Activity: Menu analysis

Examining menus is one way to learn about what a society or group considers or considered food. Whether historic or current, menus serve as a time capsule representing the tastes, values, and ingredients—the cuisine of a moment. Menus are one of many primary sources food scholars use to study food.

Primary sources are documents or objects that were created during the time under study. They provide insight on a particular event. Food-related primary sources can include original documents like cookbooks, menus, recipe cards, restaurant reviews, and diaries; creative works like paintings and art; as well as relicts and artifacts like cookware, pottery, and even buildings such as kitchens in historic homes.

This activity focuses on menus. Food scholars are increasingly turning their attention to historic menus to understand the lives and eating habits of people in the past. Chefs and restaurants also consult menus, as inspiration for their contemporary menus.[5] Major menu collections exist at The New York Public Library, The Culinary Institute of America Menu Collection, and The Los Angeles Public Library, among others.

Discussion questions

● Describe the document. Consider the size, shape, color, physical characteristics, and the content it contains. Consider the paper quality, font, illustrations, and the feel of the document. How big is the menu?

- Who was the creator(s)? Who was the audience(s) of these documents?
- What is the cuisine served? How do you know? Look at the clues provided.
- What does the document tell us about social class and status? Use listed prices, prices adjusted for inflation, menu items, ingredients, and so on as clues.
- What might these documents have meant to the historical actors who created them or encountered them?
- What kind of beliefs about the past might they provide evidence for (or against)?
- How do we know your analysis is correct?
- What information does the menu leave off? What questions remain?
- What do meals of the past tell us about what we considered "edible"? How has this changed?

Instructor's note

This activity can be turned into an essay assignment. This activity works best with paper menus, but can easily be conducted with online menus and digital collections. This activity can work with a range of menus across place, time, and space or can also be modified to focus on a theme (e.g., diners, menus from the 1950s, airline menus).

Further resources

Greenstein, Lou (1994). *A La Carte: A Tour of Dining History.* Glen Cove, NY: PBC International.
Heimann, J. (2011). *Menu Design in America: A Visual and Culinary History of Graphic Styles and Design 1850–1985.* Köln, Germany: Taschen
Wright, W. and E. Ransom (2005). "Stratification on the Menu: Using Restaurant Menus to Examine Social Class." *Teaching Sociology*, 33(3), 310–316.

Some notable menu collections

Cornell University Library
https://rare.library.cornell.edu/collections/food-wine/menus.
The Culinary Institute of America
http://ciadigitalcollections.culinary.edu/cdm/landingpage/collection/p16940coll1.
The Los Angeles Public Library
https://www.lapl.org/collections-resources/visual-collections/menu-collection.

The New York Public Library
http://menus.nypl.org.
US Navy Department Library—Menus from Ship to Shore
https://www.history.navy.mil/research/library/manuscripts/m/menus-from-
    ship-to-shore.html.
This collection focuses on naval menus and is a site to explore themed
    menus.

Morals

When I ask my students about some of the best food that they've ever eaten, invariably many of them will mention the food of maternal figures: mothers, aunts, and grandmothers. Grandmothers hold a particular place in the construction of food. People often have a tendency to equate grandmothers (and other family elders) with goodness, nurture, and other feminine qualities of empathy and care. Popular imagery and writings reinforce these stereotypes of cooking as a form of maternal care. As of this writing, a brief search on Amazon, one of the world's largest booksellers, reveals that there are 709 cookbooks with "grandma" in the title. There are also 209 cookbooks with "grandmother" in the title. Grandpa is far less popular, with ninety-one listings, and "grandfathers" only have nineteen references. Clearly, the terms "grandma" and "grandmother" evoke certain feelings about food, nurture, and care.

Grandmothers remain potent in popular discourse, especially among food advocates like Michael Pollan, because they evoke morality. Take, for instance, journalist and food writer Michael Pollan's now-infamous advice. In his book *Food Rules: An Eater's Manual* (2009), he declares that people shouldn't "eat anything their great grandmother wouldn't recognize as food" (2009: 7). This is his second rule, following his first: "eat food," by which he means avoiding what he calls "edible foodlike substances" and "industrial novelties" (2009: 5).

But what if your grandmother was none of the above? What if your grandmother was a terrible cook? In my own family, my maternal grandmother was a horrendous cook. My step-grandfather was actually the gourmand of the family, and would spend hours pouring over cookbooks and reading newspapers for food inspiration. He'd even special order cookbooks from Hong Kong, hot off the presses, so he could stay afloat with food trends. My grandmother was not to be trusted in the kitchen. Things were always underdone and under-seasoned, dishes were never washed properly, and food was never "clean." She even once started a small kitchen fire.

So what's your grandma or great grandmother like? Does she fit the romantic stereotype created and reinforced by food writers like Pollan?

Perhaps she was more like mine, who could not be trusted in the kitchen. Maybe you never met your grandmother and don't have any memories to fall on. Pollan's rule to eat like your great grandmother invokes nostalgia and romanticism for the past, overlooking the sometimes cold realities. What if your great grandmother's food was simply awful? What if she struggled to have enough to eat?

My maternal great grandmother lived in rural China, was illiterate and had bound feet, and married at fifteen in an arranged marriage, carried out from the family home in a sedan chair on her wedding day. That fateful journey, which took her from her girlhood residence to her new marital home, was the farthest she had ever traveled in her life. Her life, which spanned the first half of the twentieth century, was punctuated by wars, revolutions, famines, and bad harvests during late imperial and early Communist China. My mother recalls my great grandmother preparing meals for the family: a simple fare of rice, vegetables, and, once a month, a little meat. Under the planned economy of Communist China, all of these items were strictly rationed by the state government. Because my great grandmother's mobility was limited by her bound feet, she sent my mother and uncle to buy food as part of their chores. On one occasion she mixed up the expiration date on the family's ration tickets, and they were left to scrounge and make do with what they had until the next month's allotments were doled out. My great grandmother hobbled to the government office to plead her case to exchange her expired tickets for new ones; to have them take pity on an old woman. My mother still recalls this experience with sad bitterness, about the difficulties of this time period. Needless to say, I have no rose-tinted feelings about my great grandmother's life, food, or her diet.

Food scholars caution us to be careful with Pollan's glib claims (Laudan 2001). While sound bites from Pollan are certainly catchy, they are divorced from historical and sociopolitical context. Historian Rachel Laudan reminds us that Pollan and others celebrate culinary luddism—the slow, old, romanticized foodways of a bygone time, "a past sharply divided between good and bad, between the sunny rural days of yore and the grey industrial present" (Laudan 2001: 36). Built into his claims is an assumption that everyone's great grandmother would have had gastronomically rich diets. That their dinner tables would have been wonderfully decorated and stomachs always full and content. It is easy to disrupt this narrative by returning to facts and grounding ourselves in historical context. My point here is not to critique the use of grandmothers in food discourse but to show how morality is an important part of defining food.

At the turn of the twenty-first century, there has been a growing interest in old foodways. This is evidenced in the rise of Slow Food, an international organization founded in 1989, which states that its mission is to "prevent the disappearance of local food cultures and traditions, counteract the rise of fast life and combat people's dwindling interest in the food they eat, where it comes from and how our food choices affect the world around us" (Slow Food International 2015). There has also been growing interest in farming as an occupation among young people in the United States (see Mitchell 2015). There has also been a return to traditional food-making practices such as baking your own sourdough, baking your own bread, and preserving food. This has been described by food scholars and commentators loosely as a return of artisanal food (Cope 2014), which could be interpreted as a moral statement against the seemingly globalized, industrialized food system.

Historian Rachel Laudan calls this the rise of culinary luddites (Laudan 2001). Culinary luddies invoke romantic, nostalgic notions of the past in their culinary creations. Words like artisanal, craft, small batch, handmade, homemade, independent are moral judgements. Laudan points out that this food movement presupposes that "food should be fresh and natural has become an article of faith" (Laudan 2001: 36). As we can see, nostalgia about what food was is an expression of morality. It presupposes that the past held a better way of eating.

Laudan cautions against this rose-colored view of the past, reminding us that "natural was something quite nasty" until the recent past (Laudan 2001: 36). What concerned Americans at the turn of the twentieth century was food contamination—adulteration through human hands. Harvey Levenstein points out that food that we, today, consider to be "good" and "natural"—foods like milk—were often adulterated and dangerous to consume (Levenstein 1980).

People have long been concerned about eating what is "right." As the example above suggests, eating the right stuff is also a conversation about morality, for eating something socially incorrect might garner judgment. Today's food campaigners use morality to push and cajole the public into better eating habits. British celebrity chef Jamie Oliver, who has worked to improve school food, has been met with lots of resistance. The parents of the schoolchildren whose meals he was trying to reform pushed back—they didn't like being told their food was wrong because it felt like an attack on *them* (Hollows and Jones 2010; Warin 2011).

Manners

Imagine that you have won a contest and are invited to dine at a nice French restaurant. As you take your seat at the table and place your order, you notice the server arranging an array of objects in front of you. To your left, he places a fork, on the right, a knife and spoon. There is also a water glass and, perhaps, also a plate for bread and a knife for butter. Today, this is what one has come to expect for a "proper" and "nice" meal in a Western-style restaurant. But if we were to travel back in time to Renaissance Europe (c. 1300 to 1700) and were invited to dine at the illustrious table of some lords and ladies, we would find ourselves at a loss on how to conduct ourselves properly.

For one, we would have to "BYOK"—bring your own knives. Today, while it is acceptable in some restaurants to BYOB (bring your own beverages), often a special wine or premium liquor, or to BYOB at a casual gathering among friends, such as a barbecue or community potluck, we would never be expected to bring our own utensils to a party or to a restaurant. But during medieval and Renaissance Europe, everyone carried their own personalized eating knife in a sheath. The practice of BYOK remained firmly in place until the seventeenth century, after which hosts began to supply table knives and the shape of the knife was modified to be less threatening. These new smaller, single-edged table knives were joined not long after by their new mate, the fork. Though archeological evidence suggests there were fork-like objects used in early civilizations, the fork as we know it today was not widely accepted in Europe until around 1700. Forks allowed diners to eat without contamination—without sullying their fingers or spoiling the food with theirs—and thus safely abiding by the new standards of manners. This anecdote illustrates how manners and the concept of acceptable behaviors at dinner table have evolved over time. Our ideas of "good taste" at the dinner table are not simply about what tastes good from an alimentary sense, but what is good from a social sense—what is seen as classy as opposed to trashy.

Manners are part of the food rules, spoken and spoken, in a society. *Food rules* are cultural classifications or folk taxonomies. These rules have little or nothing to do with nutrition or health, but often fit greater ideas of what a group of people considers to be acceptable. When looking at the food rules of any given group, we quickly realize that the rules vary widely and can be, at times, arbitrary. What is good to some is bad to others.

Manners have been a source of anxiety and can lead to political snafus. A famous incident in 1939 helps illuminate this point. With Europe on the brink of World War II, the United States sought to create closer diplomatic ties with Great Britain. Then president Franklin D. Roosevelt and first lady Eleanor Roosevelt invited King George VI and Queen Elizabeth for a diplomatic visit to the United States, including a trip to their country home in Hyde Park, New York. The Roosevelts famously served hot dogs to the royals at a country picnic, despite worries from various advisors that the meal was far too informal for such dignitaries.

The menu for the infamous picnic on June 11, 1939

Virginia Ham
Hot dogs
Cold turkey
Sausages (hot)
Cranberry jelly
Green salad
Rolls
Strawberry shortcake
Coffee
Beer
Soft drinks
(Anon 1939)

For most Americans, this seems like a perfectly delightful menu that one might find at a casual picnic on a nice summer day. But for the visiting British royals, the etiquette of how to consume these items was befuddling.

The *New York Times* and the American public were seemingly charmed by King George VI's willingness to dive right in. Headlines on the next day's front page proclaimed, "KING TRIES HOT DOG AND ASKS FOR MORE; and He Drinks Beer with Them" (Belair Jr. 1939). News reports from that era note the king enjoyed his the American way, eating his hot dogs with his hands and fingers, while his consort chose to attack hers with a fork and knife.

Today, this story seems so innocent, but imagine if the picnic had not gone well. What if the British had rejected the meal? What if they had been offended at its simplicity? How might the American public have viewed the British if they did not embrace this occasion? Though this seems like but a footnote in time, historians often credit this hot dog incident as an important moment in shaping Anglo-American relations. Shortly after this picnic, Great Britain declared war on Germany and entered into World War II. Later in the war, in part due to the alliances forged during this visit, Americans also entered the war in support of our British allies.

This excerpt from history leads us into examining the importance of manners. Rules about how to eat shape our behavior around the dining table and are also a reflection of one's moral character and values. Despite being taught a new set of rules on how to enjoy a cuisine, the royals at this dinner were hesitant about jumping in. After all, doing so would be an act of consciously undoing and unlearning everything one has been taught about "proper" public behavior.

Proper etiquette, or following the right code of polite behavior in society, is important because it signals to others that you belong. The Emily Post Institute, the doyenne of etiquette and appropriate behavior in America, considers the following to be the top ten table manners. Table manners have evolved over centuries to make the practice of eating with others pleasant and sociable. With so many table manners to keep track, keep these basic but oh-so-important table manners in mind as you eat:

1. Chew with your mouth closed.

2. Keep your smartphone off the table and set to silent or vibrate. Wait to check calls and texts until you are finished with the meal and away from the table.

3. Don't use your utensils like a shovel or stab your food.

4. Don't pick your teeth at the table.

5. Remember to use your napkin.

6. Wait until you're done chewing to sip or swallow a drink. (Choking is clearly an exception.)

7. Cut only one piece of food at a time.

8. Avoid slouching and don't place your elbows on the table while eating (though it is okay to prop your elbows on the table while conversing between courses, and always has been, even in Emily's day).

9. Instead of reaching across the table for something, ask for it to be passed to you.

10. Take part in the dinner conversation.

(Anon n.d.)

Now contrast Emily Post's rules for proper American dining with those given for Chinese dining. Hsu and Hsu write (1977: 304):

The typical Chinese dining table is round or square, the ts'ai [side dishes] are laid in the center, and each participant in the meal is equipped with a bowl for fan, a pair of chopsticks, a saucer, and a spoon. All take from the ts'ai dishes as they proceed with the meal.

At the Chinese table, toothpicks are also provided at the table. It is not rude to pick through one's teeth at the table, as long as one covers one's mouth with the opposite hand.

It is important to note that the types of table manners written down in etiquette books are normally guidelines for public consumption. In the private sphere, often diners take on more informal rules. The things that would be unacceptable in a polite, public setting may be perfectly permissible, maybe even encouraged in private at home. Table manners are, in fact, "social agreements," devised to avoid violence at the dinner table (and elsewhere) (Visser 2015).

Table manners became important in Europe during the Renaissance for these reasons. Returning to an earlier discussion of the knife and the fork, both of these cutlery items were introduced to the table as ways to regulate behaviors—to promote a new sensibility about civility and manners. Codified rules, such as those presented in etiquette books and manuals, regulate public behavior and are part of the "civilizing process." Status-anxious individuals throughout history have been conscientious about learning the proper behavior to fit in.

Consider a scene from the film *Tampopo* (1985). In one vignette, a group of well-to-do ladies who lunch are taking an etiquette class. The instructor, a coiffed woman, gently instructs the group that the proper way to eat Italian pasta is with a fork and spoon. She adds that noodles should be eaten without making a sound. This is difficult for some of the women because of what they had been taught as children. In Japan, it is customary to slurp noodles loudly to show appreciation for the dish. The camera cuts away to a table with a solitary Western male diner and he is slurping and eating animatedly. The women begin happily slurping away at their pasta and reluctantly the instructor joins them.

Renaissance diners were concerned with proper eating behaviors as a reflection of their self-fashioning and proper morality. Scholars of Japan note that women in Japan today still take lessons on proper etiquette and eating, anxious about their status (White 2001). This practice is also common in the West. Many business schools in the United States send their soon-to-be graduates to mock lunch interviews. These classes teach young people how to conform to social norms of civility and acceptable behavior. In these classes, people learn things like which forks to use with what meal, where to set the bread, and also what foods should be appreciated hot and which ones cold. For instance, *gazpacho*, a cold tomato-based soup from Spain, and *vichyssoise*, a cold vegetable soup from France, should be appreciated lightly chilled. The old wives' tale often goes that some bright-eyed job seeker failed their interview because they sent the soup back to the kitchen to be reheated, not realizing that this soup is meant to be served chilled. This suggests that manners are not simply about eating properly, but also showing the right status and cultural knowledge. Not knowing that *gazpacho* and *vichysoisse* are chilled soups suggests one is déclassé (and perhaps not a "right fit" for the type of organization whose management would appreciate such dishes). Eating right is about showing you belong.

Proper eating is such a concern that it is a school subject in many countries around the world. The French are probably the most associated with the concept of lunch as a lesson. Students are taught how to set a table, dine, and appreciate food. Learning how to eat properly is also learning how to fit in to society. Of course, formal manners and etiquette are not held in the same esteem across all societies. Etiquette and manners appear to be more important in societies where there is a regular food supply. Anthropologist Alan R. Holmberg notes that among the Siriono, a seminomadic hunting and gathering indigenous group located in the forested regions of Bolivia, acquiring food is the main priority. In regard to eating habits, "People eat when they have food . . . Eating takes place without etiquette or ceremony. Food is bolted rapidly as possible, and when a person is eating he never looks up from his food until he has finished . . . The principal goal of eating seems thus to be swallowing the greatest quantity of food in the shortest possible time" (Holmberg 1977: 157).

2.4 Activity: Explaining the rules

Imagine you are on the committee to welcome international students to your campus. These students have not spent any time in the country prior to arrival and most of their knowledge about local customs and foods are from popular movies, social media, and internet videos. What are some things they should know about the unspoken food rules? What might you tell them about the unofficial rules about how we eat, the things that are seemingly normal to those who grew up in this country but are never written down in guidebooks.

A few unspoken American food rules from my students include:

- Beverages come with free refills.
- Cold beverages must be served with lots of ice.
- The five-second rule: food dropped on the floor can usually be eaten if it's picked up within five seconds.
- It is acceptable to drink coffee all day long.
- Dinner is usually served at around six p.m.

Directions

Brainstorm your own list of American food rules. Write these down on a whiteboard or a large sheet of paper for the entire group to see.

Discussion questions

1. How many rules did your group come up with? Was there agreement about the rules?
2. Did the rules cluster around themes or issues (e.g., the use of silverware versus the use of hands)?
3. Consider ranking the rules. What would be the most important? What would be the least important? Explore what the rankings reveal about American eating habits.

2.5 Activity: Historic recipe interpretation

One way to think about how meals, morals, and manners converge to become food is to look at recipes and dishes of the past. Historic recipe interpretation is a fun and thought-provoking activity. Students are pushed to assess their knowledge base, rethink their biases, and appreciate food in a different way when they are asked to recreate it and experience the past first hand.

Directions

1. Identify a series of recipes and a time period for study. Listed below are some collections of historic recipes.
2. Before cooking the recipes, read them several times over and decide on some ground rules. How faithful to the time period will you be? What is an acceptable level of substitution for ingredients, techniques, and methods? Will you simply be "inspired" by historic recipes or are you aiming for full historical accuracy?
3. Do your research on how the food would have been served and presented, as well as consumed. Consider how the final consumption setting might influence the preparation.
4. During cooking, record everything. Include cooking times, amount/volume prepared, what techniques were used, how things were cut and prepared, and so on.
5. Everything subjected to interpretation should be recorded and discussed. For instance, if there is an ingredient listed that can't be found and something else was substituted, record the substitution. If a recipe gives a general instruction like "put in pot and boil," record what size pot, how much water was added, what temperature was it boiled at, and so on.

Discussion questions

1. Before cooking: write down your thoughts on the food. What might you imagine the food tasting like? Looking like?
2. After cooking: consider how you approached the recipes. How true were you to the historical moment and context?
3. After cooking: how was it working with primary sources? What challenges did you face?
4. After cooking: what did you think of the food? How did it taste? What was familiar about the food? What was unfamiliar or foreign?

Instructor's note

This activity can be conducted with any number of time periods, but one that is especially rewarding for students to consider is ancient Mesopotamia. Most have no idea what the world's oldest recipes taste like. Because they have no reference point from which to judge, students are asked to put aside the assumptions. This activity can also be modified into a homework assignment if there is no easy access to a communal kitchen.

Further resources

Albala, K. (ed.) (2014). *The Food History Reader: Primary Sources*. London: Bloomsbury.
Bottéro, J. (2004). *The Oldest Cuisine in the World: Cooking in Mesopotamia*. Chicago: University of Chicago Press.
Hess, K. (ed.) (1995). *Martha Washington's Book of Cookery*. New York: Columbia University Press.
Simmons, Amelia (1996). *American Cookery*. Bedford, MA: Applewood.

Summary

- Food is much more than fuel.

- Food is meals, morals, and manners.

- Humans are superomnivores—we experience the omnivore's dilemma of what to eat.

- We put parameters on our food consumption, based on biology, culture, geographical access, as well as taking in our preferences, aversions, fears, and taboos.

- Food habits can—and do—change over time.

- Cuisine and national dishes are used as identity markers.

- Food takes on the tone of morality.

- Humans have ideas about how to eat and enforce these rules as a way of showing inclusion/exclusion in a group.

Discussion questions

1. Who was your great-great grandmother? Consider the details of her life. What would her life been like? Where did she live? What would she have eaten? Would you want to eat what your great-great grandmother ate?

2. Do you experience an omnivore's dilemma? What are your preferences, aversions, fears, and taboos regarding food? What are your boundaries?

3. How has your social environment or culture influenced your views of what you consider food?

Further resources

Documentaries and videos

Great Depression Cooking with Clara is an online cooking show featuring 94-year-old Clara, who came of age during the Great Depression (1929–1939). She reflects on the tastes, recipes, and memories of her life. Her life stories provide a glimpse into what one's great-great grandmother might have eaten. www.greatdepressioncooking.com.

Make Hummus Not War (2012) is about the *hummus* wars in the Middle East as different countries sought the title of the inventor of *hummus*. *Hummus* became a metaphor for other geopolitical struggles in the region.

Townsends is a YouTube channel devoted to eighteenth-century American living. Its videos show historic reenacting of cooking, technology, and lifestyles of the era. https://www.youtube.com/user/jastownsendandson/.

The Victorian Way is a YouTube channel produced by English Heritage, a charity that cares for historic sites across England. This channel has a series of videos reenacting the daily work and cooking of Mrs. Avis Crocombe, head cook at Audley End House in Essex during Victorian England. https://www. youtube.com/playlist?list=PLx2QMoA1Th9deXXbo7htq21CUPqEPPGuc.

Notes

1 The Japanese reverence for *ikizukuri*, a method of preparing and serving sashimi from live seafood, is another example of "fresh" that would be considered reprehensible to diners unaccustomed to this practice.

2 See Anderson (2013) and Carroll (2013) for more on the invention of breakfast as the most important meal of the day.

3 Chicken Tikka Masala has even become a metaphor among politicians for describing contemporary multicultural Britain. See Cook (2001).

4 *Hummus* is a popular dip made of mashed chickpeas, sesame paste (*tahini*), olive oil, lemon juice, salt, and garlic.

5 Some modern restaurants use historic menus for inspiration. Two well-known examples include Dinner by Heston Blumenthal, who takes inspiration from historic British recipes (Dinner by Heston Blumenthal in London and Melbourne is a well-regarded Michelin-starred restaurant headed by British celebrity chef Heston Blumenthal. This restaurant is inspired by historic dishes of Britain's past and the menus even cite the sources of inspiration, such as the *Forme of Curye*, a collection of medieval English recipes from the fourteenth century purportedly from the chief master cooks of King Richard II. Their approach to historic foods is inspiration as opposed to reenactment. www.dinnerbyheston.com. See www.dinnerbyheston.com), and the Four Seasons Restaurant in New York City, whose menu is a tribute to the original Four Seasons Restaurant, the home of the "power lunch" (see http://thegrillnewyork.com).

Further readings

Arndt Anderson, Heather (2013). *Breakfast: A History*. Lanham: Rowman & Littlefield.

Brillat-Savarin, Jean Anthelme (2002). *The Physiology of Taste, or Meditations on Transcendental Gastronomy*. Mineola: Dover Publications.

Douglas, Mary (1997). "Deciphering a Meal." In Carol Counihan and Esterik Van (eds.), *Food and Culture: A Reader*. New York: Routledge.

Elias, Norbert (1978). *The Civilizing Process: The History of Manners*. New York: Urizen Press.

Harris, Marvin (1985). *Good to Eat: Riddles of Food and Culture*. New York: Simon and Schuster.

Levi-Strauss, Claude (1978). *The Origin of Table Manners*. Chicago: University of Chicago Press.

Pollan, Michael (2006). *The Omnivore's Dilemma: A Natural History of Four Meals*. New York: Penguin Press.

Visser, Margaret (1987). *Much Depends on Dinner: The Extraordinary History and Mythology, Allure and Obsessions, Perils and Taboos, of an Ordinary Meal*. New York: Grove Press.

Visser, Margaret (1991). *The Rituals of Dinner: The Origins, Evolution, Eccentricities, and Meaning of Table Manners*. New York: Grove Weidenfeld.

3

Food, Identity, and Culture

Humans are an incredibly diverse species, with great variations in biology and physiology. People have tried to understand and explain these differences since the earliest of times. In this chapter, I focus on four areas of variation: kinship, gender, race, and ethnicity. Kinship, gender, race, and ethnicity are four examples of a *cultural ontology* or taxonomy, a system of classification and evaluation. Many academic fields are interested in these systems of categorization because these categories provide insight on power, access, and social relations.

Kinship, gender, race, and ethnicity also make up some of the most important parts of our social identities: how we see the world as well as how the world sees us as individuals (or as members of a group). What we see in discussing kinship, gender, race, and ethnicity is that it is not simply about defining the terms but also considering how these terms carry with them power and privilege. Furthermore, food becomes a framework for understanding these different systems of classification and evaluation, as well as providing evidence for how these ontologies impact everyday life. Anthropologist Audrey Richards pointed out that food has the greatest determination over the nature of our social groupings and the form of our activities (Richards 1932). Food and beverages can be coded with messages about who one is, where they're from, their gender, and other aspects of one's identity. As this chapter will elucidate, food can be used to bind ties or reinforce divisions. They can be used to create affiliation and belonging, or to demarcate who should be an outsider.

Kinship and commensality

Humans are social beings. For many of us, our families serve as the first point of socialization into the world. Through our families, we learn how to act and function in our given societies. They are the ones who feed, clothe, shelter, and hopefully nurture us into the people we are today.

A *family* is a group of people who are related in some way, either by ancestry or "blood" (*consanguine*), or marriage (*affine*). It can include parents, stepparents, children, stepchildren, siblings, grandparents, grandchildren, uncles, aunts, nephews, nieces, cousins, spouses, siblings-in-law, parents-in-law, and children-in-law. Living among *nuclear family*, composed of parents and their children (and possibly stepparents and stepchildren), is the likely arrangement you were born into and grew up in.

But why would humans bother to care for their young, to transmit their knowledge and values to them? Anthropologists examine how these relationships are formed and why they persist. They recognize that these relationships are essential to human survival, as they establish networks of support and aid for access to food, shelter, clothing, and other necessities. Moreover, these relationships also reflect social ideas and values.

Kinship, how family members define their affiliation with one another, is socially constructed. That is to say, it is based on learning, and varies from culture to culture. Systems of kinship reflect cultural values. For instance, if you grew up in the Western world, you likely lived among your nuclear family. In contrast, grandparents, parents, and children often share a home as an extended family in many other parts of the world. Fictive kin also play a role in families. Individuals who claim no consanguinal (blood) or affinal (marriage) ties yet are important to the family are called *fictive kin*. You may know them as the family friend who is like an uncle or aunt, or someone close to you that you consider a brother or sister. Though not all kin live together, its members may gather from time to time.

Holidays and celebrations are occasions for reuniting kin members, and food is often involved in festivities. Therefore, an important part of kinship bonding is *commensality*, the act of eating and sharing food together. Commensality can strengthen social bonds and create unity.

3.1 Activity: Cooking stone soup

Stone Soup is an old folktale that begins with the story of several travelers. This group of travelers enters a village with nothing more than the clothes on their back and an empty cooking pot. The curious villagers gather to greet the visitors, who promise to share tales of their adventures in exchange for food. The villagers are unwilling to share their food. The travelers shrug off the villagers' indifference and say they will make stone soup instead, which is made by taking a stone, placing it in the pot, filling it with water, and cooking it over a fire. The travelers proclaim they would be happy to share their soup with any villagers, but that it would taste better with some additional garnishes and vegetables. The curious villagers begin to contribute different items: a bit of seasoning, a few vegetables, each adding something to the communal pot. Finally, the stone is removed from the pot and a delightful soup is shared by the travelers and villagers—an act of *commensality*.

Equipment

Heavy saucepan or soup pot
Cutting board
Knife
Wooden spoon or silicone spatula
Stone or large rock (cleaned free of debris)

Directions

1. Gather a variety of ingredients. Get creative with the theme of your stone soup. Stone soup can be made with vegetable peelings and food trim, leftovers, and ugly vegetables.
2. Place the stone or rock in a heavy pot. Add ingredients and fill the pot with water. Cook until the soup reaches your desired taste and consistency.

Instructor's note

Stone soup can only be made through the efforts and contributions of a group. This can be assigned as a homework exercise by encouraging students to get their "contributions" from roommates, friends, relatives, neighbors, and so on.

It is probably easier to stick to a meatless version of stone soup for sanitary and cultural reasons. Meat scraps are more difficult to deal with (and carry a higher risk of food-borne illness). Some religions have prohibitions against certain types of meat (e.g., pork is especially problematic).

If done in a classroom setting without kitchen access, consider making stone soup over a hotplate, slow cooker, or an InstaPot. Start the soup at beginning of class and end class by sending everyone off with a serving of stone soup.

Discussion questions

1. The story of stone soup is often used to illustrate the concept of commensality. Explain why.
2. What ingredients does your stone soup feature? Where did these ingredients come from? What stories do the ingredients tell?
3. Who helped fill the pot? Who ended up dining from the communal pot? What might this suggest about your social networks and who shares food?

Family commensality has been idealized in popular culture. Consider the classic Norman Rockwell (1943) painting, *Freedom from Want*. In this painting, extended kin gather together at a holiday table. Fine china and a crisp white tablecloth adorn the table, around which happy faces await in anticipation. Standing at the head of the table is the matriarch holding a perfect golden-brown roast turkey. Behind her is the patriarch, his hands hovering over a pair of carving utensils, ready to cut and provision meat to his eager kin.

The popularity of this painting suggests it serves as an ideal of kinship and commensality. Television families like those on the sitcom *Modern Family* and the long-running animated comedy *The Simpsons* have parodied this scene. Artists have recreated countless renditions of this painting with Disney characters, comic book superheroes, and celebrities. But do your family celebrations resemble this painting? Does your family look like the one portrayed? Or is this only a romanticized vision? The pervasiveness of this scene speaks to the idealization of family commensality in broader culture.

Family meals have been put on a pedestal and championed as the proverbial glue that holds a family together. Eating a cooked meal at home suggests intimacy. In Western societies, family dinners have been celebrated as an important event for family cohesion (DeVault 1991; Ochs, Pontecorvo, and Fasulo 1996; Grieshaber 1997; Kendall 2008), for they suggest the presence of a "proper family" (Douglas 1972). A quick search on Amazon's US site for the phrase "family dinner" returns over 2,000 hits, with book titles like *The Family Dinner: Great Ways to Connect with Your Kids, One Meal at a Time* (David and Uhrenholdt 2010); *Dinner: A Love Story: It all begins at the Family Table* (Rosenstrach 2012); *Dinner: The Playbook: A 30-Day Plan for Mastering the Art of the Family Meal* (Rosenstrach 2014)—titles that play into the notion that home-cooked meals eaten in a domestic setting are important.

Everyday wisdom suggests that home-cooked meals eaten together would promote positive socialization and commensality, with adults helping socialize children as they transition to adulthood and adult discussion. Food advocates like Michael Pollan (2008) heavily champion family dining, focusing on its importance to the nuclear family. He writes, "The shared meal elevates eating from a mechanical process of fueling the body to a ritual of family and community, from the mere animal biology to an act of culture" (2008: 189). For Pollan, commensality is especially important for families. He argues that eating dinner together every night is the best way for children to learn how to interact with the wider world. Indeed, there is evidence to support claims that family dinners are useful for socialization (Ochs and Shohet 2006; Sterponi 2009; Blum-Kulka 2012), may promote better dietary habits and health (Gillman et al. 2000; Neumark-Sztainer et al. 2004; Taveras et al. 2005; Hammons and Fiese 2011), and help keep children from adopting high-risk behaviors (Fulkerson et al. 2006).

Many social commentators and academics have lamented the decline of family meals, tracing the source of contemporary social ills back to this activity. It is not simply the decline of the meal that is being mourned, but what it symbolizes and suggests—certain moralities and beliefs about our societies and ourselves. Eating together is suggestive of "purity" and "order"—an intact family that is harmonious (c.f. Douglas 1972).

For all of our romanticization of and interest in family meals, it is important to note that eating together is far more complicated than it sounds. It has become a source of stress in different ways. For those families already eating meals together, but perhaps on-the-go, there is the issue of time. Researchers contend that it is not simply the act of eating together that is meaningful, but that families need to spend at least a specific amount of time together for those bonds to make an impact. The amount, of course, varies depending on the research. Another consideration is that census data suggests that the nightly family meal is simply unachievable for some. To put it in context, living alone has become more widespread, with approximately thirty-two million one-person households in America. Single-parent households account for 9 percent of families in the United States. Gathering around the dinner table as a nuclear family headed by two heterosexual parents and their children is not possible (or perhaps even desirable) for a significant number of Americans. It reflects an aspirational fantasy rather than the reality of everyday life and the constraints of managing different schedules (c.f. Charles and Kerr 1988).

It is important to remember that "family" is a falsely monolithic concept (DeVault 1991: 15) and with it we assume certain moral overtones about what a family *should* be rather than what families are. For instance, this aspirational fantasy overlooks social changes to what it means to be a family, including families headed by two same-sex parents. Furthermore, there is an assumption that families are harmonious, when research shows that families may be sources of dysfunctionality. Eating together may be undesirable, as the dinner table may be a place of tension and conflict rather than respite and bonding. It is important to remember that family meals may involve eating food you dislike with relatives you don't particularly care for (Bove, Sobal, and Rauschenbach 2003; Bove and Sobal 2006).

Scholars remind us that there has been anxiety about the so-called decline of family meals for quite some time. Sociologist Anne Murcott questions this decline, making a point to separate the perceived threat from something that is felt to be lacking (Murcott 1997: 37). Additionally, Jackson et al. reminds us the myths of the family meal have persisted for decades, if not centuries (Jackson, Olive, and Smith 2009). To illustrate, Britons in Edwardian England before World War I were already worried about the decline of the family meal and what it meant for changing social mores. These worries persist in contemporary headlines today.[1] It appears that our present concern about the decline of family meals is not a new panic, but an old one that is ongoing.

Furthermore, there is an assumption that everything eaten at the family dinner table will be home-cooked, perhaps lovingly made from scratch by a family member. Yet as social norms, work patterns, and product availability have changed, the boundaries of what constitutes a family meal have been expanded. Eating together may involve incorporating convenience or even fast food products. Swedish families often choose to dine at McDonald's, as this fast food establishment serves as an ersatz home and, therefore, meals served there constitute "proper" family meals. For parents of young children, this is one of the easiest ways to maintain the ideal of family dining, and has expanded the boundaries of what "family" and "home" mean in modern Swedish life (Brembeck 2005).

Those whose eating practices differ from the rest of their family may find that they are ostracized at the dinner table. Folklorist LuAnn K. Roth observes that vegetarians are initially perceived by their families to be "unpatriotic, un-American, and even downright un-family like" for rejecting meat (Roth 2005: 188). And, of course, we assume that families like one another or that family dinners always go smoothly. There is an assumption that everyone will simply eat what is at the dinner table, an imagined commensality that is often perpetuated in popular culture. Dinner tables can actually be intense sites of conflict. Family dinners are subject to negotiation, as parents may have to cajole, beg, probe, praise, and bargain with their children to get them to eat (Ochs and Shohet 2006). Generational conflicts also come to a head at the table, where different sets of values and ideologies can clash, leading to a "contested table." Simone Cinnotto's work on Italian Americans notes that younger Italian Americans and their immigrant parents clashed over values and beliefs, but also through food. He points out that younger Italian Americans in East Harlem, New York, in the early twentieth century were likely to dismiss their parents' food habits as "embarrassing expressions of an inferior culture," and "immigrant foodways were symptoms of ignorance, backwardness, and poverty" (Cinotto 2013: 29).

It is important to remember that the act of eating together, participating in family commensality is not necessarily just about furthering social connections, promoting positive eating habits, or encouraging positive social behaviors.

For some, eating together is about survival, first and foremost. As mentioned previously, it is important to remember that family can be a falsely monolithic concept (DeVault 1991: 15), which fails to take into account the diversity of family and household arrangements today. "Family," as implied in the romanticized and idealized interpretation of the term, discussion of family meals, implies a nuclear family headed by two heterosexual parents. This Standard North American Family (SNAF) shapes people's ideal views of family life and has formed the dominant narrative of what we consider family life to be (Smith 1993). It has also created anxiety among those who do not confirm to this model and becomes a yardstick for measuring their own families (Hertz 2006; Nelson 2006). Instead, other scholars contend that it is important to remember that a " 'family' is not a naturally occurring collection of individuals; its reality is constructed from day to day through activities like eating together" (DeVault 1991: 39).

Family may in fact span several generations and even include fictive kin. In some cultures, a multigenerational family is the preferred form residence and support. Among some households it may be a way of bringing closeness between different generations of kin. But among others, different generations and types of kin, fictive and real, living together may form a coping mechanism. Poorer families are more likely to live together as a coping strategy. Multigenerational households in America are more likely to be in poverty. Forming a multigenerational family serves as a coping mechanism. It can offer a safety net for people to live and eat together, as it creates a network of social and financial resources by pooling them together. Among the urban poor, fictive kin also play an important role in family survival (c.f. Stack 1975). Sharing resources like food among a broader network of fictive kin is a noted coping strategy. Socioeconomic realities have real implications for kinship and commensality.

Eating together also creates family ties among LGBTQ[2] families, which often do not follow the SNAF model. Scholars who analyze "nontraditional" family structures contend that food help create family. Among lesbian and gay families, Christopher Carrington contends that it is the shared feeding work that denotes family rather than kinship structures. That is to say, "the work of preparing and sharing meals creates family" rather than kinship ties alone (Carrington 2008).

Ultimately, for all the uproar about the loss of family meals, researchers have found that the family meal has not disappeared, but perhaps has been reconceived. In Britain, eating out in restaurants has increased, but home-cooked meals are still integral to daily eating habits. Alan Warde and Martens (Warde and Martens 2000: 107–8) found that 82 percent of those surveyed report cooking a main family meal every day. While dining out, the same respondents (72 percent) reported that they were usually doing so with family members. What we can establish is that family and kinship are important defining aspects of identity, and food, particularly the act of dining together as a family, stands in for notions of morality, family, and kinship.

3.2 Activity: Kinship and commensality

Researchers use kinship charts to understand social relations between family members. Kinship charts are similar to family trees in that they capture lineage and descent. However, there are specific symbols and signs to denote different types of relationships (see Figures 3.1 and 3.2). The purpose of this exercise is to reflect on who you consider kin, and what role these kin members had in feeding and nurturing you—and, also, to consider your role in feeding and nurturing your kin members.

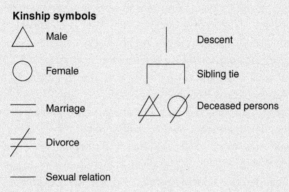

FIGURE 3.1 *Kinship symbols.*

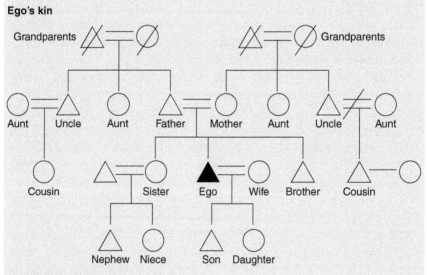

FIGURE 3.2 *Sample kinship chart.*

Materials

Paper
Colored pens, pencils, markers, or crayons
Ruler

Directions

1. Start by drawing yourself, the ego, on the kinship chart. Color "your" symbol. From there, add in the rest of your kin by following the symbols listed above. Make sure each generation of kin is aligned at the same level. Draw straight lines to denote relationships between individuals. A sample chart is given here for reference.
2. Once your chart is complete, grab two different colored pens. Don't pick any colors that have already been used.
3. Pick a color and shade everyone who fed you. It is up to you to interpret what "feeding" means. This can range from heating up leftovers in a microwave to cooking you an elaborate holiday feast.
4. Pick another color and mark everyone who you fed. It is up to you to interpret what "feeding" means.

Discussion questions

1. Who do you consider family? How far are you able to trace your kin?
2. Who were the people responsible for feeding you? How do you define feeding?
3. Who did you feed? How do you define feeding?
4. Are there any overlaps between the two?
5. What types of feeding did each person do? Were they ordinary events (e.g., breakfast) or special occasions (e.g., Christmas, birthdays)?
6. What impact does generation have on feeding and eating roles?
7. What role, if any, did fictive kin have in feeding you?

Further resources

Berzok, L. M. (ed.) (2010). *Storied Dishes: What Our Family Recipes Tell Us about Who We Are and Where We've Been*. Santa Barbara: ABC-CLIO.
Stack, C. B. (1975), *All Our Kin: Strategies for Survival in a Black Community*. New York: Harper Torchbooks.
Williams-Forson, Psyche (2008), "More than Just the 'Big Piece of Chicken.' The Power of Race, Class, and Food in American Consciousness." In Carole Counihan and Penny van Esterik (eds.), *Food and Culture: A Reader*. Routledge: New York.

Sex and gender

Next, we move on to consider gender. Sex and gender are also important aspects of identity. *Gender* is differentiated from biological *sex*. Sex is often used to refer to both biologic sex (male, female, or intersex), as well as sexuality. Nowadays, it is more common to hear the term gender used to refer to male, female, or other gender identities.

Biological sex refers to the chromosomal makeup of a person. Under most circumstances, one either possesses two X chromosomes, making them female, or one X and Y chromosome, making them male. In some circumstances (about 1.7 percent of all human births), one might possess XXY chromosomes and will be an intersex person.

Gender differs in that it is the cultural and historically invented categories and concepts assigned to people based on their physical makeup. Those who are born biologically female (XX) are expected to act in socially defined "feminine" ways, while those born biologically male (XY) are expected to act "masculine." While gender has a biological aspect, what is expected of you based on those biological aspects is the social idea of gender. There are no "natural" gender roles, but rather they are socially constructed. In other words, gender is a "performance" (Butler 1990; Moore 1994). "Doing gender involves a complex of socially guided perceptual, interactional, and micropolitical activities that cast particular pursuits as expressions of masculine and feminine 'natures'" (West and Zimmerman 1987: 132). Thus, what is considered "feminine" or "masculine" varies considerably from place to place, through different time periods, and as social norms evolve. What is constant is that there is pressure in all societies to conform to expected gender roles and identities, particularly if a society has especially rigid gender norms.

These gendered expectations appear to have been part of human social organization since our earliest times. Researchers studying our early human past explain that gender expectations even impacted our early societies. Even among early primates, they suggest, sex and gender shaped the roles people took on in sustaining everyday life. The *sexual division of labor* was present in these early societies, as men and women took on different roles and contributions (Washburn and Lancaster 1968; Gurven et al. 2009; Zeanah 2004). How labor is divided affects not only household subsistence but also society as a whole. During our earliest existence, humans acquired food through hunting and gathering (what is also termed foraging). Males were expected to hunt for food, while females collected raw foods, cooked, and also took care of their offspring.

The sexual division of labor might have arisen out of necessity. But it is distinct from biological determinism, which it is often confused with sexual division of labor. *Biological determinism*, a theory that biological differences between males and females lead to fundamentally different capacities, preferences, and gendered behaviors, shape popular discussions about gender and perpetuate the notion that gender roles are rooted in biology as opposed to cultural expectations. Biological determinism has helped perpetuate the notion that men and women are fundamentally different and suited only toward specific tasks, when archeological and historical records suggest that what each society conceives of as appropriate tasks for each gender has been subjected to change. Even among hunting and gathering societies, it was not always the case that only men hunted. Yet this pattern that men participated in hunting (and eventually, "public" work outside the home), while women took on gathering, cooking, and childcare or domestic activities, continues to shape discourse in many societies today.

Food production, food acquisition, meal preparation, and the practices of food and eating are realms where gendered ideas rise up and are contested. Frances Short reminds us that "power relations and gender roles are established, acknowledged, and represented at the dining and kitchen table" (Short 2006: 3). The work of anthropologists George Murdock and Catarina Provost (1973) helps illustrate the extent to which gender impacts the way we eat. Their systematic study of household food provisioning in 185 cultures concluded that, overall, food work is primarily a female activity. Moreover, women were the primary cooks in 97.8 societies. Murdock and Provost found there were only four societies in which cooking was spread equally between males and females or was considered a predominantly male activity. Thus, "feeding others is women's work. Women collect, prepare, and serve our daily bread. So doing, they care for us. The acts of feeding and caring, as connected to each other as earth to water, maintain and sustain the family" (Stimpson in DeVault 1991: viii).

One pattern we see clearly in the scholarship on food in the West is that the majority of cooking and feeding responsibilities are women's responsibilities. Even when employed outside of the home, women do the vast majority of household chores. Returning to the kinship structure discussed in the previous section, within a family or kinship structure, you may notice that there are certain members that take on more of the "feeding" or "caregiving" role. Among many American families, the heavier burden of buying food, cooking it, and cleaning up often falls to the female members of the family. In households headed by a heterosexual couple, the majority of domestic tasks, including "feeding," falls on the shoulders of the head female member. This is interesting given the rise of women's economic roles outside of the home. Although increasing numbers of men are becoming stay-at-home dads, opting to take on a domestic role, while more women work, their numbers remain in the minority. More significantly, many husbands and wives perceive this to be a "fair" arrangement—that women continue to take on a "second shift" of domestic work on top of their work outside of the home (Gillman et al. 2000). In lesbian and gay families, feeding tasks fall to the less economically dominant partner (Carrington 2008).

Thus, the term "work" seems appropriate to describe the activities necessary to feed and maintain a household. Sociologist Marjorie DeVault describes it as "feeding work," and it can be just that: work and drudgery (DeVault 1991: 38, 55). Moreover, this work is largely "invisible" (Matthews 1987). That is to say, this type of work is discounted as trivial even by the women who participate in it, and is largely overlooked despite its enormous importance to everyday life and the maintenance of a family. Furthermore, cooking involves more than simply getting food to a table. It is "servicing other family members and expending large amounts of energy to ensure that their likes and dislikes were satisfied when preparing those meals" (Endrijonas 2001: 169).

But it is also important to remember that cooking can also be a form of pleasure and pride among women. It is undeniable that cooking demands incredible amounts of temporal, economic, physical, and emotional labor. Social mores in the early twentieth century also dictated that women embrace their homemaking abilities as part of their feminine responsibilities (see Shapiro 2009).

Though the lion's share of feeding work has been women's work, this is not to say that men do not cook or participate in food preparation. Quite the contrary. Men *do* participate in cooking and food work, but often in different ways and to different degrees. Allen and Sachs are careful to point out that women derived power by serving as the gatekeeper of the household's food provisions (Allen and Sachs 2012), to which McIntosh and Zey add that though women are the gatekeepers, men "control their enactment" (McIntosh and Zey 1998: 126). Furthermore, Sobal contends "family meals are masculine means" as "men's food preferences dominate family food choices" (2005: 142).

Richard Wrangham reminds us that there is an important division in cooking: the type of cooking (2009: 148–55). That is to say, men's cooking tends to be public and women's cooking tends to be private and domestic. Women's cooking is done for the family and, as described above, is part of the everyday "drudgery" of running a household economy. This type of cooking tends to be "invisible" and in a private sphere, the home. By contrast, male cooking is done for the community and is public. DeVault attributes to the Industrial Revolution the rise of separate spheres in the West, which placed emphasis on men's work as earning wage outside the home and women's work as "transforming wages into goods and services needed to maintaining the household" (1991: 15).

This division in cooking and the recognition of cooking as labor may be attributed to broader cultural systems and views. Anthropologist Michelle Rosaldo contends that "what is perhaps most striking and surprising is the fact that male, as opposed to female, activities are always recognized as predominantly important, and cultural systems give authority and value to the roles and activities of men" (1974: 19). While her comments are not universally true, they are noteworthy because they do comment upon a wide range of societies and their gender divisions. In particular, Rosaldo noted that in many societies, there are clear divisions between the "domestic" or "private" sphere and the "public" one. She suggested that women are typically relegated to private or domestic spaces like the household, in part because of essentialist views about their gender and women's "nurturing" natures. While women are relegated to private or domestic spaces, they are also kept away from public spaces, which are left under the purview of men. These public spaces are also more economically and politically important.

Indeed, professional cooking—the public, visible, wage-earning type of cooking—is often considered a masculine domain. *Time Magazine*'s November 18, 2013, cover drew backlash from many readers around the globe. Splashed across the cover was "The Gods of Food: Meet the People Who Influence What (and How) You Eat." The three cover figures were American chef David Chang (best known for his Momofuku empire), Brazilian chef Alex Atala (of D. O. M. Restaurant), and Danish chef Rene Redzepi (of Noma Restaurant). The magazine's list of "13 Gods of Food" included no female chefs, although it did name four women leaders in the global food world.

In my own ethnographic work in Cantonese cooking schools in the city of Guangzhou, China, I found that women were not discouraged necessarily from becoming professional cooks. But they were ghettoized into specific types of professional cooking. Women were encouraged to take up dim sum (Cantonese snacks and pastries) cookery because instructors believed their small hands, delicate fingers, and artistic nature would make them more naturally inclined toward this type of work. Women were also encouraged to take up Western cookery because the *batterie de cuisine* of pots and pans were lighter and seen as more refined and "civilized" than the heavy carbon steel woks used in Cantonese cooking. Similar tropes have also persisted in the West about women's participation in professional cookery—that women are better suited to pastry work rather than savory cooking because of their small physical features and artistic sensibilities. However, trends are changing as women are increasingly enrolling in culinary colleges, often at a higher rate than men.[3]

Though food scholarship has tended to focus more on women's experiences and food, increasingly, scholars are turning their attention to the subject of masculinity and food (Bentley 2001; Deutsch 2005; Holden 2005; Julier and

Lindenfeld 2005; Parasecoli 2005). Notably, food can be a site of anxiety and display of masculinity. As described above, men's participation in cooking tends to be more public. To this I add that men's involvement in feeding is also more ceremonial. When I was a college undergraduate, I studied abroad in Geneva, Switzerland, for a semester. My French instructor took on the role of explaining cultural rules in addition to language rules in her course. One of her steadfast rules was that *croissants* (a type of French pastry) were only consumed on Sundays and that it was the father's job to go out and buy them from the local *boulangerie* (bakery). She explained many other rules, but this one stuck with me—that the act of buying pastries (what some might gender as a "feminine" act given that food shopping and sweets are often gendered as feminine activities) was strictly a male activity in France.

This rule is reminiscent of some of the cultural rules in America about the father's role in food. The father or the dad is the one who "brings home the bacon." He is also the "breadwinner." Popular media representations also suggest that dad's food work involves mixing drinks and cocktails or barbecuing for a crowd. Dad might also roll up his sleeves for specific meals or a "festal signature dish," such as making breakfast in bed for his wife and mother of his children on her birthday, Mother's Day, or some other special occasion and making breakfast for his family on Sundays (Adler 1981). And it is almost always the father in a heterosexual family who rolls up his sleeves to grill or barbecue, perhaps wearing a "kiss the cook" as he flips burgers for a hungry crowd.

What scholars of masculinity note is that men do not take on these roles easily. Jonathan Deutsch's work on firemen in the United States reveals how men react when they take on stereotypically feminine tasks. He surveyed this group of men who are domestic cooks, "who feel a need to and choose to cook" (Deutsch 2005: 91). His informants, all firemen at Engine 3000, are involved in feeding the firehouse "family." When cooking and doing feeding work, Deutsch points out they are "performing"—acting in ways that reinforce their identities as men. From using profanity to "masculinize" the "women's work," to speaking in falsetto in a sexualized, female-like voice, and using food and other kitchen items to "dress" in drag, their choice in language, acts, and humor are used to maintain their masculinity while doing food work.

3.3 Food for thought: ManCan

Food companies have used gender-based anxieties to sell food. Consider the product ManCan (see http://www.mancanwine.com). Wine is often heavily coded as a feminine beverage (Velikova, Dodd, and Wilcox 2013). To alleviate some of the anxieties around drinking wine, the company ManCan packaged wine in cans targeted at men. The creation of ManCan is described in the following way on its website:

> Out with a friend at a bar, Graham wished he could order wine, but didn't want a "Sauvignon Blanc" or "Pinot" in stemware when his friend had a can of beer. He bought mancanwine.com that night . . ..
>
> Wine labels are notoriously difficult to decipher. There are producers, varietals, geographical indicators, brand names, and other details on labels. Instead of having to figure out what a zinfandel from Rombauer in the Alexander River Valley means, consumers pick out white, red, or bubbly and can pop it open and drink right away. No fussy stemware, pretention, or language barriers to navigate.

It is true that in the United States, women tend to dominate in wine consumption (55 percent to 45 percent) (Thach 2012a). Wine in academic literature is often described as being more appealing to women than to men (Velikova, Dodd, and Wilcox 2013). Yet both genders had similar motivations for drinking wine, such as pairing wines to enhance food, enjoying the taste, or to relax (Thach 2012b). Yet male consumers seemed more interested in discussing the technical aspects of the wine and exhibiting knowledge of wine history and production. This scholarship appears to run contrary to the way ManCan is being sold to consumers.

Discussion questions

1. What cues (language, graphics, packaging, etc.) code this as a masculine product?
2. What aspects of masculinity does this project draw upon to sell to men?
3. Recalling Jonathan Deutsch's (2005) work on firemen and cooking, what aspects of humor and gender play are used to distinguish this product as masculine?

Further resources

Watch the commercial for DB Export Dry, "Say No to Wine" (https://www.youtube.com/watch?v=38B5K7AEmAg). This commercial for beer frames wine in similar language as that used by ManCan.

Forbes, S. L. (2012). "The Influence of Gender on Wine Purchasing and Consumption: An Exploratory Study across Four Nations." *International Journal of Wine Business Research*, 24(2), pp. 146–159.

Increasingly, researchers and activists are turning their attention to third genders and alternative sexualities and food. Scholarship on LGBTQ communities and food have explored how eating and feeding are important to the construction of sexual identities, personal identities, and community formation. Christopher Carrington's seminal work has examined what "feeding work" looks like among lesbian and gay families (2008). Among lesbian and gay households, one member of the family takes on the "planner" role—a role that in families with heterosexual parents (one male, one female) often falls to the female partner. Among Carrington's participants, that role often fell to the less economically dominant partner. This pattern replicates domestic roles headed by heterosexual partners. Furthermore, in lesbian and gay households, the woman who is not taking on the planner role is evading gendered expectations, while the partner in a gay relationship who takes on this task is also defying gender roles by taking on a "feminine" activity. As a result, Carrington contends that heteronormative gendered expectations, when placed on lesbian and gay couples, can create tension in the relationship and outside of it.

3.4 Activity: The first date

Imagine you are going on a first date. You really like this person and you want to impress them. You are planning to take them to a nice restaurant to get to know them over dinner and maybe even grab ice cream or dessert at another place after. Are there things you would or would not order to make the right impression? How many of these are determined by your own likes and dislikes or habits, and how much of this is determined by societal norms about gender appropriate behavior?

Directions

1. Take a sheet of paper and draw a line down the middle. One side would be good behaviors and the other would be bad behaviors.
2. For instance, in a heterosexual relationship between a male and female, good behaviors for a male might include opening the door for his date and picking up the check. Males might be reticent to order a salad because it is perceived to be too fussy or too feminine.

Discussion questions

1. Discuss your list of good and bad behaviors. How many of these behaviors are influenced by gender norms? How many of these are influenced by heterosexual gender norms?
2. How might the rules shift among same-sex couples or couples of alternative sexual identities?

Further resources

Amiraian, D. E. and J. Sobal (2009). "Dating and Eating: Beliefs about Dating Foods among University Students." *Appetite*, 53(2), pp. 226–232.

DeLucia, J. L. (1987). "Gender Role Identity and Dating Behavior: What Is the Relationship?" *Sex Roles*, 17(3–4), pp. 153–161.

Hasford, J., B. Kidwell, and V. Lopez-Kidwell (2018). "Happy Wife, Happy Life: Food Choices in Romantic Relationships." *Journal of Consumer Research*, 44(6), pp. 1238–1256.

Salkin, A. (2007). "Be Yourselves, Girls, Order the Rib-Eye." *New York Times*, August 9.

Race and ethnicity

Another important cultural ontology is the category of race. Sociologists and anthropologists, as well as biologists and other scientists have been interested in the study of *race*. From a biological standpoint, race does not exist as it is defined by a limited set of physical (and often arbitrarily determined) categories. For instance, hair color, eye color, and especially skin tone form the basis for determining one's race. Once we begin attempting to categorize groups of people to discrete categories based on selective physical characteristics, we realize fairly quickly how the concept of race becomes invalid, at least from a hard-and-fast biological perspective.

Scientists argue that race is not biologically valid. This is not to say race has no validity; far from it. Instead, race carries immense cultural, historical, and social meanings. One's racial categorization could mean differences in terms of socioeconomic status, political power, and access to resources and rights. In many societies, including the United States, the concept of race is shaped more by social, economic, and political forces than biology or physical attributes alone (Omi and Winant 1986: 61).

3.5 Food for thought: *The Green Book*

If you were to ask food loving people today to name what they consider to be the most respected food and travel guide, they would likely name the red book. This red book is, of course, the Michelin Guide. Created in 1900, this guide was originally printed and given away for free as a promotion item by the Michelin Company, a car tire manufacturer. It provided budding automobile enthusiasts with practical information about car maintenance, maps, hotels, gas stations, lodging, and where to eat throughout France. The intent was that people would take their cars and drive them along the newly created auto routes. Of course, the more driving that occurred, the more frequently the motorists would need to purchase tires (ideally, Michelin brand tires). Nowadays, this guide covers twenty-eight countries and is associated with the world of fine dining rather than road trips. It is most famous for its "stars": restaurants are awarded stars as markers of distinction in food and hospitality.

Now, if you had asked an African American motorist from the mid-twentieth century what they considered to be the most valued guide, they would've likely named "The Green Book." *The Negro Motorist Green Book*, as it was formally known, was first published in 1936. It was created by letter carrier Victor Hugo Green to help black travelers navigate the country at a time when segregation and intense racial discrimination made travel difficult at best, and potentially dangerous. Green was a postal worker who traveled often and found himself struggling with simple acts like finding places to eat, to fill up gas, and to stop for the night when in unfamiliar environments, in an era of heavy discrimination against African Americans. In response, he gathered entries of friendly businesses in the New York metropolitan area. This grew into a national roster of "hotels, road houses, taverns, night clubs, tourist homes, trailer parks and camps, restaurants, garages, service stations, summer resorts, barber shops, beauty parlors, dance halls, [and] theaters" (Green 1949). Ultimately, this guide served to "give the Negro traveler information that will keep him from running into difficulties, embarrassments and to make his trips more enjoyable."

For African American travelers, this was a godsend as it contained listings of businesses, restaurants, and lodgings that were friendly and would accept them as customers. Traveling under Jim Crow was incredibly risky and, in unfamiliar places, left black travelers vulnerable to prejudice and discrimination. Inadvertently entering a sundown town, a nickname for an all-white municipality with laws barring people of color, could mean harassment, jail time, or violence.

The introduction to the 1949 edition explains the rationale behind the book.

> There will be a day sometime in the near future when this guide will not have to be published. That is when we as a race will have equal opportunities and privileges in the United States. It will be a great day for us to suspend this publication for then we can go wherever we please, and without embarrassment. But until that time comes we shall continue to publish this information for your convenience each year.

This guide was published until the passing of the Civil Rights Act of 1964, which forbade discrimination on the basis of race, color, religion, sex, and national origin. Researchers contend that the book was significant, not just because it helped keep African American travelers safe, but because it also marked the rise of an African American middle class who could afford cars and consumer goods and could participate in leisure travel, and signaled the evolving changes to social and economic opportunities for African Americans.

Further resources

The Green Book Chronicles, a forthcoming documentary. https://greenbookchronicles.com.
Mapping the Green Book is a blog project that maps the landscape of race and travel post–World War II. It is based on listings in *The Green Book*. http://mappingthegreenbook.tumblr.com.
The New York Public Library has a digital collection of *The Green Book* for public use. https://digitalcollections.nypl.org/collections/the-green-book#/?tab=about&scroll=6.

In the United States, race and ethnicity are sometimes used interchangeably. Like race, ethnicity is also defined by a series of socially constructed categories. But unlike race, ethnicity is more nuanced. Ethnicity is often defined by the individual or members of the group rather than society's construction of who a person is (or is not). Ethnicity refers to the degree to which a person identifies with and feels affinity toward a particular ethnic group. Ethnicity can form an important element of someone's personal and social identity. Ethnicity can also be fluid and complex, and may shift over time.

Food is a useful lens for examining ethnicity, as it can denote ethnic boundaries. Food can be used to demarcate difference, signaling "us" versus "them" through people's foodways. Today, the French still make jibes about "*Les Rostbifs*" (the roast beefs) who live across the English Channel. This insult is derived from the British practice of feasting on Sunday roast, a traditional meal intended to be eaten after church on Sundays. A classic version of this meal features roast beef and gravy, roast potatoes, Yorkshire pudding (a type of puffy quick bread made with batter), and vegetables. In retort to being called *Les Rostbifs*, the English respond by calling the French "frogs" because of their penchant for eating these amphibians. Frogs legs or *cuisses de grenouille* remain popular in French cuisine. Other insults abound and persist. Other groups have been described in similarly derogatory manners with regard to their foodways (see de Garine 2001). In the United States, Germans are still sometimes called "krauts" and "potato eaters,"

Mexicans "beaners," and Brits are referred to as "limeys." Food is an effective way to mark another group as different, as "other."

We sling food-based insults at groups that are not like "us," but at the same time Americans love to eat "ethnic food." So what does that mean? This raises many questions about acceptance: about who belongs, about why foods may be embraced but the people making the food might not be welcomed with the same open arms. Who is ethnic? What constitutes ethnic food? What does it mean to eat in a racially and culturally conscious way? How does one appreciate food diversity without diminishing or overlooking the sovereignty and integrity of the originating communities?

Many people nowadays like to think of themselves as being culturally omnivorous. "Taco Tuesdays," "Stir-Fridays," celebrating cultural holidays through eating and drinking (St. Patrick's Day, Cinco de Mayo, Chinese New Year) reflect a multicultural sensibility. Certainly, food has the power of positive commensality, the ability to drive inclusion. But how does "eating the other" transcend a superficial experience into one that is meaningful?

Recently, chefs and restaurateurs have come under fire for "Columbusing" (see Figure 3.3). This term is a neologism, a new word coined based on an existing one. It came into usage on the internet around 2013 and quickly gained

FIGURE 3.3 *Globalization, glocalization, or Columbusing? The lines can be difficult to draw. Photo courtesy of the author.*

popular use to describe when white people appropriate or "discover" something that has existed outside of their own culture, nationality, race, or heritage but has been familiar to the community it originated from. In other words, Columbusing is another term for cultural appropriation. This act of appropriating often ignores or overlooks the originating community and does not credit that community for inventing it. Italian explorer Christopher Columbus, who is often credited for discovering the New World in 1492 even though it was already inhabited and developed by indigenous communities, inspires this term.[4]

While the term Columbusing is relatively new, the debates about who receives credit, especially economic gain, for an idea or product is an ongoing one in the culinary world. In the gastronomically driven side of food, the issues of privilege and access are raised. It calls into question who gets to be an authority on "ethnic" foods and who benefits financially from this power.

To illustrate, Chipotle Mexican Grill, a fast-casual restaurant chain featuring Mexican burritos and tacos, with locations in the United States, Canada, France, Germany, and the United Kingdom, also came under scrutiny for its lack of cultural recognition toward Mexican and Latinos. It adopted a series of packaging called the "Cultivating Thought Author Series," which featured short stories from renowned writers. It came under fire in 2014 for not featuring any authors with a Mexican or Latino heritage despite being, as it describes itself, a "Mexican grill" (see Chow 2014).

3.6 Food for thought: Are you Columbusing?

National Public Radio has created a checklist for reflecting upon whether you are Columbusing or meaningfully appreciating another culture. When feasting on food from another culture, they suggest considering:

● Who is providing this good or service for me?
● Am I engaging with them in a thoughtful manner?
● Am I learning about this culture?
● Are people from this culture benefiting from my spending money here?
● Are they being hurt by my spending money here?

Adapted from Salinas (2014). "'Columbusing': The Art of Discovering Something That Is Not New."

3.7 Activity: Food privilege checklist

This checklist was inspired by Peggy McIntosh's "White Privilege: Unpacking the Invisible Knapsack" (McIntosh 1988). McIntosh reflects, "I was taught to see racism only in individual acts of meanness, not in invisible systems conferring dominance on my group." She points out that "privilege" confers dominance because of one's identity and is a type of strength and unearned power. This seminal article has been used in schools and universities to engage students in conversations on race and its relationship to systems of power and access. This checklist relates specifically to racial and ethnic privilege through the specific focus of food.

1. I can if I wish arrange to eat the food of my cultural/ethnic heritage most of the time.
2. I can be pretty sure that my neighbors will not complain about the smell of my food.
3. I can turn on the television and see food from my cultural/ethnic heritage represented.
4. When I see representations of food from my cultural/ethnic background in the media, I see someone of that heritage cooking and explaining its practices.
5. When I am told about the food of my cultural/ethnic heritage, I am shown that people of my color made it what it is.
6. The most expensive restaurant in town serves the cuisine of my cultural/ethnic background.
7. I can eat food from my cultural/ethnic background in a public setting without experiencing embarrassment or hostility.
8. When I bring food from my cultural/ethnic background into a public setting, I can expect that statements others make about it are positive or complimentary.
9. If I cook for others and someone says something negative about the food, I can be sure it is because I cooked it improperly.
10. I can easily buy cookbooks and magazines at a bookstore featuring recipes from my cultural/ethnic cuisine.
11. I can be confident that others are interested in my cuisine because it is tasty and not because it is trendy at the moment.
12. I can easily shop for ingredients to make my cultural/ethnic cuisine, at the nearest mainstream supermarket.
13. I can be confident that restaurants and food sellers serving my cultural/ethnic cuisine are making a living wage.
14. I can name more than a handful celebrity chefs who serve my cultural/ethnic cuisine.
15. The ingredients to make my cultural/ethnic cuisine are located throughout the supermarket and not just in the "ethnic foods" aisle.
16. I can travel and find my cultural/ethnic cuisine easily accessible wherever I go.
17. Friends are not afraid to dine at restaurants serving my cultural/ethnic cuisine.

18. I can study the foodways of my cultural/ethnic background without it being seen as self-interested or self-seeking.

19. I can be sure that media representations of the foodways of my cultural/ethnic background regularly show off the best of its practices and gastronomy.

20. I have never been asked why people from my background eat exotic or unusual foods.

Discussion questions

1. Were there any patterns you noticed in your responses? Describe.

2. How might your responses change if you were to move in an area with different racial/ethnic demographics?

3. How might your experiences related to food (in terms of your racial/ethnic background) be related to broader issues of race and ethnicity in your home society?

Further resources

McIntosh, P. (1989). "White Privilege: Unpacking the Invisible Knapsack." *Peace and Freedom Magazine*, July/August, pp. 10–12.

On one end of the spectrum, there has been lively debate about the "domestication" of ethnic foods for American palates, with thoughtful discussions of what the line is between enjoyment and appropriation. On the other end, scholars have looked what it means for migrants to America to adjust to "SNAF" food habits. They question, what does it mean to become American? What food practices are adopted and what is rejected in the process of becoming American?

Newcomers to America find American food practices to be perplexing. Sociologist Krishnendu Ray points out the miscommunications and misperceptions highlighted by Bengali American migrants in experiencing American meals (2004). His informants were perplexed by domestic American foods like casseroles, stews, baked potatoes, baked beans, pies, soups, corn on the cob, as well as hamburgers, beefsteaks, salad, hot dogs, and cornflakes. Meat was especially challenging. As he points out, "The quantity, quality, and nature of meat cookery appear to be the most important markers of ethnicity for Bengalis. American food is imagined in astonishingly negative terms, perhaps echoing subconscious Hindu revulsion toward meat, especially red meat" (Ray 2004: 79).

As migrants to a country adjust to their new homelands, they find that food is one of the markers of home that is most missed. Adjusting to new foodways, which can include new ways of cooking, new products, new ingredients, and ways of shopping for food, are part of what makes the migration experience "perplexing."

Summary

- Kinship, gender, race, and ethnicity are cultural ontologies used to classify people. These categories provide insight on power, access, and social relations.

- Kin may play an important role in feeding and nurturing us, but not everyone has a traditional kin model.

- Family meals are promoted as important to kin bonding, but can also be a source of tension. Experts suggest family meals are declining. LGBTQ families are especially challenged in terms of feeding work.

- Sex and gender are connected to the division of labor in food work. Women do the lion's share of feeding work.

- Food can also be a site for displaying masculinity.

- Food can be an expression of race and ethnicity.

- Ethnic and racial foodways can be "Columbused" and culturally appropriated. Or they can be used as a point of segregation and differentiation from mainstream society.

Discussion questions

1. Consider your relationship to family meals. Were they part of your family routine? What were family meals like in your household?

2. Reflect on the division of labor in your household growing up. Who took on the burden of feeding work?

3. What kind of meals did your family eat while you were growing up? Was there a dominant ethnic or cultural bent to your food? If so, what relationship might that have to your ethnic or cultural heritage?

Further resources

Movies and documentaries

Soul Food (1997) is a film about a close-knit African American family that bonds through their weekly Sunday dinners. When the matriarch suddenly falls ill, the family struggles to adjust in the absence of her presence and nurture.

Soul Food Junkies (2012) is a documentary about the emotional, cultural, and health impacts of soul food in the African American community.

Tortilla Soup (2001) focuses on the story of three adult daughters and their father, a retired chef. They struggle to communicate their thoughts and feelings over their weekly family dinners.

What's Cooking? (2000) is filmed around the stories of four ethnically diverse American families—Vietnamese, Latino, Jewish, and African American—on Thanksgiving Day. As each family prepares its Thanksgiving meal, each family is also struggling to cope with its own troubles.

Notes

1 See "Death of the Family Meal" in *Daily Mail*, the second-biggest selling newspaper in the United Kingdom, for a recent example. It targets a female readership. http://www.dailymail.co.uk/news/article-135045/Death-family-meal.html.

2 LGBTQ stands for lesbian, gay, bisexual, transgender, and queer. Increasingly, LGBTQ+ is used to be inclusive of other sexual orientations.

3 See http://www.foodandwine.com/news/more-women-at-CIA-than-men.

4 See Salinas (2014) for more on the term.

Further resources

Abarca, Meredith (2006). *Voices in the Kitchen: Views of Food and the World from Working Class Mexican and Mexican-American Women."* College Station: Texas A&M University Press.

Counihan, Carole and Stephen L. Kaplan (1998). *Food and Gender: Identity and Power.* Cagliari, Italy: Gordon and Breach.

Harper, A. Breeze (ed.) (2010). *Sistah Vegan: Black Female Vegans Speak on Food, Identity, Health, and Society.* New York: Lantern Books.

Kalcik, S. (1984). "Ethnic Foodways in America: Symbol and the Performance of Identity." In L. K. Brown and K. Mussell (eds.), *Ethnic and Regional Foodways in the United States: The Performance of Group Identity.* Knoxville: University of Tennessee Press.

Pilcher, Jeffrey M. (1998). *Que vivan los tamales! Food and the Making of Mexican Identity.* Albuquerque: University of New Mexico Press.

Ray, Krishnendu (2004). *The Migrant's Table: Meals and Memories in Bengali-American Households.* Philadelphia: Temple University Press.

Williams-Forson, Pysche (2006). *Building Houses out of Chicken Legs: Black Women, Food and Power.* Chapel Hill: University of North Carolina Press.

Witt, Doris (1999). *Black Hunger: Food and the Politics of US Identity.* New York: Oxford University Press.

4

From Producers to Consumers

For most Americans, getting food means getting into a car, driving to a supermarket, and buying food off a well-organized shelf or refrigerated cabinet. You will probably do this once a week and buy enough food to get you through the next seven days. This way of getting food has become the norm, although it is not "natural," in the biological sense. This way of acquiring food is instead the consequence of hundreds of thousands of years of changes, both big and small. In many ways, the American way of acquiring food is a tremendous technological and cultural achievement, representing a highly complex and interconnected global food system connecting the producers, distributers, consumers, and disparate landscapes. What a group of people eat reflects evolutionary gastronomy. The food a group eats takes into account ecological, environmental concerns, as well as taste preferences, preparation habits established as a working mix responding to necessity.

This chapter traces the journey of how driving to a supermarket and shopping for the week became the norm for most Americans and residents of other wealthy industrialized nations. In particular, it raises the issue of how we went from being mostly producers of food to consumers. This shift from being a society that buys and eats food—and is largely divorced from the origins of our food supply—is a relatively recent development. Even this is a bit of a mislabeling, as we were not always the "producers" of our food, so to speak. Long before we became producers—farmers—we were "seekers" of food as foragers (also known as hunters and gatherers). Our ability to produce food rather than merely acquire it is one of several attributes that have distinguished us from other primates and creatures. How a society gets its food reveals insights into its social priorities, values, and technologies.

Ensuring regularity and continuity in our food supply has been a challenge since our earliest days as a species. Establishing a regular food supply is a fundamental problem for all societies, and failure to secure food can lead to riots and socioeconomic and political instability, not to mention delayed social growth and human illness. Even in highly industrialized nations like the United States and those of Western Europe, access to food remains a social question.

Since our earliest days as a species, we have struggled in our quest to feed ourselves in order to survive. Each subsistence system has evolved based upon a society's way of maximizing its *carrying capacity*. The carrying capacity of an environment refers to the maximum population size of a species that can be sustained given the natural resources available, such food, water, and land, without destroying the ecological system. The carrying capacity for a given area is not fixed and can change based on human interaction and interference. Humans have used technology to improve an area, but have also damaged lands, sometimes irreparably, in the quest to support a population. While the struggles have changed, even today we are struggling with questions regarding the best way to feed ourselves—what is the most efficient, price conscious, effective, productive, sustainable, ethical, or least harmful method to sustain our current carrying capacity.

Throughout our existence, humans have relied on four types of *subsistence systems*. A subsistence system is the set of practices, technologies, and techniques used by members of a society to acquire food. These four subsistence systems are *foraging*, *pastoralism*, *horticulture* (or basic agriculture), and *intensive agriculture*. Every society utilizes some combination of these subsistence systems, although there is often one subsistence system that dominates in a society. For instance, foraging and intensive agriculture coexist in many societies, including the United States. Hunting wild game remains a popular pastime in the United States, but these same hunters do not rely on wild foods alone. Many of them will also shop at modern supermarkets, buying food produced by farmers and agribusinesses. Some might also grow their own food in their own small-scale plots, practicing horticulture.

Though there are different subsistence systems, there are some universals that characterize human food patterns. As mentioned in Chapter 1, humans (*Homo sapiens*) are omnivores. We are able to incorporate a wide range of foods in our diets, unlike other organisms that may have highly specific diets. As a result, humans have been able to live in a variety of environments. Furthermore, humans regularly and extensively use tools and technology in their food production and preparation. Tools have ranged from basic stone tools to very sophisticated machinery for harvesting crops. Fire, too, is an important form of technology used in food acquisition and food preparation. Lastly, humans have the ability to be choosy about their foods. Humans have clear ideas about what is edible and what is not, based on more than simply what is poisonous and what is safe. We have preferences, aversions, fears, and taboos. These ideas about what to eat have ultimately shaped our subsistence patterns, impacting what is acquired, produced, and cooked (or not).

Ultimately, we want to look at subsistence systems because they show a connection between how people produce their food and the environment they live in. Furthermore, how people get their food reveals insights into their culture and society: how they live, what they value, how they relate to one another, and how these patterns of existence have changed over time, based upon how people acquire their food.

Foraging

Humans are *primates*, members of a zoological order with apes, monkeys, and prosimians. We share much in common with our primate cousins. In fact, humans share over 98 percent of their DNA with chimpanzees and gorillas. In terms of anatomy, primates are bipedal (two-footed) and can stand upright. They have hands with opposable thumbs able to grasp and hold, a relatively large field of vision and depth perception, and the use of fingertips to perceive touch. Primates also have large brains relative to their body size. Greater brain capacity enables primates to be capable of learning, and in terms of human, able to process complex thought and the ability to remember.

Primates live in social groups and maintain social relations. There are hierarchies among primates. Among apes, monkeys, and prosimians, there is often a dominant male in each group. Primates also rear their offspring and take care of their kin. Primates usually have only one offspring at a time (as opposed to a litter), thereby investing more energy and care. The offspring receive more attention and care, and also have more opportunities to learn than other mammals. Learned behavior is essential in primates, including humans, as it allows for resilience and adaptability to environmental conditions. In the face of challenges, primates are able to modify their behavior and social patterns while other mammals might have to wait for a genetic or physical response.

Primate food habits also bear some similarities with humans. Primates tend to subsist on primarily vegetarian diets—fruits, plants, and insects— although some also hunt and eat meat. Some primates will use basic tools to acquire food. For instance, wild chimpanzees in Tanzania, East Africa, regularly use tools to acquire food (McGrew 1987; Matsuzawa 1994). They pick and chew leaves to make them into an ersatz sponge to soak up water in difficult-to-reach places. Twigs are used to probe termite hills to acquire termites for food. Chimpanzees can also hunt for meat. In fact, chimpanzees can hunt and eat nearly as much meat as some human hunter gatherers (see Boesch 1994; Mitani and Watts 2001; Tennie, Gilby, and Mundry 2009). There are many similarities between primate food habits and early human food patterns—it is more of a difference of degree to which certain habits are executed.

4.1 Food for thought: Teeth

Ever wonder why you have sharp teeth? Take a look in the mirror at your own teeth (or if you have a willing volunteer, take a peek at theirs). Most people have four sharp pointed teeth, or canine teeth—two on the top and two at the bottom. All primates have canine teeth, as do many other mammals such as dogs and cats. These teeth were more important during our early human period, before the rise of fire use and cooking. They might have also been used as a weapon for taking prey. Over millions of years, our teeth and jaws have become smaller. This is due to the invention of fire and, later, the rise of domestication. Our ability to cook transformed our diets, making food softer and easier to chew and digest. As we domesticated wild food sources, we bred them not just for yield, size, and taste but also for texture. Flesh from domesticated animals is tenderer than wild animals, which tend to be harder to chew and digest due to their different musculature. So today, instead of needing canine teeth to grab and rip raw meat, we can use them to rip open bags of our favorite snack foods.

Humans first appeared as a species separate from our primate cousins—gorillas, apes, and chimpanzees—approximately five to seven million years ago. During our earliest days as a distinct species, we acquired food through *hunting and gathering* or what archeologists and anthropologists call *foraging*. This involved finding and harvesting wild plants and animal food resources from land and water by hunting, fishing, gathering, and scavenging, or consuming dead animals. Vegetable foods like roots, beans, nuts, tubers, and fruits were important to early human nutrition. Flowers and edible gums were also occasionally consumed. This was the only method of food acquisition until approximately 10,000–12,000 years ago. In other words, foraging has been the dominant mode of food acquisition for 99 percent of our existence as a species. Humans continue to forage today, albeit at smaller scales and in conjunction with other subsistence systems.

Foragers lived in small communities called bands. These groups, composed of about 100 people who were related through *kinship* (by blood or by marriage), lived, acquired food, cooked, and ate together. They were highly interdependent for survival and, as a result, were relatively egalitarian (although not always equal) in their social structures. Wealth, in the form of surplus food, was often shared with members of the band as the community relied on one another for well-being and survival. However, foragers did have delineations about work and social roles. Foraging included "hunting" work and "gathering" work, often split upon gendered lines, a sexual based *division of labor*. The stereotypical arrangement was that males hunted and females gathered and performed domestic tasks like childrearing. While some foraging societies did practice this type of sexual division of labor, different arrangements were present, including systems where men hunted and both men and women gathered; men and women both hunted and gathered; or men hunted but women processed the men's catch (Friedl 1975, 1978).

Foragers were attuned to seasons, migratory patterns, and climate conditions because that was the only way they could find food. Because humans were reliant entirely on wild food sources, we were at the mercy of climate and environmental conditions, and constrained by the hours of daylight available to look and acquire such food sources. Archeological records suggest that early humans likely chose their environments based on where there were relatively good food sources—in particular, substantial herds of wild grazing animals. What different groups of humans ate was highly dependent on their environmental access. Foragers had a *broad spectrum diet*, meaning their diets were based on a wide variety of food sources. Many different foodstuffs would be considered food—insects, larvae, rodents, and even sap and resins. Although early human diets varied greatly, the one commonality all humans shared at this point was that they were tied intimately to their environments. Though early humans faced food shortages in many environments, especially seasonal food shortages, data from archaeological research suggests that foragers had relatively good nutritional status (Barnard 1998; O'Keefe and Cordain 2004; Bowles 2011). Foragers did not seem to suffer from chronic malnutrition or nutrient-deficiency diseases.

Like other primates, early humans also adopted tool use and new technologies in their quest for food. Archaeological evidence suggests that humans developed stone tool use around 2.5 million years ago. Humans may also have discovered the use of fire around 1.6–1.9 million years ago (see Wrangham 2009). Fire offered protection from dangerous animals, provided light and warmth, and also enabled us to cook with heat. Scientists also suggest that the invention of fire—and the introduction of cooking—helped push along human development as it changed how and what we ate. Humans also began to eat much more meat around 1.6–1.8 million years ago, a likely consequence of fire discovery (Bunn 1981; Rose and Marshall 1996; Stanford 1999; Stanford and Bunn 2001; Tennie, Gilby, and Mundry 2009). The invention of fire as a technology will be discussed further in Chapter 5.

Although there are seemingly abundant possibilities for eating, hunter-gatherers do not consume everything in their environment. Instead, they choose from a limited range of edible foodstuffs. Each society has its set of preferred ingredients, foods that have been given different value based upon their abundance, availability, accessibility and ease of acquisition, and nutritional value (see Lee 2003: 43). Foods that were scarce and less abundant often carried higher prestige and social value than foods that were abundant and more easily acquired. Of course, it is important to remember that early hunter-gatherers also selected certain foods because they tasted delicious—foods were also selected for their flavors. Meats, fats, and sweets were especially appreciated for their tastes as well as their caloric value (White 1997; Outram 2007).

While foraging is no longer the dominant mode of food acquisition for humans, some societies continue to participate in this rapidly disappearing way of life, such as the the !Kung or Ju/hosani in Africa, Australian Aboriginal societies, the Inuit peoples of the Arctic, and indigenous Americans (Native Americans) in the United States. This way of life has persisted in areas where food production is difficult to sustain (Lee and Daly 1999). Deserts, islands, areas with extreme cold, and very dense forests are some environments where foraging persists. For instance, the !Kung Bushmen of Botswana, a landlocked country in southern Africa, maintain their hunting and gathering ways. Their home is in the northwest region of the Kalahari Desert, a semiarid area that receives less than ten inches of rainfall each year. They rely almost exclusively on hunting and gathering for their food.

However, it is important not to romanticize modern foragers as being "untouched" by modern society or developments. While modern foragers might live on the fringes of mainstream societies, sometimes forced off to marginal foraging lands, many groups now incorporate modern technologies and are impacted by changes in the global system. For instance, Inuit in Alaska and Canada now hunt seals with the aid of snowmobiles and modern weaponry. And all modern foragers live in modern nation-states and are influenced by national and international policies. Australia's indigenous population (Aborigines) and the Native Americans in the United States have been impacted by government policy, which determines where they can live and where they can practice their hunter-gatherer way of life, limited and delineated by government regulation.

Living a hunter-gatherer lifestyle remains risky. While scientists caution us that the life of a hunter-gatherer is not always a "precarious and arduous struggle for existence" (Lee 1988: 43), it is important to remember that a subsistence based upon eating wild foods always carries with it some degree of risk. The fear of poisoning is ever-present, especially when many wild species have look-alikes and eating the wrong one could mean deadly consequences. As an old saying goes, "All fungi are edible; some only once." However, because of our relatively large brains as a primate species, humans were able to learn and adapt to their environments—to quickly recognize and remember which species of plants were safe to eat, how to follow animal behaviors, and how to best acquire food. The Industrial Revolution in Europe, beginning in the late eighteenth century and stretching into the nineteenth century, introduced mass-produced convenience foods. These foods, promoted as being "safe" and "scientific" further relegated wild foods into the category of "unsafe" and "dangerous," a discussion we will return to in Chapter 5.

Common stereotypes suggest that the hunter-gatherer life was short, nasty, and hard; that early humans were always on the brink of starvation. Indubitably, life was difficult. Some hunter gatherers would spend up to seventy hours or more per week looking for food. But perhaps life for hunter-gatherers was not difficult to the extent that most people today imagine. Evidence suggests that hunter-gatherers were able to maintain food security and were knowledgeable about animal habits and plant species. Some researchers contend that "the hunter-gatherer subsistence base is at least routine and reliable and at best surprisingly abundant" (Lee 1988: 43). Anthropologist Marshall Sahlins describes the hunter-gatherer existence as "the original affluent society," suggesting that the ease of acquiring food allowed hunter-gatherers to live a relatively leisurely life. He contends:

Hunter-gatherers consume less energy per capita per year than any other group of human beings. Yet when you come to examine it the original affluent society was none other than the hunter's—in which all the people's material wants were easily satisfied. To accept that the hunters are affluent is therefore to recognize that the present human condition of man slaving to bridge the gap between his unlimited wants and his insufficient means is a tragedy of modern times. (Sahlins 1972: 1)

Sahlins's claims challenge our understanding of hunter-gatherer life. However, it is important to remember that the comfort and so-called affluence of hunter-gatherers varied widely from group to group, based on the environmental and ecological conditions they faced.

Yet despite the risks and the rise of industrial agriculture, foraging has never fully died out. Foraging remains a way to supplement food supplies or a means to obtain access to wild foods that cannot be cultivated. Consider, for instance, the popularity of wild mushrooms and fungi. As our food supply has become more industrialized in the West, it seems that wild foods are becoming fetishized for their connections to a natural world that, in some cases, is becoming more and more distant. White truffles (*Tuber magnatum pico*) are especially prized by gourmands and elite chefs for their pungent aroma and rarity. Large truffles, in particular, can fetch top dollar at the world's major auction houses. A two-pound white truffle was sold for over US$300,000. Clearly, wild foods can be valuable.

Although foraging has never stopped as a practice, in recent years foraging has come back into popularity in food-worshipping circles. Among chefs in the world of fine dining and elite cuisine, foraging has come back in vogue. Many of the world's foremost chefs and restaurants feature foraged ingredients, fetishizing them for their connection to locality and the natural world (Duram and Cawley 2012; Hall 2013). These restaurants that top the Michelin Guide, the Gault-Millau, and the San Pellegrino list of The World's 50 Best Restaurants have menus that incorporate foraged and wild ingredients. For instance, Rene Redzepi, chef of Noma in Copenhagen, Denmark, focuses on hyper-local, micro-seasonal menus, ushering a new culinary movement called "New Nordic Cuisine," which celebrated the wild foods and landscape of northern Europe. It is easy to be entranced by the use of wild foods, but it is important to remember that Noma, and other modern foragers, cannot exist without other food sources today. Though these elite restaurants highlight their local wild bounty, many of them also use items that are clearly domesticated.

Food lovers are also participating in foraging, in part because of feelings of nostalgia for a romantic past when humans lived closer to the land. It is another way of distinguishing one's personal identity as a food lover (Hall 2013). It is important to keep in mind that the type of foraging that modern chefs and food lovers engage in is not the same as the foraging of our ancestors of the past, whose only form of food and subsistence was whatever could be acquired through wild sources (see Figure 4.1).

Another unlikely group has also sung the praises of foraging and wild foods. Some scientists have suggested a return to foraging and wild foods as a way to deal with environmental problems. Ecologists have also promoted hunting and gathering as a way to control invasive species. For instance, the invasive lionfish is a predator threatening native species in the Atlantic Ocean, the Caribbean, and parts of the Gulf of Mexico. Some conservationists are working with chefs to encourage restaurants to serve lionfish. Under the slogan, "Eat them to beat them," hunting wild foods is promoted as a creative way to deal with invasive populations.

FIGURE 4.1 *Foraged wild mushrooms for sale in France. Photo courtesy of the author.*

4.2 Activity: Would you survive as a forager?

This activity allows you to experience, briefly, what it is like to depend on wild food sources alone. Would you survive as a modern forager? How many wild species of plants can you identify?

Materials

Camera or smartphone with camera
Notebook
Regional field guide (optional)

Directions

1. Take a thirty-minute walk in your neighborhood or campus environment. Take a photo and document the place and location of every item you think might be edible. Make notes of anything that might help identify whether

it may be poisonous or delicious: color, size, shape, where it is growing, other plants nearby, and so on.

2. After the thirty-minute walk, look up the different plants online or through a field guide. It is best to look at a field guide specific to your region for the best result.

Discussion questions

1. How many edible species were you able to identify? How many poisonous species did you identify?
2. How might lengthening the amount of time or expanding the radius of your foraging location impact your success?
3. Imagine you had to survive on wild plants alone. What types of skills and knowledge would you need to know to thrive?
4. How might other factors—seasons, weather patterns, geography—impact your success as a forager?

Instructor's note

It goes without saying, but do not pick or eat any species unless you are an experienced forager and know for certain that a particular species is edible. Even sampling a little bit may cause harm. Mushrooms and edible fungi are especially risky to experiment with.

Further resources

Allport, Susan (2000). *The Primal Feast: Food, Sex, Foraging and Love.* New York: Harmony Books.

Cook, Langdon (2009). *Fat of the Land: Adventures of the 21st Century Forager.* Seattle: Mountaineers Books/Skipstone.

Falconi, D. (2013). *Foraging & Feasting: A Field Guide and Wild Food Cookbook.* Accord, NY: Botanical Arts Press.

Hunter Angler Gardener Cook has an excellent list of field guides and foraging guides. https://honest-food.net/my-foraging-library/.

4.3 Food for thought: The Paleo diet

One of the most recent fad diets and health trends to emerge is the Paleo (or Paleolithic) diet. Founded by Loren Cordain, a professor of exercise science, the premise of this diet is that modern humans should only eat foods that were available to our Paleolithic era ancestors.

The inspiration for this diet trend is a period in human history. The Paleolithic age (or "the Old Stone Age") is a prehistoric period of human history distinguished for its use of primitive stone tools. The dates of the Paleolithic era run roughly from 2.6 million years ago to about 10,000 BCE. This period accounts for roughly 95 percent of human prehistory (human existence before the invention of writing and recorded existence). During this time, humans lived in small societies of roughly one hundred people each. These societies, also known as *bands*, subsisted through foraging. They also used simple tools to hunt and cook food. Stones like flint, chert, and obsidian were shaped or knapped to form basic cutting tools. Cordain's claim is that Paleolithic humans, or "cavemen," had better health, were less sedentary, and obtained better nutrition than our current cohort. In other words, they did not suffer from the "diseases of civilization" as modern humans do—diabetes, high cholesterol, hypertension, obesity, and so on (Eaton, Eaton III, and Konner 1997; Konner and Eaton 2010).

Cordain's theory has caught on. Over 100,000 copies of his book, *The Paleo Diet*, have been sold. There is an entire industry built up around the Paleo diet. Devotees can read blogs and books, buy Paleo-friendly snack foods, participate in workout regimes, and watch internet videos. Some followers have become celebrities in their own right. Michelle Tam, a Paleo diet devotee, has become an award-winning blogger for her blog Nom Nom Paleo, and *New York Times* bestselling author for her Paleo-friendly cookbooks.

Yet despite its intriguing name and catchy marketing spin, the Paleo diet is an anachronistic misnomer. The diet overlooks the fact that the foods modern humans consume today have very little in common with what our Paleolithic ancestors ate. That is to say, the foods that people purchase today from supermarkets or farmers markets, or even grow themselves are domesticated plants and animals. Even if a Paleo enthusiast were to consume only wild plants and animals, these modern species have evolved and adapted to the point where they have limited genetic resemblance to their forbearers from the Paleolithic era. Moreover, early humans had short life expectancies. And some of the foodstuffs that our ancestors ate simply do not exist anymore due to extinction. We are unable to dig into mammoth burgers.

It is also important to bear in mind that Paleolithic humans lived to only about 30–35 years of age. Modern Americans have a life expectancy of almost 79 years (78.74 years). While some scientists shown that our hunter-gatherer ancestors had better health than modern humans, modern science and technology has allowed humans to live much longer lives. Therefore, while the intentions of this diet are presumably good, as its core tenants include eschewing eating whole foods, avoiding processed foods, and exercising regularly, it is historically inaccurate.

Further resources

Cordain, L. (2002). *The Paleo Diet*. Hoboken, NJ: John Wiley.

Jew, S., S. S. AbuMweis, and P. J. H. Jones (2009). "Evolution of Human Diet: Linking Our Ancestral Diet to Modern Functional Foods as a Means of Chronic Disease Prevention." *Journal of Medicinal Food* 12(5), pp. 925–934.

Nestle, M. (2000), "Paleolithic Diets: A Sceptical View." *Nutrition Bulletin*, 25: pp. 43–47.

Nom Nom Paleo is an award-winning blog that highlights paleo friendly cooking. www.nomnompaleo.com.

Zuk, M. (2013). *Paleofantasy: What Evolution Really Tells Us about Sex, Diet, and How We Live*. New York: W. W. Norton.

Early domestication: Horticulture

If people "are what they eat," then we should think of ourselves as being only about 10,000–12,000 years old, so to speak. This is when we saw the earliest development of agriculture and this innovation changed human relationships to the landscape, geography, ecology, and also our food supply. Instead of being vulnerable to seasons and the elements, now humans were able to exert greater control over their landscape and, as a result, control the food that the landscape yielded. Some researchers suggest that agriculture was the most important of human revolutions. The invention of agriculture changed human existence: "We domesticated crops and our crops domesticated us" (Dufour, Goodman, and Pelto 2012: 61). Having the ability to domesticate plants and animals has some clear advantages over foraging. The biggest advantage was that humans were now able to exert greater control over their landscape and environment, and thus yield greater control and regulate their food supply. This quickly replaced hunting and gathering in many areas as the dominant subsistence system.

The rise of domestication coincided with climactic changes and the end of the last glacial period, more popularly known as the Ice Age. There were several ice ages, or glacials, that coincided with early human existence. During the glacials, continental ice sheets advanced in Europe and North America. Climates also cooled with each advance. There were also long warm periods between each advance called interglacials, when climates warmed and the ice sheets retreated. The last glacial period occurred from c.110,000 to c.117,000 years ago, falling within the Paleolithic and Mesolithic periods.

The melting of the ice sheet in northern Europe, covering present-day Scotland, Scandinavia, northern Germany, and Russia, marked the end of the Würm glacial—somewhere between 17,000 and 12,000 years ago. By 10,000

BCE the glaciers had changed climactic conditions in Europe so much that big game that formerly existed were no longer present. Big game species like reindeer, once the mainstay of European hunter-gatherers, had diminished. The herds that remained moved north as climates were cooler further north, and some people followed suit. Hunter-gatherers started pursuing smaller game and also had to look to other food resources. Changes in climactic conditions caused humans to make adaptations to their food behaviors and preferences.

Hunter-gatherers gradually began to move toward food production. There is no single answer for why hunter-gatherers transitioned toward food production, but scientists have several theories to explain this shift. Archeologist Kent Flannery (1969) suggests that the glacial retreats were the start of the broad spectrum revolution. Glacial retreats caused hunter-gatherers to focus less on certain foods, specifically big game, but instead to pursue a broader range of foodstuffs. Brian Hayden adds that preferences shifted from large-bodied, slow reproducing animals like mammoths to widely available and fast reproducing organisms like fish, mollusks, and rabbits (1981). Ultimately, Cohen reminds us, the question is not how domestication was "invented," but why it was adopted so widely (Cohen 2003: 49).

Researchers have speculated on why humans developed domestication, and there are no clear answers. The theories behind the reason for domestication vary. What is clear is the impact of domestication on the environment and on human patterns of subsistence. Domestication also brought on social and lifestyle changes. These changes in food acquisition strategies led to the rise of horticulture, or the extensive use of domesticated plants and some small animals. It also led to the establishment of pastoralism, the domestication of and reliance on herd animals as the primary source of food and social existence.

Around 10,000–12,000 years ago, the first domesticated crops and animals appeared, a result of human interference. Domestication was a slow, deliberate process involving choosing certain wild animals and plants and placing them within the proximity of humans. These wild species were chosen for selective breeding for specific qualities and traits desired by humans (Deur and Turner 2005: 15). This selective breeding changed the ecology, as animals, plants, and humans developed new biological relationships with one another. This changed our relationships with the land as, instead of being highly vulnerable to seasons, climate conditions, and incredibly mobile in order to access our food supply, humans began gaining greater control over nature.

This shift from foraging to farming also marked the Neolithic Revolution. This was the "New Stone Age" marked by the new types of stone tools produced during the time period. These new tools, only some of which were made of stone, were developed to support agricultural work rather than facilitate hunting and gathering. They included scythes for harvesting plants and hoes for soil. With these new tools, humans began to shape their environments more intensively and extensively by tilling the soil, irrigating the land, and making other changes to better suit their land use needs as they became the first farmers (Moore 1985; Outram 2007).

The earliest presence of agriculture occurred in what we call the Fertile Crescent of the Middle East, in what is now present-day Iran and Iraq. This area, centered on the Tigris and Euphrates Rivers, was highly fertile. Wheat, barley, lentils, peas, and chickpeas were domesticated. Goats, sheep, pigs, and cattle were also domesticated and became sources of food and fertilizer. Cattle were also used as draft animals for work. These people became the first farmers and the first herders.

Shortly thereafter, domesticated crops and animals also began appearing other parts of the world. Archaeologists believe that agriculture developed independently in as many as fifteen different zones around the world, an example of independent innovation. Agriculture developed in China around the Yangtze River Valley in southern China and the Yellow River in the north, sub-Saharan Africa, India, in the Andean highlands of Peru, in Mexico and Central America, what we call Mesoamerica, and the eastern United States.

What this means is that agriculture was not developed in the Middle East and then spread out; instead, it was invented in each zone free of the knowledge of what was occurring in another part of the world.

Staple foods were some of the first domesticated crops. They are foods eaten in regular quantities that are major sources of carbohydrates and serve as caloric staples in a diet. Staple foods can be grains and cereals, legumes, tubers, or fruits. Although staple foods may form the bulk of a diet, they alone cannot meet all the required nutritional needs. Maize, beans, and squash remain the foundation of a Mesoamerican diet, while in sub-Saharan Africa, roots and tubers like manioc (cassava) account for a substantial part of the diet.

Domestication altered the way plants and animals looked, tasted, and behaved. Plants mostly got larger, resulting in greater yields. Animals, conversely, got smaller likely because they were easier to control and tame. It is important to remember that domestication was an ongoing process— humans continued to breed plants and animals, refining characteristics to their preferences. This continues today, and will be discussed further in a later chapter on technology.

Scholars remind us that domestication is a highly selective process (Diamond 1997). That is to say, not all plants or animals were worth the effort to domesticate. There are over 50,000 known edible plants in the world, but humans rely on a small fraction. A dozen dominate modern food production: wheat, corn (maize), rice, barley, sorghum (millet), soybeans, potatoes, cassava (manioc), sweet potatoes, sugarcane, sugar beets, and bananas. In particular, wheat, rice, and maize (corn) provide 60 percent of the world's food intake.

The earliest form of agriculture is what is known as *horticulture*.[1] This type of subsistence system is a low-tech form of farming or gardening. Horticulturalists generally have limited tools at their disposal. Early horticulturalists often farmed without plows, draft animals, irrigation, or fertilizers. Horticulture continues to be practiced today, particularly in tropical forest areas with lots of rainfall and in hilly inland areas. Horticulturalists remain in parts of Central and South America, Africa, Southeast Asia, and in some of the Pacific Islands. Modern horticulturalists still incorporate techniques used by early farmers.

Unlike foragers, who were relatively mobile, horticulturalists tended to be more sedentary and stayed in a site. Horticulturalists moved primarily to look for fresh land. Because they did not use fertilizers and used only basic farming technology, land would be depleted of its nutrients after continuous farming. Thus, slash-and-burn (or swidden) cultivation was used, particularly in heavily forested areas. Forests were cut down and burned; land was cleared and the ashes of vegetation used to enrich the soil. After two or three harvests, horticulturalists would leave a site and allow it to "return to nature" to regain its nutrients.

With the invention of agriculture, humans began to stay in one place, settling down and creating permanent housing, eventually developing complex infrastructures, including governments, political systems, and religious systems. Horticulturalist societies had more extensive social hierarchies than foraging societies. There were sexual divisions of labor. Men commonly cleared land in preparation for slash-and-burn cultivation, while women planted and harvested crops. Given that horticulturalist societies tended to be more sedentary, they could build up surpluses of food and store them. As a result, horticulturalists lived in larger societies than foragers. Multiple communities, without any kinship ties, might live and work together to clear land and farm. Due to the larger population groups, leaders tended to have greater power and horticulturalist societies were less egalitarian than foraging societies. Surpluses were also used to raise social standing and could be accumulated for wealth.

The advent of horticulturalism also resulted in other social changes. Because horticulture did not require constant work due to the ability to produce storage excess, this "freed" some members of the society to develop and practice other skills like pottery, metalworking, and crafts like weaving. Religion and a sense of timekeeping also emerged at this time, often focusing on land fertility and planting cycles. Rituals and practices centered around different seasons and natural cycles of planting, harvest, and "death" in the winter.

4.4 Activity: Grow your own food

Have you ever grown your own food? Most modern consumers have little understanding of how to grow food. This activity encourages you to take a try at growing your own food. Food can be effectively grown, especially culinary herbs and small vegetables, even in small spaces like dormitory rooms.

Materials

Growing containers. Reused yogurt pots, tin cans, and food jars make excellent starter pots. Alternatively, seed trays can be purchased from any garden store.

Fresh seedling mix—avoid reusing soil from another plant or soil taken directly from the ground.

Notebook

Phone or camera to document the growth process

Directions

1. Clean your containers and fill with seedling mix. Seedling mix is available at garden stores. Do not use potting soil, which does not have the proper mix of nutrients to support growth.
2. Water your seedlings as directed on the seed packet. A gentle mist is often plenty. Plants are fragile at this state.
3. Place your seedling containers in a warm spot. On top of the refrigerator or near the kitchen oven are good options. Avoid roasting your seeds— putting it close to a radiator is too warm. Seeds are most comfortable around 65–75 degrees Fahrenheit (18–24 degrees C).
4. Seedlings will appear in a few weeks. Move to individual containers filled with potting mix when the seedlings get their second set of leaves.
5. Be sure to document the changes to your seedlings every day. Take photos and notes of daily progress.

Discussion questions

1. How long did it take for your seedlings to appear? What feelings and emotions did you experience waiting for your plant to appear?
2. How successful were you in growing your seedlings?
3. If your seedlings failed, why might that be? What factors might have impacted your success?
4. Consider if you had to grow all of your food. How much effort might that take out of your day? How might that influence your daily schedule and patterns?

Early domestication: Pastoralism

While horticulture focused on the domestication of plants and some small species of animals, other societies focused on animal husbandry and livestock. The rise of animal domestication also led to *pastoralism*, a subsistence system that centers on domesticated animals as food, fuel, transportation, wealth, and power (and even in religious rites). Pastoralism is more commonly called "ranching" or "herding." Pastoralist communities exist in many different landscapes. Most of the world's pastoralist communities are on the African continent, although pastoralists also roam Central Asia, Tibet, Scandinavia, and Siberia.

This type of subsistence first arose in the Middle East approximately 12,000 years ago, where sheep and goats were among the earliest domesticated animals, providing milk, meat, hides, wool, and hair for weaving (Kiple 2007: 16). It is a common misconception that livestock was reared for meat. In actuality, meat was often the last choice food—eaten after an animal had been sacrificed for religious purposes or had died from natural causes. Keeping an animal alive was more valuable in the long run. Milk was transformed into butter, yogurt, and cheese and in some pastoralist societies, milk products accounted for the majority of their caloric intake. Fur and wool could even be sold. The whole animal was utilized: blood was used as food and, in some religious rites, bones could be transformed into tools and decorative objects; even dung could be used as a fuel source or as building material. Like horticulturalists, pastoralists did not live off their harvest alone. Pastoralists could supplement their food by hunting and gathering. They could trade with farming communities to gain access to foodstuffs and goods they could not produce themselves.

Pastoralist communities tended to be centered upon one animal rather than multiple animals. For instance, cattle is the primary animal among pastoralists in East Africa. Common animals include cattle, sheep, goats, llamas, horses, camels, yak, and pigs. The types of animals herded depends on the landscape and ecology.

Pastoralist societies tended to be more nomadic than horticulturalist societies. Mobility was shaped by seasonality: terrain, seasons, available grazing land, and water access influenced where pastoralists lived and moved. Some pastoralist societies were nomadic, or always on the move. Others tended to be seminomadic and moved only with the seasons. Like horticultural societies, pastoralists also lived in larger communities formed of different groups of non-kin members. Many pastoralist societies tended to be patrilineal—descent determined through the male line—and patriarchal. Men tended to dominate in public life. Though pastoralist societies often lacked formal government systems, leaders emerged, often powerful men with large herds, and these men looked after their own communities and sometimes made alliances with other pastoralist communities.

The concept of property and ownership is incredibly important in pastoralist societies. One's herd is an immense source of pride, status, and prestige. Though herds tended to be owned by one individual, family lineage was important to pastoralist social organization. Herds are part of lineage property and the wealth of an individual is reflective of the larger lineage's wealth. The prestige and power of a lineage is based upon their collective herds. Those with larger herds are often accorded higher social status and thought of as being more knowledgeable and powerful than those with smaller herds (see Sutter 1987).

4.5 Activity: Butter

Butter is an important food item among pastoralists. Butter is a way of extending the shelf life of milk, which spoils quickly. The process of making butter transforms cream into a solid, storable food. The earliest butters likely would have been made from sheep or goat's milk; this recipe is for butter made from cow's milk.

In some pastoralist societies, butter is more than food—it is also a source of oil (for heating and lighting) and is sometimes used in religious rites and ceremonies. For instance, traditionally Tibetans herd yak, a long-haired domesticated bovid native to the Himalayas. Yak milk is transformed into yogurt, butter, and cheese. Yak butter is burned as a source of heat and light, and is also used in Tibetan Buddhist rituals. Yak butter lamps are used to help focus the mind and aid in meditation, and pilgrims bring offerings of yak butter to monasteries and temples.

Equipment

Sturdy glass jar with a lid, cleaned and dried. Old food jars work well for this task
Glass marbles, cleaned and dried (optional)
Extra storage container

Ingredients

Heavy cream (ideally 35 percent fat or higher). Consider buying locally produced cream for extra freshness, if available.
Salt

Directions

1. Fill the cleaned jar no more than halfway with cream. If using marbles, add them to the jar.
2. Place the lid and tighten. Shake vigorously until the cream thickens and forms a ball. Continue shaking until the liquid separates from the ball of butter. Shaking will take several minutes.
3. Open the jar and drain the liquid into a separate container. Don't throw this liquid away—it is buttermilk and can be used for dishes like pancakes or marinating chicken.
4. Take the butter and gently knead under cold running water to remove the remaining buttermilk. This is an important step, as the butter will spoil quickly unless the buttermilk is removed.
5. If desired, knead salt into the butter. Store the butter in a cleaned jar or container in the refrigerator. Butter can also be frozen for later use.

Instructor's note

This can be assigned as homework. This activity can be completed in any space as long as there is access to running water to rinse the buttermilk.

Discussion questions

1. Have you ever made butter before? What was it like making butter? Has making your own changed your appreciation for butter?
2. Imagine being a pastoralist. Why might butter and other storable products be useful? Why would it be important to transform milk and cream into other products?

Further resources

Butter (2011) is a comedy about the dark side of a butter sculpture competition in Iowa.

Bhatia, A. (2012). "Milk, Meat and Blood: How Diet Drives Natural Selection in the Maasai." *Wired*. https://www.wired.com/2012/09/milk-meat-and-blood-how-diet-drives-natural-selection-in-the-maasai/.

Kerven, C. (1987). "The Role of Milk in a Pastoral Diet and Economy: The Case of South Darfur, Sudan." *ILCA Bulletin*, 27, pp. 18–27.

"What do pastoralists produce and how do they market it?" Food and Agriculture Organization. http://www.fao.org/docrep/005/Y2647E/y2647e06.htm.

Intensive agriculture

Intensive agriculture, which dates back 5,000–6,000 years, has had the most significant impact on our diets, our lifestyles, and social structures. Intensive agriculture led to the rise of large-scale societies, or what we call *civilizations*. The concept of ownership and social status also emerged with the rise of civilizations. Intensive agriculture is differentiated from horticulture in the intensity, frequency, and size of production. Intensive agriculture can support a large population in less space than other systems. With the invention of agriculture, humans began to stay in one place, settling down and creating permanent housing, developing complex infrastructures including governments, political systems, and religious systems.

There are four key characteristics that distinguish intensive agriculture from horticulture. There is an increasing tendency to rely on a single plant species, to practice monocropping. Monocropping is an efficient system of production, as it allows for large yields with relatively low costs because the inputs and growing methods all the same. However, it has downfalls for human diets and for the ecology. Monocropping tends to privilege certain species—often staple foods like wheat, rice, and maize. Furthermore, it is often just a few varieties within certain species are grown. To illustrate, maize (corn) is a common staple food indigenous to the Americas. Though there are thousands of *heirloom* varieties, most commercially grown corn comes from just a handful of varieties, much of it *hybridized* or even *genetically modified* (see Figures 4.2 and 4.3).

Hanging in the balance is also the risk of malnutrition in a society due to the sameness of food sources. Humans need a diverse range of nutrients (often only attainable through consuming a variety of foodstuffs). And this impacts our ecological diversity, as bad climate conditions and plant diseases and pests can wipe out an entire harvest. Thus, humans still face precariousness and risk as the loss of harvest could potentially lead to famine and malnutrition. Monocropping is especially prevalent as a practice in twenty-first-century industrial agribusiness, the consequences of which will be discussed in the next section.

The second characteristic is that intensive farming led to huge increases in human population, in terms of population size and population density. Archeological records indicate that human communities grew rapidly upon the advent of agriculture. Larger population sizes and density also led to the third characteristic of agriculture. Though humans have practiced some form of division of labor since our earliest existence, intensive agriculture facilitated the emergence of specialized occupations. Because agriculture ensured consistent and high yields of foods, especially staple crops, it meant that not everyone had to farm. Instead, people began to take on different tasks

FIGURE 4.2 *A popular hybridized apple sold in a commercial North American supermarket. Photo courtesy of the author.*

FIGURE 4.3 *Blue agave (*Agave tequilana*) cultivated for tequila and mezcal production in the Yucatan Peninsula, Mexico. An example of monocrop. Photo courtesy of the author.*

and roles in a society, adopting specialized knowledge and skills, including nonagricultural knowledge.

This leads into the fourth aspect of intensive agricultural systems. Specialized knowledge and skills, as well as the ability to store (and control) surplus as wealth, led to social stratification. While it is true that all human societies have had some type of hierarchies, even among hunter-gatherer groups, intense social stratification emerged with intensive agriculture. Differentiated roles and wealth accounted for the origins of social class and inequality. Some scholars contend that agriculture has been the most ruinous subsistence system. Jared Diamond (1997) has commented, "The adoption of agriculture, supposedly our most decisive step toward a better life, was in many was a catastrophe from which we have never recovered").

The modern agricultural system

Modern industrial agriculture emerged in the mid-twentieth century and is the basis for food production and consumption in the developed industrialized world. In the developed industrialized world, few people are "producers" of food. Most, instead, are the "consumers"—the people who buy food rather than have some hand in growing it or making it. This shift from producer to consumer has had different consequences for our societies. In particular, I draw attention to three main areas: lack of food knowledge, long and complex food chains, and the rise of food waste. These three issues are not isolated from one another, but are connected as part of our present focus on serving the consumer rather than becoming producers.

Food knowledge

Consumers in industrialized nations like the United States know surprisingly little about the origins of their food, how it is grown, and where it comes from. A survey of 1,000 people conducted by the Innovation Center for US Dairy found that 7 percent of Americans polled think that chocolate milk comes from brown cows (National Dairy Council 2017). Admittedly, this was a relatively small sample from a survey conducted by the dairy lobby. And some respondents may have selected this answer as a joke. But it points to how little many Americans know about their food system. Researchers studying fourth, fifth, and sixth graders in a major metropolitan area of California found that urban schoolchildren are deficient in agricultural literacy. Of the children surveyed, only 28 percent knew that a hamburger bun was made of flour/wheat. Only 22 percent knew that pickles were made from cucumbers. One respondent stated that pickles come from lions and tigers and that bread comes from an unidentified animal (Hess and Trexler 2011).

Census data provides some insights as to why Americans know very little about their food. Less than 2 percent of Americans live on a farm, roughly 650,000 people out of a population of 323 million. So, while "farm-to-table" and "local" eating has grown in popularity, Americans may be very interested in so-called farm fresh food but may know very little about how their food is produced or about life on a farm (Birkenholz 1993). This lack of agricultural literacy is not simply an American problem but seems to be symptomatic of all food systems where there are stark divisions between the consumer and producer (see de Magistris and Gracia 2008; Fonte 2008; Hansen and Woronov 2013).

Of course, the food industry and the long global food chain makes it increasingly difficult for consumers to know about the origins of their food and the production methods. It is in the food industry's interest to keep consumers in the dark, so to speak, to avoid having to disclose information about the production methods, food miles, and other issues consumers may want to know about.

Though there are efforts to "demystify" the industrial food chain, consumers are still left largely in the dark about where their food comes from. There have been some efforts, however, to clarify the source of food. The UK, for instance, has started instituting better tracking measures for British-produced eggs. Eggs produced in Britain by farms involved in the British Lion scheme have a special lion stamp etched on each eggshell. Through British Lion Egg Tracking,[2] consumers can access their website and enter in a specially printed code to learn about where their eggs are from. A downside to this program is that this information is primarily limited to whether it is an egg produced in the UK or in the European Union. It is also used as a promotional tool to support the British egg industry rather than a knowledge tool for consumers to learn more about their producers.

Food chains

Our modern diets are organized around a *world system*, a complex web through which goods circulate around the globe. Among the goods that travel around the globe are agricultural products known as *commodities*. The journey a product takes from the place of production, like the field, to eventually end up on your dinner plate reveals much about the present world system (see Figure 4.4). During our hunter-gatherer days, the journey food took was fairly straightforward. Hunter-gatherers would locate their food source and acquire it themselves. Today, commodities can move through dozens of hands and even

FIGURE 4.4 *A sign from a cheese vendor showing the food chain of its product as it moves from its production in Comte, France, to Borough Market, London. Photo courtesy of the author.*

travel across oceans and continents to get to the consumer. Products might travel from producers to exporters, importers, distributors, and eventually to retailers where they are sold to consumers. As we have become further removed from our food source, we are asked to "trust" many anonymous actors in our *food chain.*

What is striking to many modern consumers is just how "foreign" our food supply is. That is to say, many of the foods we consume are from elsewhere. To illustrate, some of the most iconic foods of Italian cuisine hail from outside. When we think of stereotypes of Italian life, we think of people sipping espressos at a coffee bar, diners enjoying dishes like pasta in a red sauce, potato *gnocchi* (soft dumplings), *risotto* (creamy rice cooked in broth), or a velvety dish of *polenta* (a ground corn porridge similar to American grits), or savoring hand-crafted chocolates. These iconic Italian foods all have ingredients whose origins are outside of Italy (and even beyond the European continent). Coffee beans are native to the Arabian Peninsula; wheat for pasta is from the Middle East; corn, tomatoes, and potatoes are from the Americas; rice was first cultivated in China; and that delicious Italian chocolate is made with cacao, which originated from Mesoamerica. While a plant or animal might have been originally domesticated in one area, they have also spread to other parts of the world—a product of *diffusion*. In the modern food system, it is common to have products from all over the planet shipped to our supermarkets and in front of us on our dinner plates. This will be discussed further in Chapter 6 on globalization.

4.6 Food for thought: As American as apple pie?

To be as American as apple pie is to be wholesome, natural, and to represent the best that America has to offer. But what if apple pie wasn't actually American? The ingredients that make up apple pie hail from places outside of the United States. Apples originated from Central Asia, likely from the area known today as Kazakhstan. Apples eventually moved into Western Europe through trade, where they eventually became incorporated into "local" European dishes. Apples arrived in America via European colonists. Native American fruits like the pawpaw were rejected in favor of the apples, and pawpaw trees were ripped out to plant apples instead. Apple orchards were planted widely across the United States due, in part, to the efforts of a man named John Chapman, who is more popularly known as Johnny Appleseed. Chapman cleared land and planted appleseeds across the Midwest for forty years. This fruit became integral to the early American diet because they were easy to grow, easily stored, and also provided a good source of nutrients. Other ingredients used to make apple pie are also foreign: wheat, used as flour in making the pastry crust, originates from the Middle East; sugarcane to sweeten the pie originates from South or Southeast Asia; and butter made from cow's milk is made possible by the transfer of cattle from Eurasia during the Great Exchange.

4.7 Activity: Checking the food chain

A *food chain* includes the processes and actors as food moves from its production point to its final consumption point. It takes into account the food producers, the distributors, and consumers involved. Food chains can be incredibly short—if you grow or acquire your own food, you might know exactly where your food is from and under what conditions it was raised. But if you buy food from a modern supermarket, it may be very difficult to obtain information about its origin point. The information about the original source may be lost or even obscured as the food moves through the many hands and miles to get to the consumer.

Increasingly, many companies are trying to make their food chain more transparent. They highlight their sustainability practices and claim that they can tell you where their food is from.

Just how long is the food chain? To get some first-hand insight, we will investigate the food chain of coffee beans, an important *commodity*, an economic good that can be bought and sold, and the reason many of us are able to wake up for morning classes.

Coffee is a popular morning beverage and is sold at many food establishments. Some of the most popular coffee vendors in the United States include Starbucks, McDonald's, Dunkin' Donuts, and Whole Foods Market. There are countless other regional chains. Additionally, each of these companies has had recent campaigns explaining their corporate social responsibility—their efforts to ensure that their food products are acquired fairly and transparently.

Select one or more companies to call and speak to a customer service representative. Their phone numbers are:

- Starbucks 1-800-782-7282
- McDonald's 1-800-244-6227
- Dunkin' Donuts 1-800-859-5339
- Whole Foods 1-844-936-8255

When you get someone on the phone, identify yourself. Start with a line like, "Hi, I'm (your name). I'm a student at (your institution) and I'm working on a class assignment about the food chain. I would like to know more information about your house blend coffee."

Request the following information from your customer service representative:

- Where is the product from? Country, state/province/region, city/town/ village, farm, and farmers' names, if possible.
- What varietal(s) are grown? What are the growing methods? How long does it take for the product to reach maturity and harvest? Are pesticides used? If so, which ones?
- What are farmers paid for their labor?

Instructor's note

This assignment can be completed with other commodities. Try calling the same companies about their house-blend teas; chocolate manufacturers about their cacao beans; or snack food companies about the provenance of their corn.

These telephone numbers are correct at the time of publication. Do check that they remain in service.

Discussion questions

1. How much information were you able to discover from the customer service representative? Is it possible to trace coffee to its original source?
2. What insights does this interaction shed about the food chain? How long is it?
3. Are you able to trace the entire chain? Where does the chain break?

Further resources

Black Gold (2006) is a documentary about the global coffee trade.
Fridell, G. (2007). *Fair Trade Coffee: The Prospects and Pitfalls of Market-Driven Social Justice.* Toronto: University of Toronto Press.
The International Coffee Organization maintains a list of the prices paid to coffee farmers. http://www.ico.org/coffee_prices.asp.
Pendergrast, Mark (1999). *Uncommon Grounds: The History of Coffee and how It Transformed Our World.* New York: Basic Books.
Talbot, J. M. (2004). *Grounds for Agreement: The Political Economy of the Coffee Commodity Chain.* Oxford: Rowman & Littlefield.

Inequality

Although we fetishize "fresh," "local," and "farm-to-table" foods, most modern American consumers know very little about those who grow their food. We may drool over beautiful images of farms and farm fresh-food, but far less often do we see representations of workers and producers toiling to produce our food. When we do see images of landscapes and agricultural zones, they tend to be devoid of the workers in these scenes. Scenes of California, the proverbial "Golden State," the sixth-largest economy in the world if taken alone, is also one of the biggest agricultural states in the United States. When we see advertisements to visit California and sample its unique agricultural products, we don't see any pictures of the workers in the fields. Pictures of California's wine regions, for instance, show happy consumers drinking wine with shots of pristine, rolling vineyards in the background. The laborers, especially migrant workers from Mexico and Central America who come north to work the fields, are nowhere to be found.

Farmers and farm workers see low financial returns for their work. Because food producers are at the very start of the food chain, their distance from consumers keeps them "invisible." Furthermore, it is often the food retailer at the end of the food chain that reaps the financial benefit from agricultural production. The retailer is the name, the brand, the logo that consumers associate with products, as opposed to the anonymous farmers. To illustrate, coffee farmers earn somewhere around $1.40 per pound for their coffee beans. Starbucks, one of the world's most iconic coffee retailers, sells those same beans for between $10 and $20 per pound to consumers.

Environment

Indubitably, the modern agricultural system has changed the landscape and ecologies to produce food. The plant and animal species we eat have little in common with their wild ancestors. Consider modern-day poultry. Chicken is one of the most popular types of meat worldwide. Modern chickens are domesticated birds that have been bred for certain traits. Chickens are believed to have descended from the red junglefowl (*Gallus gallus*), a bird native to Southeast Asia. Modern chickens have little in common with their wild ancestors. For one, modern meat chickens, what supermarkets often call "broiler chickens," are bred for their meat content. A bird can mature to full size in five weeks' time. These birds are hybrids, bred to grow rapidly to a large size to fulfill modern consumer demands for meat. Similarly, modern turkeys have little in common with their wild cousins. Modern turkeys are also often hybrids and are raised for meat consumption. In particular, modern turkeys have very large breasts, which makes it difficult for them to fly or even move around.

But one consequence less considered is the waste produced. Much of what is grown in the modern agricultural system is thrown out—never so much as passing the shopping baskets of consumers. Consumers also throw out a tremendous amount of food. In the United States, food waste is estimated to be between 30 and 40 percent of the food supply. This means roughly 133 billion pounds and $161 billion worth of food is thrown out, sent to landfills instead of feeding people. Furthermore, the resources needed to produce food—land, labor, energy—also add to the total cost of waste.

Moreover, the foods that modern humans consume produce a tremendous amount of packaging waste. Think about your trip to the supermarket. Most people will buy a mixture of fresh produce, meats, dairy products, and dry foods. You will likely bag your fresh produce in plastic bags. Your meats have been wrapped in plastic wrap. Milk is sold in plastic jugs. Dry foods like cereals, grains, and snack foods come packaged in plastic bags and plastic trays. Eating in the modern food system means generating waste.

4.8 Activity: Tracking your food waste

Back in 2014, Lauren Singer's story went viral on the internet and was profiled by many media outlets. Her claim to fame? Singer, a young British woman, managed to whittle her waste footprint down to what many consider an impossible small amount. All of the waste she produced over a year fit into a 16 ounce glass jar. This feat seems astonishing, and Singer went on the record explaining the many conscientious efforts she took to meet this objective, including shopping in bulk or package-free stores, recycling, and composting her food waste. Her website, http://www.trashisfortossers. com, chronicles how she accomplished this feat and how others can also minimize their ecological footprint.

This challenge is a take on this. Can you fit all of your waste during one day (24 hours) into a small jar? What lifestyle changes and efforts would you have to undertake to fulfill this challenge?

Materials

16 ounce glass jar (pint jar)
Plastic garbage bag
Notebook
Camera

Directions

For 24 hours, document (photos and written notes) your waste. Track and note everything you throw away—paper, food packaging, food scraps, and so on. Be sure to include time entries to note your waste producing patterns. Place your waste into your jar. If you manage to fill up your jar, note the time. Continue to collect the waste but deposit it into a plastic garbage bag.

Discussion questions

1. Did you fill up your jar? How long did it take to fill it up?
2. Are there certain patterns to your waste production? For instance, do you produce more waste at certain times of day? Do you produce certain types of waste at different moments?
3. How much of your waste was food waste (e.g., food packaging, unfinished food) versus other waste?
4. Did tracking your daily waste output change your waste patterns? For instance, did you become more inclined to recycle or reuse certain products (e.g., plastic bags, disposable cutlery, plastic straws)?
5. What insights did you gain about your waste habits?

Summary

- Our subsistence systems have consequences on the way we live.

- The journey from the seekers of food, to the producers, and now consumers of food is one that has stretched over millions of years.

- Foraging (hunting and gathering), horticulturalism, pastoralism, and intensive agriculture are the main systems of food acquisition.

- How we acquire our food has consequences for our lifestyles.

- The modern agricultural system has decreased food knowledge, lengthened the food chain, promoted inequality, and has had a significant environmental impact.

Discussion questions

1. Would you have survived as a hunter-gatherer? What types of knowledge about animals, plants, your local ecology, and the seasons would you need to know to be successful?

2. What are some of the advantages of the modern agricultural system? What are some of the disadvantages?

Further resources

Documentaries

Food, Inc. (2008) is a documentary about corporate agribusiness in the United States and its impact on human and environmental welfare.

King Corn (2007) is a documentary that follows two friends as they move to Iowa to grow and farm an acre of corn. Their film takes on the growth of agribusiness, the industrialization of farming, and the shift toward commodity crops like corn.

The Plow That Broke the Plains (1936) is a historic short documentary on what happened to the Great Plains region of the United States and Canada during the Dust Bowl. It exposes the dangers of uncontrolled agricultural practices and overfarming.

Polyfaces (2015) is a documentary about an Australian family who moves to the United States to create a sustainable farm.

Rancher, Farmer, Fisherman (2017) is a documentary on how ranchers, farmers, and fishermen are involved in an unseen fight for environmental activism and sustainability.

Websites

Third World Farmer (https://3rdworldfarmer.org) is a simulation game. Players experience the life of a farming family on the African continent and learn about the difficulties of subsistence horticulture in the modern world.

Notes

1 Horticulture is also used to refer to serious amateur gardening.
2 See http://lioneggfarms.co.uk.

Further resources

Cook, Langdon (2009). *Fat of the Land: Adventures of the 21st Century Forager.* Seattle: Mountaineers Books/Skipstone.

Harper, Charles and Bryan LeBeau (2003). *Food, Society and Environment.* Upper Saddle River, NJ: Prentice Hall.
Howell, Nancy (2010). *Life Histories of the Dobe! Kung: Food, Fatness, and Well-Being over the Life Span (Vol. 4).* Berkeley: University of California Press.
Pincetl, Stephanie S. (1999). *Transforming California: A Political History of Land Use and Development.* Baltimore: Johns Hopkins University Press.
Roberts, Paul (2008). *The End of Food.* New York: Houghton Mifflin.
Wiessner, Pauline (1996). "Leveling the Hunter: Constraints on the Status Quest in Foraging Societies." In P. Wiessner and W. Schiefenhövel (eds.), *Food and the Status Quest: An Interdisciplinary Perspective.* Providence, RI: Berghahn Books, pp. 171–191.

5

Food and Technology

There's a well-known American saying, "The best thing since sliced bread." This phrase expresses excitement about a new technology or invention. Given all of the technologies we have today, it makes us wonder, the best thing we can have is . . . presliced bread? Calling something the best thing since sliced bread sounds antiquated today, something your grandmother might say. But at one point in our recent past, presliced bread was a radical technology and was the so-called best thing. It represented convenience, modernity, and efficiency—values that consumers held in high importance in the early twentieth century.

Bread is the proverbial staff of life, a staple food that nourishes much of the world. For much of bread's existence as a foodstuff, it was sliced as needed: piece by piece from a larger loaf. The first bread-slicing machine was invented in the 1860s, although it did not catch on in wide commercial use until the late 1920s when other technologies came along to reinforce its necessity. This is typical of new technologies. Scholars have observed that technologies rarely emerge alone; they come in "clusters" (Wilson 2012: xx). When a new technology is introduced, others are needed to support or facilitate. This was certainly new in the case of bread. No one had—or more appropriately, knew they had—a need for perfectly uniform slices of toast until the invention of the electric toaster in 1893. Previously, bread was toasted in a metal frame on a long-handled toasting fork held over a fire or a kitchen grill. The introduction of the toaster made the bread slicer relevant. Presliced bread quickly caught on and, by the 1930s, commercial bread makers adopted the bread slicing machine.

Through this brief exploration of the phrase "The best thing since sliced bread," we can quickly establish that technology is a term that must be considered in its historic and sociocultural context. What was the height of innovation at one point, such as sliced bread, can become quotidian by the next generation. Today, the technology cycle moves even faster: new phones, gadgets, computers are released each year (if not more frequently). The "upgrade cycle" is a nonstop hamster wheel that keeps turning, urging consumers to keep up with the latest and greatest for fear of losing out and falling out of touch.

We live in a supposed "technological age" (Wilson 2012: xiv). Never have we had such access to sophisticated science, technology, and modern machinery. And never before has it been so integrated into our lives and everyday existence. Food writer Bee Wilson reminds us that this phrase is a pithy way of proclaiming "we have a lot of computers" (2012: xiv). She cautions us to remember that every period in history had its own technologies. In its own way, every period in time was a technological age. Humans use technology to make life easier. After all, invention is the mother of necessity.

When we pair the pair the words food and technology together, our minds might tend to think about cutting-edge inventions or modernist cooking techniques. We might think about the popularization of *sous vide*, a method of slow cooking that ensures consistent temperatures. We might think of the coolest avant-garde chefs working in Michelin-starred restaurants, whose dishes made of foams, gels, and spherifications look more like abstract art than food. Or our minds turn toward genetically modified organisms and the value of bioengineering in our food supply.

But what if we took a step back and considered how some of the most mundane, everyday objects around us are *also* forms of technology. At one point, these inventions were new and revolutionary. The most versatile and most timeless inventions are usually the most basic. Many of the everyday culinary objects and tools that we take for granted today were novel during their advent. Consider the fact that cutlery, mortars and pestles, knives, wooden spoons, pottery, cooking vessels, and fire were all new at one point and have endured to change how we eat, cook, and share food. These, too, are technologies.

Contemporary scholars use the phrase "technological age" to mean that we are aware that science, technology, and society are "intermeshed with one another" and impact our lives in many different ways (Kranzberg 1991: 234). When they write about our present "technological age," they are not simply marking the presence of new gizmos and gadgets, but are showing awareness of the impact that the said objects can bring upon our everyday existence. Furthermore, they are careful not to pass judgement but to observe. "Technology is neither good nor bad; nor is it neutral" (Kranzberg 1986: 545). Technology must be considered in terms of both its short and long range impacts (see Braudel 1992). After all, "technological capabilities do not necessarily determine our actions" (Kranzberg 1986: 559). What seems like a terrible technology in the short term may have overall benefits in the long term—and vice versa. Our charge here is to consider how technology interacts "in different ways with different values and institutions, indeed, with the entire sociocultural milieu" (Kranzberg 1986: 548).

This chapter is an exploration of technology and how it has affected the way we get our food, what we eat, how we eat, and how food shapes our lives. The purpose of this chapter is not to create an essential list of what is and is not technology. That would be a futile effort, in part because some of the things to be discussed on this list may be outdated by the time you read this. Instead, this chapter is to think about broad categories—ways in which technology has impacted our world and the types of technologies that have had the greatest impact on our food, and about the short and long range impacts of technology on how we eat, cook, and produce food, and what we think about our food acquisition systems.

Tools

Imagine an object with three or four tines and a long handle. You likely have seen it in many places—in cupboards, in kitchens, on tables. Sometimes they are left in other places like park benches, on the side of the street, or in a garbage can. To many people, this object is a fork. Its understood purpose is to move food from an eating vessel (like a plate) to the diner's mouth without having to soil one's fingers. Yet, not everyone would look at this object and think the same thing.

A scene from Disney's *The Little Mermaid* exemplifies how an object, when taken out of its usual context, can mean something different. Ariel, the mermaid, brings up objects she finds at the bottom of the sea, to her friend Scuttle, the seagull. The wise and knowing seagull, a self-proclaimed expert on human habits, explains what the objects are. He pulls out what most of us consider a fork and proclaims it to be a dinglehopper. He tells her that the dinglehopper is used for grooming, and he twirls the tines of the dinglehopper around the feathers on his head to style it into a hairdo. Later in the film, when the mermaid has been transformed into a human and is living on land, she finds herself at a dinner table with her romantic interest and his family. She recognizes a familiar object and recalls its use. Ariel reaches for the dinglehopper and twirls her hair around its tines, just in the way she'd seen before. Her romantic interest and his family give her an odd look as they tuck into their dinners with their forks. As this movie scene illustrates, a tool is never just a tool but takes on whatever meaning the user wants it to have. A three- or four-tined object could be a fork for eating or a dinglehopper for hairstyling.

Many animal species use tools. Bottlenose dolphins use sponges to protect their rostrum as they hunt for food on the bottom of the seabed. Sea otters use rocks to break open shellfish. Elephants will use tree branches as flyswatters. Beavers fashion dams out of logs, sticks, plant matter, and rocks. Chimpanzees, our evolutionary cousins, will use sticks to gather insects or chew up leaves and wad them up as a sponge to gather water. Clearly, tool use is not unique to humans. But tool *making* is. Humans make tools with foresight—they do so in anticipation of something and make tools to serve specific needs. "Man could not have become Homo Sapiens, 'man the thinker,' had he not at the same time been Homo faber, 'man the maker'" (Kranzberg 1986: 557).

Tools have been part of the human world since our earliest days as a species. The earliest tools were likely rocks, stones, and sticks gathered from the natural environment and used to make food acquisition simpler. Tool use was important to early humans because they helped facilitate hunting and gathering. Because humans stand upright and are bipedal (two-legged), humans can easily carry things for long distances. Tools made it easier to hunt and gather food, particularly in pursuing big game and butchering it for consumption. Humans also use tools far more systematically than other species; we possess the widest range of tools.

Archeological evidence suggests that stone tool manufacture may date as far back as 2.5 million years ago. Rock fragments dug from Ethiopia, one of the oldest inhabited areas of the world, show that rocks were deliberately smacked together to form a knife. Fossil records from this time also show bones with deliberate cut marks—evidence of tool use. Knife making suggests "planning, patience, cooperation, and organized behavior" (Wrangham 2009: 4). In other words, tool making was a deliberate practice. Around 1.5 million years ago, humans developed a new type of stone tool made by shaping rock cores or large stone flakes into a symmetrical teardrop shape. The Acheulean hand axe and similar types of tools were produced to serve specific needs. In this case, the Acheulean hand axe became the "Swiss Army Knife of the Paleolithic" (Tattersall 1999: 138). They were all-purpose instruments that helped advance society. These hand axes were used for digging up roots and bulbs, butchering animals, cracking nuts, breaking small animal bones, and even chopping wood. Early humans carried them everywhere and used them for various tasks.

The advent of stone tools had a meaningful impact on our diets and our evolution as a species. Our diets changed once humans were able to more efficiently capture and prepare meat. The addition of meat into human diets resulted in bigger brains and bodies, as meat provided the calories necessary to fuel human brain growth. Human brains demand roughly 20 percent of a body's resting calories and more if involved in stressful or strenuous tasks.

The rest of our bodies also followed suit with changes after the advent of new stone tools. Chiefly, our teeth became smaller since we were able to cut meat down into smaller pieces. Researchers have found that simply slicing meat and pounding it to tenderize would have enabled early humans to chew meat into smaller particles, thus making it easier for meat to be digested (see Zink and Lieberman 2016). Because we no longer needed large teeth to rip meat, our jaws and chewing muscles also shrank over time. Over time, this also affected our digestive systems. Our guts also decreased in size following the change in diets due to stone tools.

One might assume that tools were simply invented. That one fateful day, an early human picked up a piece of rock, bashed it with another one, until it reached the shape and sharpness that they desired. Perhaps that is what happened roughly 2.5 million years ago. But for something to become effective as a tool, it took a lot of time to refine these technologies. At times, this process happened incrementally over many successive generations.

New tools and technologies arise because there is some type of need or social shift. For instance, the invention of pottery emerged in societies as they became more sedentary. Pottery facilitates a variety of tasks. It enabled early humans to carry water, store food, and cook and prepare foods. But pottery can be difficult to transport given its weight, fragility, and size. And it can be time and labor intensive to produce, making it incompatible with highly mobile lifestyles like those of foragers. Pottery production became more prevalent as human societies shifted away from foraging lifestyles and toward semipermanent (and eventually permanent) settlements.

Moreover, pottery allowed humans to cook different types of food, specifically food of a drinkable consistency. Soft, easily consumed, and digestible liquid foods became part of human diets and some scientists suggest that this helped extend human lifespans. Liquid diets allowed the elderly and those who could not chew to continue receiving nourishment, whereas prior to the invention of pottery as cooking vessels there was only the option to eat whole foods that were difficult for those with limited chewing ability to consume.

5.1 Activity: Grinding ancient grains

It is easy to overlook "simple" technology like mortars and pestles. Yet, they have been and continue to be some of the most important tools for processing food. A mortar and pestle can mash, grind, and pound food and medicine. A good mortar and pestle must hold up to the repeated pounding action. It must be made of material that is hard enough break down food items, while at the same time not chipping away and leaving residue in the ingredients. The material should also not leech flavors or odors into the food.

It is also easy to take for granted how physical and laborious the act of using a mortar and pestle can be. Grinding hard food items, like seeds and grains, or very sticky, starchy food items like tubers, can be taxing. The arms, neck, shoulders, and back can ache if this is done for hours on end.

Materials

Rocks
Ancient grains—popcorn, wheat, chickpeas, barley are some possibilities
Large paper plates
Measuring cups (optional)
Kitchen scale (optional)
Cell phone or timer
Newspaper or tablecloth (optional)—to aid with cleanup
Broom and dustpan (optional)—to aid with cleanup
Earplugs (optional). This can be a very loud exercise.
All-purpose flour (optional). This serves as a point of comparison to the flour students are making.

Directions

1. Take a walk in your local area and find rocks you think would make good grindstones.
2. Return to your work area and cover with newspaper or a tablecloth (optional).
3. Measure (by weight or by volume) some of your ancient grains. Pour onto a large paper plate.
4. Start your timer to track how long it takes to turn your ancient grain into a useable flour. Continue grinding until you feel you have produced a sufficient amount of flour.

Instructor's note

Before starting this activity, spend time researching the local rocks in your area. Ideally, students will bring a variety of rocks with different properties into the class. This becomes a conversation point, as not all rocks are suited to be grindstones. For instance, my area (the Hudson Valley in New York) has a lot of slate, which chips and flakes easily. This becomes a discussion point for how early humans had to figure, through trial and error, which rocks would be suitable for this type of task. It also becomes a way of discussing co-technologies, as students raise questions like, "Would a sieve be invented to sift out rocks?" Or "Could we roast the grains to make it easier to grind?"

Discussion questions

1. How much flour were you able to produce?
2. Compare the texture of your flour to that of industrially produced all-purpose flour. What are the differences?
3. What insights does this activity give you about the invention of tools and technology?
4. In many parts of the world, people still grind grains by hand. Discuss how this would change the workday and food production if you had to produce flour by hand.

Further resources

Blogs

Laudan, Rachel. "It's the Shear Bloody Work of It (Sic). Grinding." *Rachel Laudan*, November 20, 2009, www.rachellaudan.com/2009/11/its-the-shear-bloody-work-of-it-sic-grinding.html.

Further resources

Henry, A. G., H. F. Hudson, and D. R. Piperno (2009). "Changes in Starch Grain Morphologies from Cooking." *Journal of Archaeological Science*, 36(3), pp. 915–922.
Laudan, R. (2012). "Mastering Grain Cookery, 20,000–300 B.C.E." *Cuisine and Empire: Cooking in World History*. Berkeley and Los Angeles: University of California Press.
McGee, H. (2004). "Seeds: Grains, Legumes, and Nuts." *On Food and Cooking: The Science and Lore of the Kitchen*. New York: Scribner.
Piperno, D. R., E. Weiss, I. Holst, and D. Nadel (2004). "Processing of Wild Cereal Grains in the Upper Paleolithic Revealed by Starch Grain Analysis." *Nature*, 430(7000), p. 670.
Revedin, A., B. Aranguren, R. Becattini, L. Longo, E. Marconi, M. M. Lippi, N. Skakun, A. Sinitsyn, E. Spiridonova, and J. Svoboda (2010). "Thirty Thousand-Year-Old Evidence of Plant Food Processing." *Proceedings of the National Academy of Sciences*, 107(44), pp. 18815–18819.

Modern kitchens exemplify this point well. Modern kitchen design is meant to incorporate the principles of modernity, science, and efficiency. Consider all the changes from a nineteenth-century home kitchen to a twentieth-century environment. Down-hearth fireplaces were replaced with freestanding cookstoves powered by coal and later gas (see Figure 5.1). Home-canned preserved foods and store-bought foods replaced the need for root cellars, where root vegetables were once stored for later consumption through the year. Indoor plumbing and indoor faucets made water pumps obsolete. Similarly, candles were replaced by gas lamps and later by electric lights.

Contemporary kitchens in the industrialized world are filled with countless gadgets and tools. Browse through any cookware or home goods store and you will see pots, pans, knives, cutting boards, and small appliances. You will also see gizmos you never knew you had a need for: a vegetable spiralizer that turns vegetables into strands of "noodles," an avocado slicer, a self-twirling spaghetti fork, and more. They were likely invented to fulfill some purpose or serve some need. Yet they have not become mainstays in our kitchens and retain an air of novelty rather than practicality.

This is typical. The simple presence of a new tool or technology does not mean it will be adopted or incorporated. Many household tools were ostensibly invented and introduced to households to make life easier, particularly life for the keeper of the home. Yet, the tools do not seem to have made life much easier. Instead, as historian Rose Schwartz Cowan notes, it is a "strange paradox that in the face of so many labor-saving devices, little labor appears to have been saved!" (Cowan 1983: 44).

Tools have shifted what we eat. Seventeen staple foods dominate our modern food system: rice, wheat, maize, sorghum, millet, rye, oat, potato, sweet potato, taro, yam, cassava, sago, arrowroot, teff, bread fruit, and barley. Among those food items, wheat, maize, rice, barley, oats, and potato are the six major staples in industrialized Western societies. While we may rely on just a few handfuls of staple foods, with tools and technology these items can be transformed into a seemingly endless variety of food items. Wheat, the predominant grain in Western societies, can be transformed into bread, cookies, crackers, pretzels, doughnuts, breakfast cereals, pasta, cakes, noodles, scones, shortbread, and many more items. As we can see, "modern man has replaced plant species variety (as in the case of the hunter-gatherer) with food variety (foods made from single plant species into diverse foods)" (Henry 1997: 587).

Tools have also impacted whether or not certain crops and foodstuffs made headway into a society. That is to say, cultivation techniques alone cannot be accountable for the delay of crop adoption. A lack of processing equipment can mean that a certain crop will face difficulties integrating into local foodways and food systems. Helen M. Leach (1999) points out two examples of how food processing technology can either help or hinder the adoption of staple foods into a society. She makes the case that the less a society has to invest into new culinary technologies, the easier it will be for a new staple to be adopted.

Wheat was introduced to the Maori, an indigenous Polynesian people of New Zealand, during the early nineteenth century by missionaries. Wheat became highly prized as a crop among the Maori, in part because it was difficult to transform into a useable product. Processing wheat requires a mill, sieves, different cooking containers, and other technologies that were not part of the Maori's technology set at the time. In contrast, corn (maize), was easily processed with the tools and technologies already available. Furthermore, corn could be cooked in ways familiar to the Maori—roasting corn in its husks was similar to the existing practice of cooking food in leaf wrappers. While wheat went on to become highly prized, in part because of its rarity, corn holds lesser status because it adapted more easily into Maori foodways.

Similarly, the adaptation of the potato into Scottish and Irish foodways tells a similar tale. Leach points out that potatoes were widely embraced in these two societies because they were easily incorporated into existing food practices. In Ireland, traditional hearth cookery techniques of boiling in a cauldron and baking in the embers were well-suited to the potato. The Scottish practice of simmering vegetables in broth meant potatoes were a welcome addition to the diet. The potato became successful because it was "technologically undemanding and economically important" in these two countries (Leach 1999: 137).

FIGURE 5.1 *A view from the kitchens at Hampton Court Palace, the residence of Henry VIII. This kitchen is typical of an elite home in Tudor England (1485–1603). Photo courtesy of the author.*

Tools transform people's knowledge base. Tools are not "passive instruments, confined to do our bidding, but have a life of their own" (Cowan 1983: 9). Tools require new skills and knowledge to be formed. Returning to our example of the sliced bread, the advent of the toaster meant that people needed to learn how to run an electric toaster, a skill no one had until its invention in 1893. But it also meant that other skills were lost. The practice of toasting a slice of bread over an open flame with a long-handled toasting fork gave way to knowing how to operate an electric toaster.

Furthermore, it is important to consider the social institutions that "mediate the availability of tools." What this means is that how the available tools are priced and how they are distributed impacts who has access, who can use them, and for what purposes, and all this is shaped by the institutions around them (Cowan 1983: 11). Tools are often meant to be social levelers, allowing some action to be improved upon to make life easier. But they can also be social dividers. Many technologies can be slow to be adopted because of their cost and other impediments to their widespread implementation. To illustrate, many Americans could not afford the newfangled electric appliances that were introduced to households during the early twentieth century. Particularly during the years of the Great Depression (1929–1939), widespread poverty and limited access to reliable electricity sources outside of urban areas made it prohibitive for most Americans to purchase things like electric toasters. Only large business and urban zones had access to reliable electricity. It was not until after World War II—with rising incomes, the expansion of electrical grids, and changes in wealth and affluence—that these objects became available on a wide scale.

Ultimately, tools are "not something apart from humanity." Instead, "all technical processes and products are the result of human creative imagination and human skills, hands and minds working together" (Kranzberg 1991: 236). Tools and technology are human activity. Tools and technology are part of food.

5.2 Activity: Tortilla making

Tortillas are a type of unleavened flatbread commonly featured in Mexican and Central American cooking. Tortillas are often made from finely ground maize (corn) that has been nixtamalized. This corn has been treated in an alkaline solution of mineral lime or calcium hydroxide, which then helps improve the nutritional value of the maize. Corn tortillas are frequently made with either white, yellow, or blue maize. Tortillas can also be made with wheat, but wheat tortillas are far less common (with the exception of Tex-Mex and other American adaptations of Mexican cuisine).

Ingredients

2 cups masa flour (masa harina)
½ teaspoon Kosher salt
1 ½ cups room temperature water

Equipment

Large mixing bowl
Spoon
Wax paper or parchment paper
Skillet or frying pan

Directions

1. Mix the masa, salt, and water in a large mixing bowl. Stir together until a dough forms. The dough should be stiff like putty.
2. Grab a hunk of dough the size of a golf ball and roll it into a ball. Place the ball of dough on top of a sheet of parchment paper or wax paper. Place another sheet of parchment paper or wax paper on top. Press flat with a skillet.
3. Carefully remove the top sheet of paper. Set the tortilla, parchment side up, on a hot skillet. Let the tortilla cook for 20–30 seconds; remove the parchment paper and continue cooking until brown spots appear. Flip and cook for another 30 seconds. Repeat until all the dough has been cooked.
4. Stack warm tortillas on a plate and wrap with a clean dishtowel to keep warm. Tortillas can be reheated for a few moments on the skillet as needed.

Discussion questions

1. Consider the experience of making tortillas. What is it like to make this without the aid of a mechanical press? How long did this take you? How long might this take you if you had to make tortillas by hand three meals a day?
2. How might this process change if you were to have a mechanical press to aid in tortilla making?
3. Corn tortillas are a mainstay on many Mexican and Central American tables. What types of factors (cultural, social, and environmental) have allowed corn to achieve such an important status?

Fire

The mastery of fire is one of the most important technologies to humankind because it revolutionized our diets and our relationship to the world around us. Fire changed our relationship to time and how humans organized their day. Fire provided warmth and light. It illuminated our dark, cold nights. It provided protection from dangerous animals. It helped dry clothes. It impacted our social lives and may have contributed toward the sexual division of labor during early human existence.

In terms of food, fire allows humans to cook with heat. As was the case with stone tools, cooking enabled humans to have bigger brains and smaller guts. Cooking boosted brainpower because it made food more digestible (see Gibbons 2007). Cooking also changed our relationship with the landscape around us, making us dependent on fuel to make fires.

It is difficult to ascertain the exact moment that humans harnessed the power of fire. Part of this difficulty is the lack of evidence—fossil records, pottery shards, hearth remnants, and other clues that would help scientists. Primatologist Richard Wrangham speculates that humans controlled the use of fire around 1.6–1.9 million years ago (Wrangham 2009). Other scholars counter that this date is likely too far back—its systematic use in cooking is likely more recent (Gibbons 2007; Shipman 2009; Roebroeks and Villa 2011). The oldest credible evidence of human-controlled fire dates back to 790,000 years ago. Researchers discovered burned seeds and wood, as well as flint fragments at a site at Gesher Benot Ya'aqov in Israel. They did not, however, find evidence of a hearth (Goren-Inbar et al. 2004). Evidence of a stone hearth or clay cooking vessels is important to scholars because it suggests regular and habitual use of fire. The best evidence of hearths in southern Europe dates back to 250,000 years ago. Other evidence of hearth use in Europe—charred bones, stones, ash, and charcoal—are still too recent to fit Wrangham's hypothesis. Sites in Hungary, Germany, and France suggest that hearth use may have been in place 300,000–500,000 years ago. Nevertheless, when humans discovered fire, it changed the way we related to the world around us.

Though we do not know the exact date that fire became incorporated as a culinary technology, what we do know for certain are its impacts. Tool use in conjunction with fire helped to make foods more digestible and usable. Cooking helped expand human brainpower. Cooking also changed our facial structures. The common thesis is that fire helped transform our diets because it made meat more digestible. Wild species of meat are notoriously tough and difficult to eat. By cutting the meat down to size and by cooking it, early humans were able to maximize the nutritional value of meat.

While meat was a much cherished food source, it was not the only food source. It is important to remember that we were hunter-*gatherers*: that foraged foods provided a significant caloric resource, especially during the times when meat was not available. Gathering involved far more than just gathering food—it also involved gathering other resources like water or firewood. Gathering can be "just as critical as hunting because men sometimes return with nothing, in which case the family must rely entirely on gathered foods" (Wrangham 2009: 7). Recently, scholars have shifted their thinking to suggest that fire was useful for more than meat cookery. Scientists contend that fire was used to cook tubers, which helped spur the evolution of our brains. A new theory suggests that tubers helped prompt an evolutionary change in humans, resulting in larger brains, smaller teeth, and modern limb proportions, and also encouraged male-female bonding (Pennisi 1999).

Cooking also helped humans develop leisure time because it made cooking and eating more convenient. Consider this: much of what we eat in the modern industrialized world is domesticated. That is to say, it has been bred to meet our taste and aesthetic standards of texture, flavor, consistency, and edibility. Early humans ate wild species of meat that were often much tougher, less fatty, and much stringier than our modern counterparts. Chewing raw wild meat would be time-consuming and much more tedious on the digestive system. Cooked food enabled humans to be more productive in many ways. Cooked food is far more easily chewed and digested than raw foods. Heat changes the physical properties of food. Cooking gelatinizes collagen in animal flesh. In plants, heat loosens the tightly woven carbohydrate molecules, making plant matter easier to absorb.

Consider testing this hypothesis yourself: take two pieces of a similar size and weight of the same food item, one cooked and one raw. Try this experiment with meat and plant foods. Time yourself and see how long it takes to chew each item until it reaches the consistency of a fine mush. The cooked item is always easier to chew and process.

From a sociocultural standpoint, cooking is important because it suggests the presence of human culture. Drawing on mythology and linguistics, anthropologist Claude Lévi-Strauss (1969) theorized that cooking reflects human ability to control nature. His theory is presented in the form of the culinary triangle (see Figure 5.2), a diagram showing the processing through which raw natural ingredients are transformed into food by "culture" through cooking or become rotten through natural transformation and decay. Lévi-Strauss points out that humans do not have to cook food—we could easily consume our food raw. However, we choose to cook food. This makes a statement about humans' difference in the natural world and distinguishes our species from other animal species in the world. "Not only does cooking mark the transition from nature to culture, but through it and by means of it, the human state can be defined with all its attributes" (Lévi-Strauss 1969: 164).

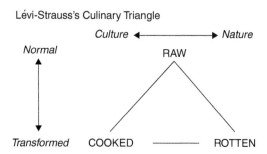

FIGURE 5.2 *Claude Lévi-Strauss's culinary triangle.*

The symbolic importance of cooking, specifically fire, remains pertinent to how humans live. Fire took on a symbolic importance in our homes. Specifically, the hearth became central to home design. The hearth became the center of the home. Families gathered around the hearth for warmth, light, to cook and prepare food, and to live out their lives. Hearth technology remained largely unchanged throughout much of human history. Until the advent of the cook stove, a wood or coal burning stove with a flue to allow for smoke dispersal was in use. During the Industrial Revolution, cooking technology remained largely stagnant. Because the hearth remained unchanged, so did cookware and cookery techniques. The advent of freestanding cook stoves changed cookery skills and knowledge, as cooks learned new ways to control fire. It also changed the associated cookery technologies—cookware, new cooking implements and tools—and even resulted in new ways of cooking and new techniques that were impossible with hearth cookery (Gdula 2008). Nowadays, heat-based cooking may not involve the presence of an active, open fire. Microwaves cook foods quickly via electromagnetic radiation. Induction cooktops utilize magnetic induction instead of thermal conduction from a flame. *Sous vide* cooks food in vacuum-sealed bags placed in water baths and avoids one of the long-standing problems of fire-based cooking: overcooking or burning food.

Even though we no longer gather around the hearth and may no longer cook over a direct flame, we continue to feel the impact of fire on our lives. What is undeniable is that cooking led to immense changes in the human diet, shaping human food preferences and transforming human bodies.

5.3 Activity: Chew your heart out

Archeological evidence suggests that tool use—cutting tools and fire, specifically—helped make food more easily digestible. Because food could be cut to size and cooked down in texture, it could be more easily processed in our mouths and guts. Heating further changed the physical properties of food, making it softer or more tender and also more easily consumed.

Materials

Raw carrots
Cooked carrots
Cups or plates
Cell phone or timer

Directions

1. Prepare your raw carrots and cooked carrots by cutting them all to a similar size and shape. Baby carrots cut to size and canned carrots or defrosted frozen carrots can be used for convenience.
2. Take a piece of raw carrot and chew it to a fine consistency (a puree or mush). Count the number of chews it takes to reach this point. Also take note of the time it takes to chew it to this texture.
3. Repeat this activity with a piece of cooked carrot. Count the number of chews and note the time it takes to reach a fine texture.

Discussion questions

1. How long and how many chews did it take to reach a fine consistency for a piece of raw carrot? How about for a cooked carrot? What were the differences in chews and length of time?
2. How did cutting the carrots make it easier to chew? What if they were left in whole, large chunks?
3. Imagine if this exercise had been conducted with meat and you were asked to chew a hunk of raw beef versus cooked beef. Discuss.

5.4 Activity: How many of your foods are cooked?

Cooking has altered human diets and human existence. While we do consume foods raw, many of the things we eat nowadays are cooked.

Directions

1. Track the number of cooked foods versus uncooked foods you eat in a 24-hour span.

Discussion questions

1. What percentage of your diet is made up of cooked versus uncooked foods?
2. What types of foods tended to be cooked versus uncooked? In particular, what was the percentage of uncooked animal protein you consumed?
3. Were there other trends you noticed about cooked versus uncooked foods? For instance, certain cuisines may have a preference toward cooked versus uncooked items.
4. Does your personal background (religion, dietary needs, diet plan, taste preferences) influence your consumption of raw versus cooked foods?

Food processing

Food processing has changed the quality and content of food. At times, food processing has enhanced the nutritional quality of food and improved its texture, taste, look, or smell. But scientists are also careful to note that processing has also reduced or degraded the quality of whole foods by reducing it to nutrients and calories rather than considering the overall product. Food processing has been used to change the food supply—to make it more secure, safer, and healthier, or to extend its lifespan.

Traditional food processing methods often revolved around preservation or ways to extend the lifespan of food. Basic preservation included sun drying, oven drying, smoking, salting, pickling, and fermentation. Today, food preservation includes a litany of techniques, including aseptic processing, irradiation, extrusion cooking, freezing and chilling, membrane processing, and the use of modified atmosphere packaging (see Kwon et al. 2004).

The advent of agriculture is often cited as one of the important developmental stages in human society. But it is important to note that an "equally profound revolution had passed unnoticed": the revolution in food processing and technology (Henry 1997: 855). It was not simply enough to cultivate a steady supply of food through the domestication of plants and animals. It was also the matter of what to do with all of this food: how to preserve and store surplus for later consumption. Unless food is properly preserved, it spoils and becomes inedible.

Until the nineteenth century, food preservation relied mostly on preventing microbial growth. Salt, sugar, spices, or acid were added to foods to inhibit microbial growth. Foods were also preserved in acid, or fermented. Sometimes they were cured and dried to extend shelf life. The biggest change to preservation was the invention of canning.

Canning became an important food preservation and processing technology in the nineteenth century. It was invented by Nicolas Appert, a Parisian confectioner, who developed a method of preserving food by placing meats, sauces, fruits, vegetables in milk in glass bottles, heating the containers in boiling water, and sealing them. His invention was a response to a call from the French government. Faced with the challenge of feeding a global army, as the French empire expanded its reach, the French government offered a prize of 12,000 francs to an inventor who could develop a method of preserving food that could withstand long journeys to its far-flung colonies. Although Appert was unsure of why his method worked, as modern science had not yet discovered the role of microorganisms in food preservation, his method became the basis of canning. It continued to be refined throughout the nineteenth century in Europe and the United States, becoming cheaper, more efficient, more transportable, and safer over time.

Canned food became a global commodity because of its prestige, price, and convenience during the nineteenth and early twentieth centuries. Canned foods helped feed hungry explorers like William E. Parry, who subsisted on canned foods during his expedition to the Arctic in 1819. Canned goods also fed armies in Europe, America, and Asia throughout many wars and conflicts, from the American Civil War on through to World Wars I and II. Though canned goods were expensive at their first introduction, by the 1920s they were much cheaper and more plentiful in variety. Canned goods changed American diets because they provided year round access to fruits and vegetables. This access was significant as new nutritional and scientific knowledge at the time revealed that fruits and vegetables are a good source of vitamins and minerals. Home canning also became a method for home cooks to preserve their seasonal harvests, to keep a surplus for the lean months of the winter, and to savor the flavors of spring and summer all year long.

Contemporary food preservation techniques are far more sophisticated than their pre-nineteenth-century predecessors. Canning remains an important food technology today. However, food scientists have moved beyond canning alone. Today, most methods focus on changing and avoiding microorganisms in food spoilage. Food can be altered through physical methods by heating, freezing, or dehydration. Chemical methods like changing the pH levels, adding preservatives, or adding carbon dioxide can also be used. Or some combination of both physical and chemical methods can be applied.

5.5 Activity: Making fruit preserves

Making your own fruit preserves used to be a common household activity. This form of preservation is a useful way of saving the season—of extending the availability of what would otherwise be a limited fruit season. Making preserves is also good way to give new life to ugly fruit. Fruit that no longer looks its best can be cooked down into sugar to make a spreadable treat. Many fruits work well as preserves, especially berries, citrus fruits, and apples.

Equipment

Heavy saucepan
Nonreactive spoon or spatula (wood or silicone)
Clean jam jars with lids. Jars can be sanitized by washing and drying on high heat in a dishwasher or heated in an oven for twenty minutes at 250 degrees Fahrenheit before use.

Ingredients

2 pints strawberries (roughly 5 cups). Other fruits may be used.
1 ½ cups sugar
½ lemon

Directions

1. Wash, hull, and cut strawberries into large chunks.
2. Place berries in a heavy saucepan with sugar. Heat gently over a medium flame, making sure to mash and stir the berries from time to time.
3. Bring to a rolling boil. Squeeze the lemon juice and stir in. Cook a few minutes more.
4. Gently spoon into sanitized jars. Let cool to room temperature. Screw on lids and put in the refrigerator to store. The preserves can keep for 3–4 weeks in the refrigerator.

Instructor's note

This recipe is for making small batches. Small batches are useful for using up leftover fruit. This can be completed as an at-home assignment. Students can bring in their preserves to share their results.

Discussion questions

1. Consider American foodways before the widespread availability of fruit. Why might food preservation be important?

2. Until recently, many households made their own fruit preserves. What skills and knowledge are needed to make preserves? What types of skills and knowledge might have been lost now that this is no longer widely practiced?

As our food chains have expanded and our food preservation and processing technologies have improved, so have our taste preferences. Preserved foods were once the way to extend the lifespan of food or to gain access to foods out of season. Foods from distant lands were also made accessible through food preservation. Take the example of pineapples. Pineapples are an exotic fruit once associated with faraway vacations to Hawaii and other tropical climates. Though pineapple consumption is roughly the same as it was in the 1970s, the type of pineapple available to American consumers has shifted. During the 1970s, Americans consumed primarily canned pineapple. Nowadays, Americans eat mostly fresh pineapple (see Bjerga et al. 2017). This switch from canned (or frozen) to fresh has occurred with many foods: orange juice, spinach, even meats and fish.

As global food chains have expanded and more sophisticated methods of preserving and transporting foods have come about, consumers in the industrialized world have shifted their taste preferences toward fresh foods. This is further evidenced in produce aisles in grocery stores that now look like eternal summer: a diverse range of fresh fruits and vegetables are available all year round to consumers. Furthermore, so-called exotic foods like avocados, coconuts, limes, and mangoes are no longer oddities but have become supermarket mainstays. In fact, most of the fruit consumed in the America is imported: in 2016, 53.1 percent of the fruit we consumed was imported (as opposed to only 23 percent in 1975). The steady rise of imported fruit reflects the changes to American foodways and dietary preferences (as well as changes to the food chain).

Of course, in other locales canned and preserved foods remain important to local foodways. Perhaps one of the most interesting examples is presented through the story of Spam (see Matejowsky 2007). A brand of canned pork luncheon meat produced by Hormel Foods Corporation, it was first introduced in 1937 and gained worldwide popularity during World War II. Spam was shipped from the United States to feed American troops in Europe and in the Pacific. During the war, Spam was prized as a taste of home—wholesome, nutritious, and even patriotic. After World War II, American consumers turned away from the meat product. However, it remained popular as an American import where American troops were stationed. Hawaiian cuisine has incorporated Spam as a mainstay, featuring in dishes like *musubi*, a rice ball topped with a slice of Spam and wrapped with *nori*, a variety of black seaweed. In the Philippines, a former American colony, Spam became symbolic of modernity and took on a valued status in local foodways. Spam is prized to the extent that is even given as a gift during holiday seasons in places where it took on a lauded status.

Food processing and preservation technology also changed the way we acquire food. Modern grocery stores and supermarkets, and their large-format cousins, the hypermarkets, have come to dominate the food retailing landscape in the industrialized world. They are recognized by their brand names like Carrefour, Walmart, Tesco, and Kroger.

Before the advent of grocery stores, supermarkets, and hypermarkets in the mid-twentieth century, consumers often had to go shopping at different stores. Consumers would have to go to the proverbial butcher, baker, and candlestick maker for these items. These large-format retailers changed shopping habits. Instead of visiting three stores for three items, everything was now one stop shopping. Furthermore, the retailing format encourages large-volume buying. Instead of stopping by and picking up a few things for a day or two, a visit to a large format retailer encourages buying for the week—or weeks at a time. These stores sell fresh produce but the majority of the store is filled with processed and preserved foods including snack foods, soft drinks, candy, and other treats. Consumers are enticed to buy these foods, which nutritional and health experts claim contribute toward obesity and other lifestyle diseases.

5.6 Activity: Supermarket sweep

How much of your local supermarket is devoted to processed and preserved foods as opposed to fresh foods?

Directions

1. Visit your local supermarket.
2. Count the number of aisles/floor space devoted to fresh products. Be sure to separate the types of fresh products (e.g., fruits, vegetables, meat, dairy).
3. Count the number of aisles/floor space devoted to processed and preserved foods. Be sure to list the categories of processed and preserved foods.

Discussion questions

1. Which section of the supermarket were you directed toward when you first entered the store?
2. What categories of food dominate the retail space?
3. What is the ratio of preserved or processed goods to fresh goods? How might the availability of certain types of goods influence consumer preferences and shopping habits?

5.7 Activity: You can pickle it—Refrigerator pickles

Pickling vegetables in salt is an old method of food preservation. This recipe is for quick cucumber pickles. This recipe is ready in less than an hour.

Ingredients

4 medium Kirby or small pickling cucumbers (approximately 13 ounces)
1 tablespoon Kosher salt
3 tablespoons sugar (preferably white granulated sugar)
Large bowl
Resealable container

Directions

1. Cut the cucumbers into slices and place into a large bowl.
2. Add sugar and salt. Mix to combine.
3. Place the cucumber mixture into a resealable container and cover. Refrigerate for at least forty-five minutes before eating. The cucumbers will last up to a month in the refrigerator.

Instructor's note

This recipe can be completed in even the smallest cooking spaces as long as there is a clean surface and a refrigerator. Consider making this recipe and the lacto-fermented pickles recipe to create a point of comparison.

Discussion questions

1. Imagine making this recipe one hundred years ago before the widespread popularity of refrigerator. How might this recipe be modified to suit those living conditions?
2. Today, many people eat pickles for the taste and texture. Discuss the reasons why pickles were popular before the advent of modern refrigeration.

5.8 Activity: You can pickle it—lacto-fermented pickles

Pickling vegetables in salt is an old method of food preservation. This recipe is for lacto-fermented pickles—pickles made by creating an environment made with lactic bacteria. Lactic bacteria contain probiotics and are routinely promoted as good for digestive health. Lacto-fermentation is one of the oldest forms of fermentation, pre-dating the rise of modern refrigeration (although a cool space is still needed to properly ferment food). This recipe is ready in one to two weeks depending on the climate.

Ingredients

4 medium Kirby or small pickling cucumbers (approximately 13 ounces)
Kosher salt or plain sea salt
Room temperature water
Large bowl
Resealable container—ideally a glass jar

Directions

1. Prepare the cucumbers. Leave whole or cut into spheres (or rounds) if they are large.
2. Mix salt and water until dissolved to create a brine. The ratio is for every two cups of water, mix in one tablespoon of salt. Use as much brine as needed to completely submerge the cucumbers.
3. Place the cucumbers and brine into a resealable container and cover with a lid. Store your pickles in a dry spot at room temperature. Test the pickles on day five. Transfer to a refrigerator to slow down fermentation after they reach your desired level of sourness.

Instructor's note

This recipe can be completed in even the smallest cooking spaces as long as there is a clean surface and a refrigerator. Consider making this recipe and the refrigerator pickles recipe to create a point of comparison.

Discussion questions

1. Imagine making this recipe 100 years ago. How might this recipe be modified to suit those living conditions? How would this recipe change given the advent of modern refrigeration?
2. Today, many people eat pickles for the taste and texture. Discuss the reasons why pickles were popular before the advent of modern refrigeration.
3. Why might salt-based preservation be useful? How does salt-based preservation change pickling (as opposed to the use of vinegar and refrigeration)?

Scientific food

Around the turn of the twentieth century, food took a new direction. Following the *Industrial Revolution* (late eighteenth to mid-nineteenth centuries), the industrialization of the food supply changed people's relationships with food. Prior to widespread industrialization, most households in America produced their most of what their households consumed. Women, in particular, would spin, weave, and sew their own clothes, grow their own fruits and vegetables (and preserve them), butcher and preserve their own meat, make candles and soap, and complete countless other tasks necessary for everyday survival. Instead of being producers of food and household goods, we shifted toward a consumption model where we bought foods as more industries took over. We began buying the very items we used to produce ourselves. New technologies and implements to help with housework were adopted into homes. Combined with the onslaught of new food advertising and marketing, consumers were sold a new bill of goods. Homes became industrialized. Households became "part of a larger economic and social system; and if it did not constantly interact with this system, it could not function at all—making it no different from the manufacturing plant outside the city or the supermarket down the street" (Cowan 1983: 6).

"Scientific" and technologically driven discoveries about food began to impact the way people thought about food, produced and packaged their food, got their food, cooked it, and ate it. Science and scientific discovery was associated with progress and modernity, values that were important to the industrializing societies of the world. "Science and technology were gaining the aura of divinity: such forces could do no wrong, and their very presence lent dignity to otherwise humble lives and proceedings" (Shapiro 1986: 4). This new scientific approach to food and cooking shared the values of the industrial food industry from its onset. It promoted the technology of food production and food distribution (see Shapiro 1986). Processed foods like canned goods, packaged foods, and, later, frozen meals were championed as nutritious, hygienic, and efficient time economizers. Advice manuals on domestic management borrowed from the lexicon of modern industry.

Scientific cookery was not simply about improving nutritional outcomes or making food better. Science and technology took on a tone of morality, particularly as it applied to women's work and the domestic sphere. Women were often the focus of this new scientific approach to food, cooking, eating, and home management. This new approach had a name: it became the field of domestic science. Cooking schools, domestic science magazines, clubs, cookbooks, household management manuals, etiquette guides, and the field of home economics all emerged through this new interest in a more scientific approach to running the home. Evidence of this new scientific approach can be seen in the advice dispensed to women through cookbooks and domestic manuals. For instance, standardized recipes, including the use of level measurements to ensure precise results, became the norm (Shapiro 1986: 4).

Women in industrializing America—specifically middle-class and well-to-do women—were expected to become "angels of the home" and create a domestic haven for their husbands and children. These new domestic havens were expected to be well-oiled machines, to run like modern factories, with no stone left unturned in terms of proper management. Laura Shapiro makes the case that as "women's traditional responsibilities became less and less relevant to a burgeoning economy, the sentimental value of home expanded proportionately" (Shapiro 1986: 13).

The field of *nutritional science* also emerged in the nineteenth century. Nutritional science reflected attempts among scientists to quantify calories and nutrients necessary for growth and the prevention of diseases. Nutritional advice based on scientific knowledge of vitamins and minerals was dispensed to the public, and women, as keepers of the home and the targets of this new scientific way of living, were expected to dispense this type of nutritional advice to their families and children. It has become the dominant paradigm of nutrition science and has framed scientific research and how we discuss food and dietary health. The way food is labeled, regulated, marketed, and engineered is a consequence of this ideology of nutritionism. The dietary advice that consumers receive prioritizes the consumption of specific nutrients and vitamins—while systematically decontextualizing how these nutrients and vitamins work and relate to broader systems of health and well-being.

The field of nutritional science also has a tendency to focus on what was good for the eater rather than what people liked (Levenstein 1980: 370). Scholars point out that this "ideology of nutritionism" is "characterized by a reductive *focus* on the nutrient composition of foods as the means for understanding their healthfulness, as well as by a reductive *interpretation* of the role of these nutrients in bodily health," and possibly conceals or "overrides concerns with the production and processing quality of a food and its ingredients" (Scrinis 2013: 2, author's emphasis).

We can see the convergence of the principles of scientific eating, domesticity as morality, and nutritional science in the advent of infant formula and baby food. The rise of infant formula and canned baby food, an outcome of late nineteenth and early twentieth century, show the impact of these new cultural ideas pervading into our foodways. In the preindustrial Western world, the overwhelming majority of children were breastfed—some estimates suggest around 95 percent. These children were fed by their mothers or by wet nurses, women who would feed and care for another's child. While breastfeeding was the norm, there were exceptions to the rule. Some mothers could not produce milk and had to rely on other means to feed their babies. Others supplemented their milk with additional food sources. Babies were dry-nursed or brought up by hand. Infants were sometimes fed animal milk. However, babies who were fed in this manner failed to thrive, suffering from malnutrition or falling ill from contaminated animal milk or water (Bentley 2014: 20). Good mothers were encouraged to "embrace commercial baby food as modern and convenient" (Bentley 2014: 7).

The baby food industry encouraged Americans to use formula and, later, solid baby foods. This shift toward industrialized foods contributed to a decline of breastfeeding in the twentieth century. Amy Bentley suggests that early consumption of processed baby food may have helped to "prime Americans' palates" toward industrial foods (2014: 6). Commercial baby foods contain high amounts of sugar, fat, and salt, and the introduction of these foods early in life may be linked to the ongoing preference for these tastes and processed foods through the later stages of life.

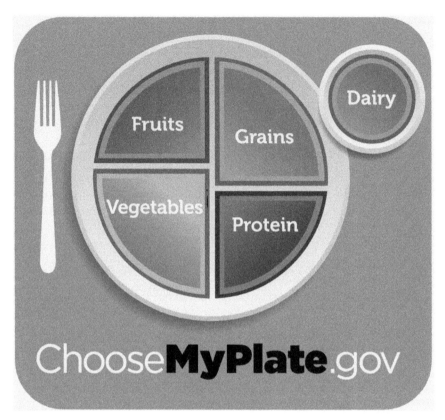

FIGURE 5.3 *The United States Department of Agriculture dietary guidelines, MyPlate.*

5.9 Activity: MyPlate

In efforts to promote better eating and healthier lifestyles, many countries around the globe have some type of food pyramid or food plate. In the United States, MyPlate is meant to illustrate what are the appropriate types and portions of food to eat (see Figure 5.3). MyPlate is based on nutritional science and presents a model for eating, but is often times an aspirational model and not realistically achievable. It can also overlook the taste preferences of individual consumers, including dietary restrictions, religious prohibitions, and cultural preferences. Many other countries around the planet also have some similar nutritional template and their models are based on their aspirational versions of eating.

Materials

Paper
Art supplies—colored pencils, markers, crayons, and so on

Directions

1. Draw what you would consider to be an ideal healthy meal.
2. Use colors and shapes to represent different food items on the plate—be sure to label all the components.
3. Compare your plate to the USDA MyPlate. Does your plate fit their suggested model?

Discussion questions

1. How does your plate compare with the MyPlate template?
2. How often do you eat a meal like the one you drew?
3. What does the MyPlate model overlook or ignore in terms of people's everyday habits and preferences?
4. Would your plate "match" if you examined plates from other cultures? For instance, if you have a strong Jamaican heritage, would your plate pass in Jamaica? (Look up the plates for other countries on Google.)
5. How is the ideology of nutritionism reflected in modern nutritional advice, such as through the MyPlate model?

Instructor's note

Consider incorporating examples of plates from around the world. These other plates serve as useful comparisons and allow the discussion to bring in considerations of the cultural constructions of health, nutrition, and wellness.

Further resources

Fieldhouse, Paul (1995). *Food and Nutrition: Customs and Culture*, 2nd edn. London: Chapman and Hall.
Mudry, Jessica (2009). *Measured Meals: Nutrition in America*. Albany: SUNY Press.
Scrinis, Gyorgy (2013). *Nutritionism: The Science and Politics of Dietary Advice*. New York: Columbia University Press.

5.10 Food for thought: Bread

Bread is one of the most important global foods. It is portable, relatively stable, and, depending on how it is produced, can be high in nutrients. In Judeo-Christian beliefs, bread takes on a symbolic importance as "the staff of life." Christians, in particular, consume communion wafers, a little slice of bread representing the body of Jesus Christ, who Christians believe to be their savior.

Bread is the consequence of domestication and agriculture in many ways. The domestication of grains to something edible represents one form of human accomplishment. But it also represents what domestication and agriculture gave rise to—permanent civilizations—where people ostensibly had the time and ability hang around and create permanent ovens and stoves, the ability to let grain sit and catch wild yeast and ferment, and the time to wait for their bread to rise, proof, and bake—social accomplishments that were unheard of during our more itinerant foraging and hunting and gathering days.

Bread itself represents a social and cultural achievement (see Counihan 1984). Harold McGee reminds us that "bread represents the culinary domestication of grain, an achievement that made possible to extract pleasure as well as nourishment from the hard, bland seeds" (McGee 2007). Bread production requires tools, technology, fire, and scientific knowledge.

Though bread is a staple in many societies, it is rarely produced at home nowadays in wealthy industrialized nations. Until the twentieth century, most Americans baked their own bread. This bread is what many call a sourdough (although the sourness of the bread varies depending on the local yeasts). Water and flour are mixed together in a vessel and allowed to sit out at room temperature. Over the course of several days, this mixture would be fed amounts of water and flour. It would also gather wild yeasts from the local environment. Once the starter has gained sufficient strength, it is used to bake bread. This type of bread takes on the local flavor, what some call the *terroir* (the "taste of place") of the environment, its structure capturing the microbes of the area. Sourdough bread bears very little resemblance to its industrialized cousin, "American white bread." By this, I mean the type of commercially made bread that is sold presliced and bagged. This bread has a soft, pillowy texture and is made with highly processed white flour and commercial yeast. Commercial white bread tastes the same—its genius is in its uniformity, its sameness. Sourdough, by contrast, can vary dramatically from loaf to loaf depending on humidity, climate, yeasts, and other environmental and human factors.

Because of its sameness, white bread is sometimes used as a euphemism to describe blandness. In *Remember to Remember*, author Henry Miller commented that Americans "eat bread without substance, . . . without flavor, . . . without vitamins . . . without life" (Miller 1952: 35).

Although industrialized bread is enriched with vitamins, it is still considered bread without substance, flavor, without personality. Consider the insult "white bread." This term is used to describe anyone who is bland, boring, rather conventional and utterly unremarkable. This insult invokes Miller's comments that white bread is "without life." Similarly, fashion icon Diana Vreeland once famously proclaimed, "People who eat white bread have no dreams."

Scholar Aaron Bobrow-Strain is quick to point out that American industrialized white bread does embody dreams—just not the right dreams, the stuff that a fashion doyenne would deem acceptable (Bobrow-Strain 2012). In fact, this type of bread was used to "save the world" in a way. Following the American occupation of Japan and Korea after World War II, cheap white bread (and other industrialized products) were promoted as an alternative to labor and agriculturally intensive rice.

Wonder Bread, manufactured by Flowers Foods in the United States, is one of the most popular industrialized brands of breads sold in the United States today. Its marketing promotes that "Wonder Bread Builds Strong Bodies 8 Ways." It is a modern "wonder," so to speak, in the way that historian Rachel Laudan has framed it (Laudan 2001).[1] Wonderbread represents the intersections of human adaptation, industrialization, and nutritional engineering.

Increasingly, this style of bread has begun to be criticized for its lack of nutrients, its cheapness, and its lack of taste. This shift away from industrial bread was part of the larger counterculture movement of the 1960s and 1970s and its pulling away from industrialized processed food as symbolic of a rejection of the status quo. Warren Belasco points out that

> whiteness meant Wonder Bread, White Tower, Cool Whip, Minute Rice, instant mashed potatoes, peeled apples, White Tornadoes, white coats, white collar, whitewash, White House, white racism. Brown meant whole wheat bread, unhulled rice, turbinado sugar, wildflower honey, unsulfured molasses, soy sauce, peasant yams, "black is beautiful." (Belasco 1989: 48)

"Artisan" breads and other handcrafted baked goods have come back into style, in part because of the shift in values that occurred during the counterculture movement. Some consumers have pivoted away from industrialized, commoditized foods toward small, handcrafted products. These breads can be found in independent bakeries, and increasingly in supermarkets. This rise in demand for crusty, handcrafted bread can be linked to broader changes in health preferences, consumer demands, and dietary awareness. This type of bread is also reflective and representative of values and morals. As an antidote to industrialized, commercialized processed food, "artisan" breads suggest craft, heritage, and workmanship.

5.11 Activity: Making a sourdough starter

Many Americans grow up eating white, pillowy soft industrial bread. It's bought in large presliced loaves stuffed in bright plastic bags. This bread tastes the same, more or less, for a week or two. Sourdough-bread bears little resemblance to its industrialized white bread cousin.

Making sourdough is inherently a simple process, but one that takes time, patience, and a willingness to experiment. This is a basic recipe for a sourdough starter. Making a sourdough starter is the first step toward making "real" bread. Sourdough relies on wild yeast, which is what gives sourdough bread its funky, sour taste. Some claim that the *terroir*, the climate and geography, will influence the quality of the bread. San Franciscans are quick to defend their version of sourdough bread, arguing there is nothing like a San Francisco sourdough because of the local yeast that inhabit their bread. A way to think of the importance of wild yeast is this: "Blues is to jazz what yeast is to bread. Without it, it's flat" (Carmen McRae).

Instructor's note

Don't forget to name your starter. Like any other pet, you will have to feed it and take care of it every day.

Ingredients

All-purpose or plain flour, preferably organic and whole grain. Do not use cake flour, Wondra flour, or an alternative flour (like almond or rice flour).
    Filtered water

Equipment

Large nonreactive bowl (glass, plastic, or stainless steel)
Spatula or wooden spoon
Kitchen scale (preferred)
Measuring cups
Dishcloth

Directions

1. Start with one cup of flour (120 grams) and one cup (236 ml) of filtered water. Add to a large bowl and mix well. Cover loosely with a dishcloth to allow wild yeast to permeate.

2. Add a little more flour and water every day for the next fourteen days—about half a cup of each per day. The mixture will start bubbling and develop a sour smell. This smell indicates the presence of wild yeast.
3. When the mixture has developed a lot of bubbles and a robust yeasty smell, it is ready for baking.
4. Do not panic if your starter is ready sooner or later depending on the time of the year and the temperature. Give it a little patience and breathing room.
5. The final step is to take your sourdough starter and use it as the basis of your bread. There are countless videos on YouTube to help you through the process.

Discussion questions

1. Describe your experience growing your own starter. What does it feel like to cultivate wild yeast for baking? How does this compare to buying a sachet of yeast from the supermarket?
2. Consider the labor and time involved in baking bread the slow way. What does this tell you about cooking?
3. What insights does this activity provide on the reception of industrialized foods during the late nineteenth and early twentieth century?

Summary

- Every age is a technological age. Technology must be understood in context of the time period.

- Although humans are not the only species that use tools, we are the only species that participate in tool making.

- Tool use and fire helped change human bodies and spurred on human evolution.

- Tools and technology are invented to fulfill social needs.

- Food preservation and processing helped extend the lifespan and usability of foods.

- A scientific approach to food and cooking emerged in the late nineteenth and twentieth centuries and continues to shape our eating habits and understanding of health.

Discussion questions

1. After reading this chapter, what does the term "technological age" mean to you now?

2. Discuss how human existence might be different if we did not develop the capacity for deliberate tool making.

3. How does the ideology of nutritionism shape our current eating today? Consider examples beyond baby food.

Further resources

Movies and Videos

Hungry for Change (2012) is a documentary on the diet industry. It addresses the food industry's role in shaping perceptions of health, wellness, and nutrition.

Kitchen Stories (2003) is a Swedish film about an unlikely friendship between a researcher and his subject. This film takes place in post–World War II Sweden, as researchers at the Home Research Institute are conducting studies to understand kitchen habits and develop more efficient kitchen designs for the modern Swedish home.

Modern Times (1936) is a silent comedy by Charlie Chaplin featuring his iconic Little Tramp character. The film is a commentary on survival in the modern, industrialized world (particularly the conditions many experienced during the Great Depression).

The SuperSizers Go . . . (2008) and *The Supersizers Eat* (2009) are BBC television series about the history of food in Britain. The show puts food in context, showing the cuisine, the technologies, homes, and lifestyles at specific periods in British history.

The Townsends channel on YouTube covers life in the eighteenth century. This channel includes videos on the food, cooking, and the technology of the eighteenth-century home kitchen. https://www.youtube.com/user/jastownsendandson.

Note

1 See also Laudan's blog post on why our ancestors preferred white bread to whole grain breads. http://www.rachellaudan.com/2017/01/why-did-our-ancestors-prefer-white-bread-to-wholegrain-bread.html.

Further resources

Bailey, Britt and Marc Lappe (eds.) (2002). *Engineering the Farm: Ethical and Social Aspects of Agricultural Biotechnology.* Washington, DC: Island Press.

Blaxter, Kenneth and Noel Robertson (1995). *From Dearth to Plenty: The Modern Revolution in Food Production.* Cambridge: Cambridge University Press.

Freeman, June (2004). *The Making of the Modern Kitchen.* Oxford: Berg.

McFeely, Mary (2000). *Can She Bake a Cherry Pie: American Women and the Kitchen in the Twentieth Century.* Amherst: University of Massachusetts Press.

Myhrvold, Nathan, Chris Young, and Maxime Bilet (2011). *Modernist Cuisine: The Art and Science of Cooking. Kitchen Manual, Volume 6.* Bellevue: Cooking Lab.

Horowitz, Roger (2006). *Putting Meat on the American Table: Taste, Technology, Transformation.* Baltimore: Johns Hopkins University Press.

Wrangham, Richard (2009). *Catching Fire: How Cooking Made Us Human.* New York: Basic Books.

6

Globalization and Food: Here, There, Everywhere, and Nowhere?

Many years ago, I popped into a busy Starbucks located on London's Oxford Street, a major shopping thoroughfare filled with all the trendiest labels and popular clothing retailers. It was a scorching hot day and my friend and I wanted to escape the crowds for just a minute and grab cold drinks. We joined the queue (a very British thing to do), which was several people deep. We inched along, drawing closer to the counter, and finally we were almost there. At the counter was a group of three adults placing their order. My friend and I paid them no mind until we realized it was taking an unusually long time for this group to finish up their order. We stopped chatting and we started listening in on their conversation with the barista to see what was holding up the line. They were pleading back and forth with the barista that they wanted Starbucks cups—the disposable paper cups that Starbucks fills their beverages to go. They were uninterested in ordering coffee or any other beverages; they simply wanted the cups to take home. They were trying to explain this in halting English and it became clear in the exchange that they were tourists visiting from abroad. Eventually, the barista figured out what they were asking for and gave them a few paper cups, free of charge. The happy group thanked the barista and headed out the door. My friend and I ordered and took our drinks outside. Again, we saw the group; they were talking animatedly. They were thrilled that they got Starbucks cups and carefully wrapped them in a plastic bag and placed it in one of their shopping bags, presumably to take home as a souvenir of their trip, and disappeared into the crowds on the busy street.

Most people would not have paid any mind to this encounter or, at best, would have thought it was a bit strange and left it there. From a Food Studies perspective, there is much to glean from this moment. Starbucks is one of the most beloved (and reviled) of global food brands. Originally founded in 1971 in Seattle, Washington, it has become a global brand with 24,000 stores in seventy countries. To many consumers in the industrialized West, Starbucks is part of everyday life. It is mundane and routine; perhaps you even sneer at it for its corporate approach to coffee. But this anecdote reminds us that for many around the world, consuming Starbucks is a privilege. It is still a status marker and a sign of prestige: its cups are worth taking home as souvenirs. We could say the same for many other products that have become both a prized status symbol as well as a source of disdain: McDonald's, Western fast food, and more. Drawing on the title of this chapter, these foods and products are here, there, and everywhere—and seemingly from nowhere at the same time, present in major cities around the globe, all seemingly familiar yet without a local identity or core. This memory of Starbucks has stayed with me over the years and speaks to some of the issues in our global food system to be discussed in this chapter. This anecdote leads us into the subject of this chapter: globalization.

Globalization is a word that we often hear in public discussions—on the news, on the internet, and floating around on social media. It is lauded as a social achievement for connecting the peoples of the world together and at the same time vilified for contributing to social, environmental, cultural, economic, and political ills. But what does this term actually mean?

Food is good to "think global" with (Bell and Valentine 1997: 190). This is because "the manifold meanings and universal significance of food, and also its concrete presence in human life afford a vantage point to explore globalization, which is pervasive by its very nature, yet at the same time abstract and elusive. Wherever globalization spreads its tentacles, food and foodways are major local concerns, providing a basis for the comparative study of globalization" (Walraven 2002: 167–8). This chapter will take a broad look at globalization, attempting to give some parameters to its definitions, and will assess how globalization has impacted our current world system. In particular, it will focus on how globalization has impacted our foodways and food system.

What is globalization?

Globalization can be defined in many ways; there is no single definition. In many ways, it is more appropriate to speak of globalizations in the plural. There are different types of globalization: economic, political, social, and cultural.

There is a tendency to think of globalization as a new phenomenon. However, history shows us that extensive cross-border exchanges have been part of our societies for millennia. In particular the, cross-border exchange of food is not a new phenomenon. Food—ingredients, cooking techniques, flavor principles cuisines—have been exchanged for many centuries, sometimes across great distances. Scholars note that food has been systematically traded and exchanged since the dawn of stratified civilization, going back to the days of the Roman Empire, the Ottoman Empire, and the transcontinental exchanges of the Silk Road. Traders on the Silk Road transported goods to China across Central Asia and Persia. Sugarcane, spinach, lettuce, almonds, figs, grapes. China exported silk, fine porcelain wares, gunpowder, tea, and the printing press, which made their way across the Eurasian continent.

There has been much debate over the origins of globalization. This chapter will focus primarily on globalization in the modern period.

Experts have made many attempts to define globalization and the exact moment it appeared in world history as a process. Many have conceded that it is difficult to determine the exact moment when it began. However, there are clearly moments in world history where human interaction was connected on an international level. Many consider the "Age of Exploration" (the period of contact between the Old World and New World, starting in the 1500s to the nineteenth century) to be the start to globalization because it was no longer centered on commercial exchange but also involved political exertion of power. Though many place globalization as a relatively new phenomenon, in fact different societies and civilizations across the world have exchanged goods, services, ideas, and technologies with one another for millennia. Evidence of wide-scale international exchange

The Columbian Exchange (now commonly known as the Great Exchange) was the widespread transfer of plants, animals, culture, peoples, technology, and ideas between the Americas (the "New World") and Western Europe (the "Old World") during the fifteenth and sixteenth centuries. The Columbian Exchange was precipitated by the European colonization of the Americas following the voyages of Christopher Columbus. This term first came into common use in 1972 in Alfred W. Crosby Jr.'s book, *The Columbian Exchange: Biological and Cultural Consequences of 1492*. The Columbian Exchange is named after Christopher Columbus, an Italian explorer, navigator, and colonizer. Though not the first European to reach the Americas, he is perhaps the most associated in popular imagery with the start of the transatlantic connections between the Old World and New World. Funded by the Catholic Monarchs of Spain, Columbus and his crew were driven to find new spice routes to Asia. The Dutch had already achieved access to the East Indies (South and Southeast Asia), and the Crown of Castile also wanted access to territories, resources, and capital.

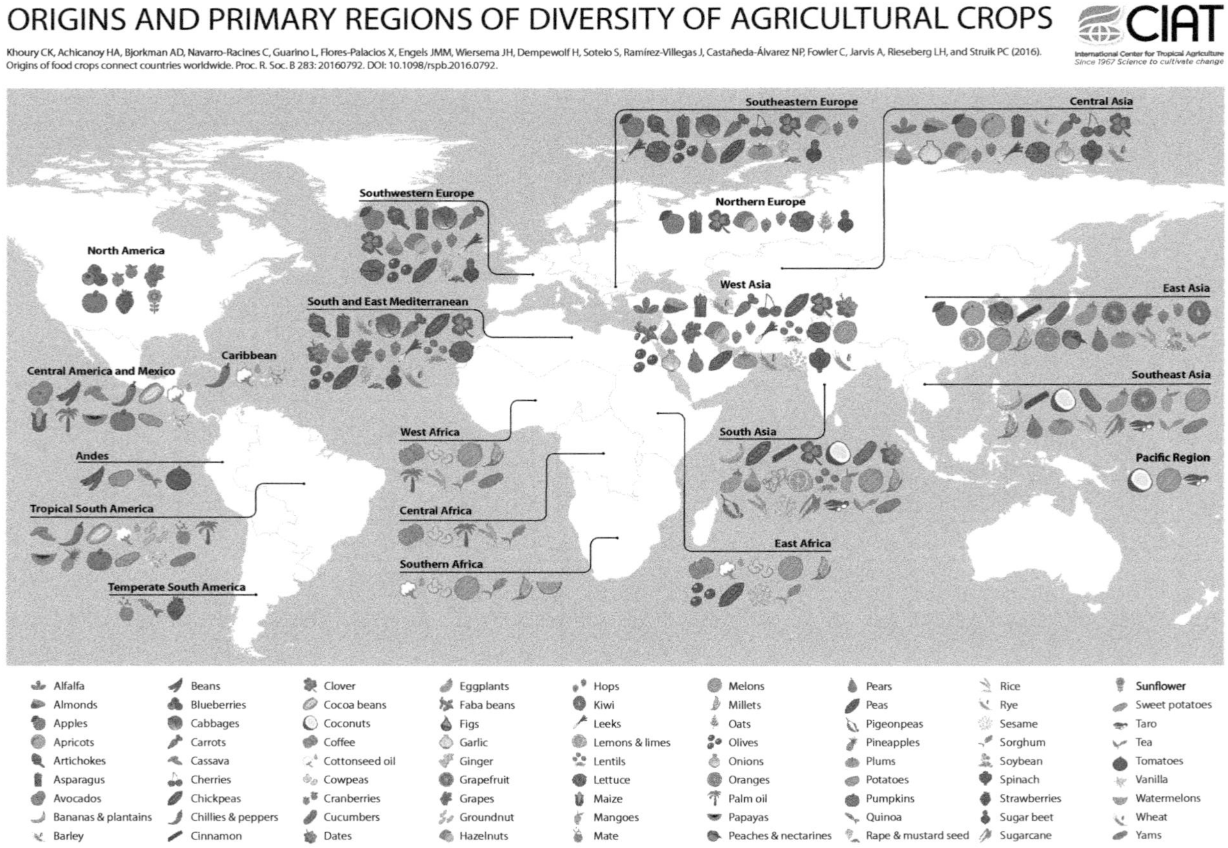

FIGURE 6.1 *Origins and primary regions of diversity of agricultural crops. CIAT. Open Access.*

The impacts of this contact between Old World and New World changed the course of human existence (see Figure 6.1). Diseases from the Old World, notably smallpox, the plague, measles, typhus, and influenza, took hold in the New World and decimated the population that had no immunity to these diseases. Old World crops and animals were brought to the New World, in part because the colonizers did not want to eat the local foodstuffs. New World crops and livestock were also eventually taken back to Europe, where they were slowly adopted. Tomatoes, potatoes, chilies, cacao (for chocolate), corn (maize), and turkey were eventually incorporated into European foodways.

What differs from these historic exchanges of the past and the twentieth- and twenty-first-century exchanges is the extent, intensity, and efficiency of exchange in modern times. Contemporary globalization is often spoken of as a twentieth- and twenty-first-century phenomenon. Many date contemporary globalization to the period immediately after World War II and the founding of various international organizations. This led to the establishment of the United Nations in 1945 and its various umbrella organizations and agencies like the International Monetary Fund, the International Bank for Reconstruction and Development (which later became the World Bank), and also the early origins of the World Trade Organization. These organizations have had a strong impact on creating an international dialogue, and connecting disparate nations and peoples together through international policies and trading regimes. These organizations, which will be discussed later in this chapter, have been praised and criticized. Neoliberalism is rooted in political economic theories and practices that propose that the well-being of society should be rooted in advancing free-market principles. Free-market economics tends to favor privatization and strong private property rights, deregulation, and free trade.

In particular, I draw attention to the modern jet age starting in the 1950s as a reference point for thinking about globalization, our contemporary food system, and the establishment of neoliberal international organizations and policies that have impacted our modern system of trading and exchange (our modern economic system). Standardized container shipping and refrigerated shipping helped move products around the globe more efficiently. Products that once had a limited shelf life could now be preserved through refrigerated shipping. Standardized container shipping (containerization) also allowed ships and trains to be loaded more efficiently, making the transition from different modes of transportation and different locales more seamless.

Places like Rungis Market in Paris, Merca Madrid in Madrid, and Tsujiki Market in Tokyo are working examples of globalization in action. These are large, wholesale markets that feed entire cities and arguably even countries. A walk through any of these markets shows just how complex and integrated our global food system is nowadays. Rungis Market, located on the outskirts of Paris, replaced Les Halles, the wholesale food market that writer Émile Zola once described as "the belly of Paris." Rungis workers start in the middle of the night and are finished before day. Thousands of products move through the airport-sized complex. Items from all continents are shipped in each day. Fish and seafood from every ocean also fill the chilled wholesale rooms. From a gastronomic perspective, these sites are celebrated and touted as evidence of globalization as a positive factor. Gourmets can feast on fresh food from everywhere—distant lands, faraway oceans.

Twentieth-century innovations like standardized shipping containers and refrigerated boxcars allowed products to be moved long distances more cheaply and efficiently, and to stay preserved as they traversed the long distances, making it possible for us to eat like a global gourmet. At the same time, critics denounce these sites for the tremendous waste they produce in terms of the resources and labor required to get products from all over the globe flown into these locales.

The system that we see today is far more complex, integrated, and expansive than what our ancestors could have imagined. The food supply is now global and we have a complex global food chain. Thus thinking about globalization and food requires thinking about power and control: who has it, who does not have it, and how do people make sense of these new balances of power and control in this interconnected world we live in.

Homogenization

In *Fight Club* (1999), in one scene, a seemingly soulless protagonist, Tyler Durden, is making photocopies in his office. His eyes are vacant and soulless, and, while he does this, he is sipping from a large Starbucks cup. In the background are other robotic office workers doing similarly mundane things: making copies, tapping away at computers, taking phone calls, all while drinking out of large Starbucks coffee cups. This scene is evocative of what scholars have called the "homogenization" or "flattening" of the world through globalization. Products like Starbucks are commodities of modern blandness.

The "flattening" of world society is an argument largely associated with *New York Times* reporter and social commentator Thomas Friedman, who published a book in 2005 called *The World Is Flat*. This book addresses the issue of globalization and claims that the world is "flat." Not in the literal sense, as was once hotly debated in the medieval period, but in the figurative sense of things being available everywhere. That borders and boundaries have fallen way to allow for a flat, borderless existence. This view of globalization might explain the presence of Starbucks everywhere and gives one explanation to the story I provided at the start of the chapter. It has made Starbucks a covetable good throughout the planet.

Another way describing this gradual "flattening" of the world is the "McDonaldization" of the world. Coined by sociologist George Ritzer in 1993 in his book *The McDonaldization of Society*, this theory quickly spread among scholars as a way to interpret this process of homogenization and globalization around the world via the expansion of fast food (or other mass market food products). This concept has also been used to explain the homogenization of cultures and cultural forms. McDonald's is seemingly *everywhere*. Indeed, the Golden Arches gleam across 36,000 outlets in more than 100 countries worldwide. But to describe the arrival of goods from elsewhere in a society as simple flattening is not enough. Instead of local foodways being entirely displaced by McDonald's and other Western fast food chains, the presence of foreign fast food revealed another process: *glocalization*.

Sidney Mintz points out that to understand the arrival of new foods, one must consider "what the foods meant to people, and what people signaled by consuming them," including how foods were associated with social differences such as age, gender, class, and occupation, as well as the "will and intent of the nation's rulers, and to the economic, social, political destiny of the nation itself" (Mintz 1996: 151). We must look to both the "inside" meaning—what he describes as "the meanings people indicate when they are demonstrating they know what things are supposed to mean" (Mintz 1996: 151), as well as the "outside" meanings—what something can "signify for a society as a whole, and especially for those who rule it; how those who govern or control the society perpetuate their status and profit from the intensified diffusion of the inside meanings, and of the consumption which the validations of these meanings entail" (Mintz 1996: 153).

Scholars have explored the issue of glocalization through the spread of different foods: Mexican cuisine and tacos (Pilcher 2012), sushi (Bestor 2004), pizza (Ceccarini 2011), and others. Historian Jeffrey Pilcher makes the case that "following a single commodity from the soil to the table and beyond provides a comprehensive view of the interrelations between technologies of production, social relations of labor, and diverse cultures of consumption" (Pilcher 2008: 532).

"Whether we have in mind an ingredient, a plant, an animal, or a cooking method, or some other concrete culinary borrowing, when such things spread and they come into the hands of the receiving farmers, processors or cooks, they have been detached from some particular cultural system; and when they are taken up, they become reintegrated into another usually quite different one" (Mintz 2007: 207). Put simply, what is sent from the "original" or "home" is different from what eventually takes root in its new destination or new home. Globalization is a "process that stimulates a surprising richness of local responses" (Walraven 2002: 173).

At the same time, scholars contend it is not simply globalization but also, simultaneously, processes of glocalization. Glocalization is a portmanteau of the words "globalization" and "local." What it suggests is that material objects (things), ideas, and values are being spread around the globe; they are also undertaking transformation at the same time. Products localize and adapt to the environment: to local tastes, needs, and trends. It suggests that there are still unique local and situated forms that grow out of the effects of widespread and global processes. A way to understand glocalization is to look at the example of McDonald's.

McDonald's has been maligned because of what it represents: American capitalism, industrialized processed food, the proliferation of a monoculture, and so on. But anthropologists and food scholars feel that McDonald's has taken on new meanings as it has glocalized in the new societies where it finds residence. In post-socialist states, McDonald's came to represent a newfound freedom. Upon its introduction to China in the 1990s, shortly after China resumed relations with the West and adopted a series of socioeconomic and political reforms, foreign businesses like McDonald's were allowed to open, and curious urban consumers flocked to these new eating establishments to see what the fuss was about (see Figure 6.2).

A quick glance at McDonald's menus around the globe give further support that McDonald's is not the same McDonald's the world over. Instead of Big Macs and other beef-based burgers in India, McAloo Tikki is a popular choice. Beer is served at McDonald's locations in Germany while in France, French pastries like croissants and macarons can be enjoyed. These are, of course, corporate-driven forms of glocalization. McDonald's executives would be ill-informed to put beef on the menu in India, a Hindu-dominant country where much of its population avoid beef consumption due to religious beliefs. In Muslim-majority countries like Malaysia and Saudi Arabia, locations are certified *halal* in recognition of local dietary restrictions. Similarly, Israeli outlets are certified kosher. It is also wise to take into account local cultural preferences, such as the German custom of pairing beer with their meals, or recognizing local taste preferences, like the taste for mango and taro instead of apple as pie fillings in the Philippines.

Other adaptations are driven from the ground up by the people making sense of new cultural forms and ideas in their own ways. The attraction to Coca-Cola in Trinidad is an example of how local meanings are impressed upon global products. Coca-Cola became coded with ethnic and socioeconomic identities in Trinidad, as well as the feeling of modernity. Coca-Cola is classified as a "black sweet drink" as opposed to the more traditional "red sweet drink" (Miller 1998). Even though it has been produced in Trinidad since 1939, it remains forever young because of its association with America and with global cosmopolitanism (as opposed to traditional drinks, which are more aligned with traditional Trinidadian values and culture). Ted Bestor's work

FIGURE 6.2 *A Ronald McDonald statue outside of a McDonald's branch in Guangzhou, China. Photo courtesy of the author.*

on sushi also highlights how food can take on new cultural meanings. Sushi has a Japanese identity throughout the world, but as it has been transported throughout the planet, it has changed and modified into local tastes. This includes how sushi is perceived and how it is eaten, to what can even be in sushi. For instance, the California roll—a type of rolled sushi made inside-out and filled with cucumber, cooked imitation crab meat, and avocado—is a supposed Californian invention. This roll is one of the most popular sushi bar items around the globe and has even made its way back to Japan.

Inequality

Many critics of globalization contend that it deepens socioeconomic inequality, increasing the divide between the "haves" and "have nots" in the world. The north-south divide provides one explanation to world inequality and poverty. The *Global North* is a term used to refer to the wealthy industrialized nations of the world, such as those of Western Europe and North America. Many of these nations are located in the northern hemisphere. These countries are also sometimes called "First World" countries or "developed countries."

The *Global South* refers to the poorer nations of the world, many of which are located in the southern hemisphere. These nations are the low income countries of the African continent, Central and South America, and Asia. These nations are also referred to as the "Third World" or "developing countries." Many of these countries were also formerly colonized by European powers.

The boundaries have been redrawn as some countries—such as Hong Kong, Singapore, South Korea, and Taiwan in the intervening years after World War II—have "graduated" from the south to north due to rapid industrialization and economic development. Australia and New Zealand, while located in the southern hemisphere, are considered members of the Global North. Scholars have questioned whether this remains a useful way to think about poverty and inequality (see Therien 1999). However, this north-south divide remains useful for examining the global food production, particularly in the context of old colonial relations.

The United Nations has aimed to diminish the divide between north and south through the Millennium Development Goals, which sought, among other things, to eradicate extreme poverty and hunger and ensure environmental sustainability. These goals were set for the year 2015 but have still not been completely achieved.

Global production patterns are also split along north/south lines. Countries of the Global South are more likely to be depending on commodity production: making raw agricultural goods that are eventually sent up to the Global North for processing, packaging, and eventual retailing. They produce primary products. The Global North also sees the largest cut of profits, while producers in the Global South often receive marginal pay for their labor and products.

This north-south divide is a socioeconomic and political divide. The Global North is home to roughly a quarter of the world's population, yet this is where the world's wealth is concentrated. Four-fifths of income earned anywhere in the world is controlled in the Global North. The Global South is home to three-quarters of the world's population but collectively they only have access to one-fifth of the world income. Nearly all of the world's manufacturing industries (90 percent) are also owned and located in the north.

Agribusiness and major food corporations are increasingly controlling the world's land resources.

As agriculture is the single largest employer throughout the world, agricultural issues and access to land are critical to understanding the north-south divide. About 40 percent of the global population works in agriculture. Among poor rural households, this is often the only means of making a living.

The majority of consumers—the people at the end of the food chain buying products—are also more likely to be in the Global North.

It is important to remember that divisions also exist within a country. Poverty and social inequality exist within countries, even the wealthier ones. Food workers, regardless of their locale in the Global North or the Global South, tend to experience higher levels of income disparity and greater risk in their working conditions. Even in a wealthy industrialized nation like the United States, food jobs are among the most dangerous and have the highest number of fatal occupational injuries. Many of the riskiest jobs are those at the start of the food chain. Farming, fishing, and forestry—a category that includes agricultural workers and ranchers, fishing and hunting workers, and forestry and logging—rank among some of the most dangerous jobs. Also in their company are food manufacturing laborers, as well as truck drivers who transport goods like food (Bureau of Labor Statistics 2015).

Minimum wage is the lowest payment permitted by law. The purpose of a minimum wage is to protect workers against low pay. Minimum wage often disproportionately impacts lower wage workers, such as those paid on an hourly basis, rather than salaried workers. These are "McJobs"—a byword for characterizing routinized jobs with low wages and low job satisfaction (Leidner 1993; Reiter 1996). Increasingly, the discussion has shifted from minimum wages (the lowest payment permitted) to living wages—payment that adequately reflects the cost of living in a community.

In the United States, minimum wages were first implemented during the Great Depression (1929–1939) to help protect workers and ensure that they could maintain a livelihood. The Fair Labor Standards Act, signed in 1938, introduced provisions that many American workers recognize as basic worker protections. The FLSA included a mandate of a forty-hour workweek, a national minimum wage, protection for minors as employees, and provision for overtime pay. Nowadays, many critics contend that minimum wages do not adequately cover daily necessities, hence the need for a living wage that more adequately reflects the cost of living in a community, including food, housing, shelter, and transportation. Living wages can be seen as a way to help overcome poverty and reduce inequality in a community.

Guarantee of minimum payment is believed to help protect workers and ensure their livelihood. However, there are loopholes in this scheme. Farmworkers in the United States are not generally bound by minimum wage laws. Food workers contend that minimum wages are not living wages. Tipped workers in the United States, a category that includes restaurant servers and other front-of-house hospitality positions like bartenders, also receive a far lower minimum wage under the excuse that tips would bring this category of workers to the minimum wage (see Jayaraman 2013). Food workers throughout the food chain have been advocating for better wages, and many of them have been advocating for living wages in different ways. A growing movement among fast food workers calls for the Fight for $15, a rally to provide living wages to a low paid occupation.

6.1 Activity: Calculating a living wage

Most people have a sense of what the minimum wage is in their community, but few have an idea of what a living wage is. A living wage is enough to support a household and pay for necessities: housing, food, transport, and other basic material needs.

Directions

1. Calculate your monthly budget for basic upkeep. Write down your monthly budget for rent/mortgage, grocery, health insurance, car insurance, car payments, electricity bill, gas and home utilities, water, automobile payment or other transportation costs, automobile insurance (if applicable), automobile repairs and gasoline (if applicable), phone, television and streaming services, internet, and any debt you have, including credit card debt and student loan payments.
2. Take the total number and divide it by 160—the average number of hours a salaried worker labors per month. This is your hourly wage.
3. Look up the minimum wage in your community at https://www.dol.gov/whd/minwage/america.htm.
4. Look up the living wage for your community at http://livingwage.mit.edu.

Discussion

1. What is the minimum wage in your community? What is the living wage? What is the wage you would need to support your current lifestyle?
2. Consider how your income needs might change if impacted by other factors: additional family members, illness, accident, or unanticipated expenses.
3. How might earning only a minimum wage affect one's ability to climb up the socioeconomic ladder?

Further resources

A Place at the Table (2013) [film], dir. Lori Silverbush and Kristi Jacobson, USA: Magnolia Pictures.

For farmers in the developing world, Fair Trade has been proposed to raise livelihoods. *Fair Trade* is a social movement intended to help producers in developing countries achieve better trading conditions and to promote sustainable farming. Fair Trade targets producers of export commodities, products that are exported from developing countries to developed countries. The premise is that producers should receive fair prices for their commodities.

Common Fair Trade commodities include coffee, sugar, tea, and cacao (chocolate), and bananas. Products or companies can be Fair Trade certified to show that they were made with these values in mind. The root of the problem is social justice.

6.2 Activity: North or south?

Look at your food labels, especially labels for packaged foods. What is the country of origin? Where was it packaged or bottled? Where is the distributor located? Where do these different nations fit in the north-south divide?

Materials

World map
Push pins or sticky notes
Notebook or journal

Directions

1. List each individual item you eat and track the countries of origin. Do this with all the food you consume for a day. Try to get specific locals, if possible (village, city, state, or province). If you do not know the country of origin, write down the food item but put "unknown" for the place of origin.
2. This includes individual ingredients that contribute toward a larger dish. For instance, if you make vinaigrette for salad, note the origins of the olive oil and the vinegar.
3. At the end of the day, track all of your food items on a map. Use sticky notes or push pins to identify all the origin points.

Discussion questions

1. What are some trends you notice about your food consumption chart?

> **2.** What percentage of your food is local (within a certain radius of your current location)? What percentage of your food is national—from the country you are residing in? What proportion of your food is from abroad?
> **3.** Were certain foods more likely to be local, national, or imported from abroad? How might your map change if you lived in a different region of your current country? Or if you lived in different country altogether?

Food security

The United Nations has some starting predictions about our future. First, the United Nations predicts that the world population will exceed nine billion people by 2050. Second, in order to feed all nine billion people, global food production will need to increase dramatically. Food production will need to increase by at least 60 percent to feed the planet, or more comfortably double to ensure a secure food supply.

What the United Nations predicts is a *Malthusian crisis*. Thomas Malthus (1766–1834), a political economist, cautioned that we needed to mind our food. Malthus warned that if population growth were to outpace food production, we would face starvation and collapse. Though Malthus's predictions have not quite come true, many still argue that we face a potential Malthusian crisis if we do not mind our food supply.

Right now there are 795 million people (one in nine) living in hunger on the planet. That number is predicted to rise to two billion living in hunger by the year 2050. The majority of these malnourished people live in developing countries. The Asian continent suffers the most, with two-thirds of the population experiencing malnutrition and hunger. The area of South Asia alone has roughly 281 million undernourished people. Poor nutrition has consequences, including stunted growth, developmental problems, and, in dire cases, even death. Hunger remains an ever-important global issue, exacerbated by the fact that much of the world's food is wasted and never eaten.

Experts claim there is finally enough food for everyone (Smil 2000). This feat is impressive, considering our battle as humankind to secure our food since our earliest days as a species. However, the battle is not over because many remain undernourished and receive inadequate access to food. At the same time, we also have a population that is overnourished. *Food security* remains a problem. Just over a handful of countries are the net exporters of food. There are many other exporters, but they export commodities like coffee, tea, and cacao and not staple foods that form the basis of diets.

The definition of food security has continued to evolve since its inception in 1974 at the World Food Conference. Originally, food security was conceived of as a supply issue. The United Nations put forth that food security meant "availability at all times of adequate world food supplies of basic food stuffs . . . to sustain a steady expansion of food consumption . . . and to offset fluctuations in production and prices" (United Nations 1975). Over time, the definition evolved.

The question of how to define food security is "widely debated and much-confused" (Braun 1992: 5). A basic definition of food security is, having enough to eat. On the international level, food security has been conceptualized and reconfigured since its first usage in 1974 at the World Food Conference. Food security was first conceived of as a supply problem.

Food security is not simply about having enough to eat. But instead, as Johan Pottier points out, it is a concept concerned with "interconnected domains," taking into account questions of "agriculture, society, environment, employment and income, marketing, health and nutrition, and public policy" (Pottier 1999: 11). But as its definition has evolved, food security has expanded to recognize that social, cultural, economic, and political issues are also bound up with the definition.

Food security is often seen as a top-down definition, drafted by governments and international organizations. Scholars have shifted their definition to recognize that food security should focus on livelihood and economic security rather than on food itself. Pottier reminds us that "it is relations—economic, social, political, religious, all interwoven—that determine who will eat and live well, and who will not" (Pottier 1999: 27). In other words, food security goes beyond securing food. Kathleen DeWalt argues that projects and programs "often fail to appreciate the complex nature of the relationships between agricultural production, income, and food consumption and nutritional status. These relationships are social, cultural, and economic, as well as biological and ecological" (DeWalt 1991: 126). Peasant and smallholder farmers—those who are at the proverbial bottom— have countered with their own definition. Instead of fighting for food security, often they demand food sovereignty.

Related to food security is the issue of *food sovereignty*. Like food security, food sovereignty also focuses on rights and power: the ability to control the food supply. This term is often attributed to *La Via Campesina*, "the peasants' way." This social movement was founded in 1993 in Mons, Belgium, as a meeting of small-scale producers from Africa, Asia, Europe, and the Americas. This original meeting addressed farmers' concerns about agricultural policies and the agribusiness that were displacing and overriding small-scale farmers. Over time, it has grown into a movement of 200 million farmers from seventy-three countries around the world. *La Via Campesina* introduced the term "food sovereignty" at the World Food Summit in 1996. Today, the definition the organization uses contends:

Food sovereignty is the right of peoples to healthy and culturally appropriate food produced through sustainable methods and their right to define their own food and agriculture systems. It develops a model of small scale sustainable production benefiting communities and their environment. Food sovereignty prioritizes local food production and consumption, giving a country the right to protect its local producers from cheap imports and to control its production.[1] It includes the struggle for land and genuine agrarian reform that ensures that the rights to use and manage lands, territories, water, seeds, livestock and biodiversity are in the hands of those who produce food and not of the corporate sector.

Sovereignty signifies "control, autonomy, democratic participation, and agency" (Andrée et al. 2014: 4). *La Via Campesina* contends that corporations, neoliberal organizations like the World Trade Organization, and free trade agreements do not recognize—or sometimes actively work against—the needs of small farmers. Andrée et al. call this a "paradox," that while there has been "increasing food production and access to affordable food for many, especially in urban areas, that has brought land grabs and dislocations, hunger and food shortages, obesity, food contamination, and environmental impacts that threaten the very resources upon which that food production depends" (2014: 3). The negative outcomes disproportionately impact the poor living in the Global South, particularly peasant and smallholding farmers.

The issue of food sovereignty has become more pressing amid the rise of global land grabs. Land grabs occur, whereby large parcels of land are purchased or leased by corporations, governments, and sometimes individual landowners. This land grab also extends to water rights and access to water. The global land grab disproportionately affects the Global South, where large parcels of land are being purchased for their natural resources such as minerals, forestry, and its fertility for food production and biofuels production.

Land is increasingly concentrated in the hands of a few. This is especially true in the United States where agribusinesses own the majority of farmland. This happens in both, wealthy nations and poorer ones. Of course, the problem is felt more deeply in poorer nations where smallholders do not have enough access to land. Global land grabs have resulted in the displacement of local peoples and these communities have not always been adequately consulted or compensated for the use of the land. Some of these landholdings are being used for large-scale agriculture, which may permanently change the ecosystem of the area.

Food insecurity can be easily dismissed as a Third World problem or a problem for lesser developed countries. It is easy to think of food insecurity as being a problem "over there," so to speak. Indeed, the prevailing stereotype we have of hunger is that of it being a foreign problem for people living in a land far away. Different types of food insecurity afflict different communities. Food insecurity exists in all nations, even among industrialized Western nations. Consider the United States, the most affluent nation in the world. Even in this prosperous country, forty-five million people or 14.5 percent of the population lives below the poverty line. The federal poverty level is $12,140 in annual income for an individual or $25,100 for a family of four.[2] Hunger and regular access to food are real problems for those below the poverty line.

Today, scholars and food activists are also engaging with food security at home. That is to say, food security is often thought of as a global issue, something happening "over there" or "elsewhere." In the United States, there is a phenomenon Raj Patel calls "stuffed and starved" (Patel 2007). Food security also means having access to the right types of food. We can be "stuffed" yet "starved" at the same time. Lifestyle diseases are on the rise in industrialized nations—obesity, diabetes, high cholesterol, heart disease, and other afflictions caused by poor diets and lifestyle choices. Poor food quality is certainly one culprit. The strong food industry in the United States, increase in the amount of sugar, low cost of processed foods, and strong food marketing and advertising have exacerbated this phenomenon (Nestle 2013).

But this is not simply a Western affliction. The World Health Organization notes that obesity is now increasing at a faster rate in the developing world.[3] Some have suggested that the loss of indigenous foods and "globalization and modernization" have further changed food habits.

Consider the rise of instant ramen noodles. Instant ramen, a staple of many college students, has become one of the most widely consumed foods throughout the world. Instant ramen is not the healthiest of foods—high in sodium and low in nutrient value, it's also fried in palm oil, which is what allows it to retain its texture and moisture. The popularization of instant ramen in many environments has had consequences for local foodways as well, with locals choosing to eat instant ramen over indigenous foods because of its cheaper cost (Errington, Fujikura, and Gewertz 2013).

Food safety issues are also no longer isolated to one place or locale. What originally started as a few dogs and cats getting sick in the United States unfurled to be a global food scandal. Pet owners in the United States noticed that their cats and dogs were falling ill, prompting the United States Food and Drug Administration to investigate. What federal investigators discovered was that the pet food was contaminated with melamine—an industrial additive used in the production of fertilizers and plastics. This additive was put into pet food to fake a higher protein content (Nestle 2008).

As the food chain grows and we become further and further divorced from the origination point, it becomes harder and harder to trace our food. We live in what anthropologists call a "risk society"—where the risks of living include blindly trusting the people ahead of you in the food chain.

6.3 Activity: Understanding inequality

This is a useful exercise for explaining inequality and how structural factors impact the likelihood of success.

Directions

1. Take a wastepaper basket and put it in the front of the classroom.
2. Ask every student to take a sheet of paper (waste paper is fine), write their name on it, and crumple it into a ball.
3. Without moving from their seats, ask students to toss their ball into the wastepaper basket. Have the entire class do it together at the same time.
4. Look into the wastepaper basket to see who made it in and won the game.

Instructor's note

This is a classroom activity and works especially well in a large lecture hall.

Discussion

1. Who was able to make the shot into the wastepaper basket?
2. How did one's location and proximity to the wastepaper basket impact their chance of success?
3. What impediments were there to success—other students, furniture, room layout, and so on?
4. What does this activity illustrate about inequality and structural impediments? Who had the best chance of success?

Biotechnology

The Green Revolution brought a change to agricultural productivity, particularly in the poorer nations of the world. Many have blamed the Green Revolution as the source of what ails peasant and smallholder farmers in poorer nations.

Colonial landholders favored cash crops over food crops. The Green Revolution furthered this preference. The Green Revolution has further eroded crop genetic diversity by making environments "uniform" (Amanor et al. 1993). That is to say, local crop varieties and their wild relatives are no longer planted. Instead, a limited number of varieties, often hybridized varieties, have taken over.

Genetically modified organisms (GMO) seeds are another source of worry for small farms on the grounds of biodiversity as well as economic livelihoods. Commercial seeds, including GMO seeds, are developed by corporations like Syngenta and Monsanto. Farmers sometimes take on loans to buy these seeds, and can find themselves in debt to pay back the loans for seeds and other agricultural materials like fertilizers and pesticides. Indian activist Vandana Shiva has criticized the proliferation of genetically engineered seeds, claiming that in addition to degrading the land, it also degrades farmers and their rights. Seeds have to be purchased over and over again, as they cannot be saved (Shiva 1992: 157). Farmers in the Global South are also labeled "*competitors* in terms of innovation and rights to genetic resources" (Shiva 1992: 157).

The United Nations estimates that 75 percent of crop diversity has been lost from farmers' fields. Farmers worldwide used to grow "traditional" varieties. Potatoes are native to the Andes Mountains and traditional varieties included those good to look at, good to store, and good to market (Brush, Carney, and Humán 1981; Van der Ploeg 1990). Traditional varieties of millet and sorghum have been replaced by maize (corn) in Zimbabwe. Of this maize, just two hybrid varieties account for 90 percent of all maize planted.

Once again we see that power is at the core of this discussion. "Labour and seed are at the heart of the claim: farmers are losing control over the allocation of resources, including their own labour, and over their products of their labour, which is the food and seed they produce" (Pottier 1999: 124).

Development planners and policy makers carry the assumption that farmers in the Global South lack scientific agricultural knowledge. Among planners and policy makers there are two opposed epistemologies: scientific Western knowledge and nonscientific indigenous knowledge. There is an underlying belief that Western scientific knowledge carries greater authority and justification than the supposed nonscientific, indigenous knowledge of farmers in the Global South (Fairhead 1993: 200). This "reductionist view separates local knowledges (plural!) from the specific social, economic and political contexts in which they have emerged" (Pottier 1999: 125). Farmer knowledge is seen as singular.

Local farmers have rejected traditional varieties because they are not "modern" or seen to be productive and efficient enough. The work of agricultural scientists and biotechnologists has been given preference over peasant farmers worldwide, for their work is seen to be more efficient and knowledgeable. These seeds are often also controlled intellectual property, owned by the seed companies or biotechnology firms that developed them. Some intellectual property laws make it illegal for farmers to sell seeds to their neighbors or even to save seeds for the next planting season. Peasant farmers are cast as "ungrateful, 'primitive' competitors whose contributions should be confined to the supply of valueless raw materials" (Pottier 1999: 128–29). Slowly, however, peasant farmers have begun to regain power.

Although bioengineered foods have been presented as a solution to our food supply, genetically modified foods have not been met with universal embrace. Several countries and regions have banned the use of genetically modified seeds in their lands, including the sub-Saharan nation of Zambia. All genetically modified foods were banned from the country in 2012, including food aid sent to help provide famine relief. Then President Levy Patrick Mwanawasa proclaimed, "We would rather starve than get genetically modified foods" (Annear 2004). This case raises an interesting issue of inequality. Christopher M. Annear points out that this rejection of genetically modified foods was a critical moment for Zambians and other sub-Saharan Africans, as it shows how countries at the receiving end of food aid should have the ability to make food decisions. He points out that the "privilege of choice is present only in prosperous industrialized countries," and Zambia's example subverts the notion that the "beggars can't be choosers" (Annear 2004).

Corporations and biotechnology firms have been charged with biopiracy. It is a term used to explain the appropriation of biological resources and knowledge of these resources for purposes that do not meet the approval or have the consent of groups or individuals who have some prior claim to the resources or knowledge. At the heart of biopiracy is the claim about control: about the ethics of who gets to control food resources, biologic life, and access to knowledge.

The globalizing world of high-tech farming and agribusiness is an appropriate illustration. True, globalizing processes have produced broad, recurring patterns in farming technology and organization on the ground (e.g., more women worldwide are not engaged as part-time workers in agriculture and in food processing industries), but, equally true, none of these transformations have been uncorruptedly imposed. The challenge is to appreciate how the different actors involved (e.g., peasant smallholders, commercial farmers, transnational companies, policy makers, banks and various agrarian organizations) struggle to negotiate outcomes.

6.4 Food for thought: Ancient foods as superfoods

"Ancient foods" have become incredibly popular in the industrialized west. Grains and pseudo cereals have been popularized and mass marketed, among them amaranth, quinoa, millet, sorghum, teff, freekeh, chia seeds, faro, spelt, and kamut. These foods are said to have been less developed and bred than other varieties.

Quinoa, arguably the grain of the moment, has probably had the most explosive rise in popularity. This grain is native to the Andean highlands and is grown in Peru and Bolivia, where it has been a staple in the diet. Cheerios, a popular brand of breakfast cereal, has even jumped on the bandwagon with a Cheerios + Ancient Grains version of its product featuring quinoa. Yet the demand for these products is not benign.

Quinoa has had an environmental impact on the soil. Some researchers suggest that soil is worse than before the quinoa boom. Land that used to be allowed to rest as fallow between harvests is now being worked more intensively to allow for higher yields and greater crops. As a result, the soil quality has eroded and lost some of its nutrient quality. Farmers following traditional methods used to fertilize their lands with llama manure. To have more land for quinoa cultivation, farmers have reduced the size of their herds, resulting in less manure for fertilizer. Due to its recent popularity, quinoa is now being planted in other environments too, such as China, India, and Nepal, as well as the United States and Canada.

News reports also state that the price of quinoa is now so high that it is no longer consumed as a staple food among the communities where it is grown. Instead it has become a cash crop. Indigenous farmers who grow quinoa now eat other foods instead—foods like instant noodles. This begs the question: Who is better off with quinoa?

Further resources

Cherfas, J. (2016). "Your Quinoa Habit Really Did Help Peru's Poor: But There's Trouble Ahead." *National Public Radio.* http://www.npr.org/sections/thesalt/2016/03/31/472453674/ your-quinoa-habit-really-did-help-perus-poor-but-theres-trouble-ahead.

6.5 Activity: Seed bombs

Seed bombs are a great way to plant seeds in a variety of places. Seed bombing has become a popular practice in urban spaces as a way of reclaiming and beautifying lands such as disused sidewalks and abandoned lots. Many seed bombers prefer to use heirloom seeds or native seeds to their environment, thus encouraging the flourishing of the local ecology over bioengineered seeds.

Materials

Seeds
Potter's clay powder (available from a craft shop or pottery supply store)

Peat-free compost
A large bowl
A large tray
Towels

Directions

1. Mix the seed, clay, and compost together in a bowl: roughly three parts clay, five parts compost, and one part seed.
2. Slowly add water to the mixture and mix until it just holds together and is malleable.
3. Take clumps of the mix and roll into small balls the size of ping-pong balls.
4. Leave out in a sunny spot to dry overnight.
5. When ready, toss, wait for it to rain, and check for growth in a few weeks' time.
6. You can get creative with the seed bomb shapes—hearts, flowers, stars; some even make bomb shapes.

Instructor's note

Pollinator seeds are an especially good choice. They help attract bees. Native wildflowers also help restore native species. A local gardening store can recommend good pollinator plants for your area.

Climate change

Climate change is transforming the world food supply. Climate change is not a new phenomenon—the earth goes through periods of heating and cooling. If we recall from Chapter 3, the last major climate change happened roughly 10,000 years ago. The gradual warming of the climate changed human food acquisition patterns. As big game died off, humans turned more and more toward domesticated plant and animal sources, leading to the start of domestication and agricultural production. This, resultantly, also changed human settlement patterns and foodways.

The climate change is progressing at an unprecedented rate, exacerbated by human activities. Some of the likely impacts of climate change, some of which are already occurring, include: more frequent and intense extreme weather events like hurricanes, floods, and heat waves; weather-related deaths, forced migration due to rising sea levels and natural disasters; and food and water-related shortages.

At the present moment, scientists argue that the planet is once again warming and will result in changes to the way we live and eat. Climate change will disproportionately impact the world's poor and food insecure. According to the Food and Agriculture Organization (FAO), 75 percent of the world's poor and food insecure rely directly on agriculture and natural resources for their livelihoods. Climate change is projected to change ecosystems and reduce the availability of arable land. This will likely result in a shrinking of food supplies and an increase in food prices. In areas where there is already a high level of hunger and food insecurity, such as in sub-Saharan Africa and the South Asian subcontinent, these changes are predicted to be especially harmful.

Globalization has also meant that one people's problems are no longer that—they quickly become everyone's problems. Climate change is emblematic of how food issues are now everyone's issues. Climate change will only further exacerbate issues in the global food chain.

The way we currently produce food has been cited as a contributor toward human-induced climate change. For instance, our taste for meat is cited as an incredibly non-environmentally friendly habit.

Some common foods that are threatened by climate change include avocados, coffee, cacao beans (the raw ingredient used in chocolate), corn, mangoes, maple syrup, cherries, and seafood, wine grapes, and wheat. Demand for animal-based protein and byproducts like meat, eggs, fish, dairy, and cheese has remained consistent in wealthy nations. As poorer nations have industrialized, they too have also developed a taste for animal products. Demand for animal protein places increased pressure on resources to produce this food, including pressures on the land, water, and emissions into the atmosphere. Livestock, especially cows, contribute heavily to greenhouse emissions. In the United States, red meat (beef, pork, and lamb) and dairy production account for roughly half of the greenhouse gas emissions associated with the food supply chain (see Engelhaupt 2008; Weber and Matthews 2008).

Greenhouse gas emissions are produced at all parts of the food chain. Production accounts for the largest percentage of emissions (83 percent). Transportation, moving food from production point to warehouses and storage facilities and eventually on to the retail point account for another 11 percent. Retail finally accounts for 5 percent. Wasted food also contributes to climate issues. Roughly one-third of the food produced is lost or wasted. The FAO estimates that global food waste amounts to $2.6 trillion per year, including $700 billion of environmental costs and $900 billion of social costs. Food waste accounts for the largest component of solid waste in landfills and incinerators (21 percent) (Environmental Protection Agency 2014). Food buried in landfills will break down over time, releasing methane into the atmosphere.

Water resources are likely to be altered by global climate change. While we tend to think of land as being the most important resource in our food supply, water is just as integral—as a source of irrigation or as the source of aquaculture. As the world's average temperature rises due to the increasing accumulation of greenhouse gases in the atmosphere, water will be impacted. Precipitation patterns are impacted, with some areas receiving more and others less rainfall than in the historical past. Rising temperatures are predicted to impact the world's oceans. Catches of the world's main species are likely to decrease by 40 percent, as the waters will be too warm for species to survive in their original habitats. Sea levels are also rising and warmer temperatures in these seas are impacting the species that live within the waters, with many species migrating to different areas in search of cooler habitats.

Even though our planet is covered with water, much of this is salt water and unfit for human consumption. Almost 70 percent of the earth's surface is salt water, while fresh water accounts for under 3 percent of the world's total water supply. A large part of this 3 percent is frozen in glaciers and polar ice caps or deep underground in aquifers. In total, only 0.01 percent of all the water on earth is truly available for human use (Commission on Sustainable Development 1997). This is problematic, as humans need an incredible amount of water to survive. Water is necessary for drinking, sanitation, cooking, and food production. On average, taking into account all of our water needs, a person needs 1,000 cubic meters (265,000 gallons) per year to survive. Irrigation is especially critical in areas that receive little rainfall, such as North Africa, Southwest Asia, and the American Southwest.

As the global population continues to climb, this puts additional pressure on our already limited water resources. The amount of water available per person grows smaller as the population continues to climb. People living in developed societies also tend to use greater amounts of water—think about the amount of water used to water green lawns and landscape buildings, maintain indoor plumbing systems, and power modern conveniences like dishwashers and washing machines. Additionally, people living in developed societies also tend to consume more meat, which is more water intensive to produce than plant foods.

6.6 Activity: A dinner party without dinner

This activity is inspired by filmmaker and producer Seth Kramer. Kramer screened his film *The Anthropologist* on campus at the Culinary Institute of America. The film is about climate change as told through the eyes of an American teenager traveling the world with her mother, a professional anthropologist. My students had many questions for Kramer. One student's question, in particular, stood out. They asked, "What is the best way to explain climate change to those who are on the fence or didn't believe in it?" Without hesitation, Kramer replied, "Have a dinner party without food."

Directions

1. Plan a three course menu consisting of a starter, main course, and dessert.
2. Consider the items listed.
3. Invite friends and members of the community attend your dinner party. Set the table with dishware, cutlery, and glasses. Don't forget to decorate the table.
4. Provide everyone with a printed menu. Explain what would have been served if climate change had not altered current agricultural systems and food systems.

Further resources

The Anthropologist (2015) [film], dir. Seth Kramer, Daniel A. Miller, and Jeremy Newberger, USA: Ironbound Films.
Burke, I. (2017). "29 of Your Favorite Foods That Are Threatened by Climate Change." *Saveur.*

Summary

- There are many different types of globalization, including economic, political, social, and cultural.

- Food has been globalized since at least the 1500s and the Columbian Exchange (The Great Exchange).

- Modern globalization has contributed to homogenization of goods and services, rising inequality among food workers and between producers and consumers, food security challenges, and the rise of biotechnology as a solution to the food system.

- Our demand for food has also contributed to global climate change. Climate change is also impacting our food supply.

Discussion questions

1. Consider the argument that the world is "flat" and that foods, goods, and services are homogenous. What are arguments in favor of homogenization? What are arguments against?

2. Experts argue that food security and income equality are interrelated. Discuss.

3. Scientists are worried about the loss of biodiversity. Why is this a pressing concern?

Further resources

Movies and documentaries

Bitter Seeds (2011) is a documentary on the plight of cotton farmers in India. It examines the structural issues leading to a growing rash of farmer suicides across the country.

Food Evolution (2016) is a documentary on our food system focused on dispelling myths about the food system.

The Fruit Hunters (2012) is a documentary about exotic fruit cultivators and preservationists. It shows the quest of exotic fruit hunters in protecting the biodiversity of the world's fruit species.

Soylent Green (1973) is a classic film. It takes place in a post-apocalyptic future where food is scarce and resources are limited.

The World According to Monsanto (2008) is a documentary on the agri-giant's business practices and its role in the world food supply.

Notes

1 See https://viacampesina.org/en/international-peasants-voice/.
2 These are the figures for 2018.
3 See http://www.who.int/nutrition/topics/obesity/en/.

Further resources

Bailey, Britt, and Marc Lappe (eds.) (2002). *Engineering the Farm: Ethical and Social Aspects of Agricultural Biotechnology.* Washington, DC: Island Press.

Bestor, Theodore (2004). *Tsukiji: The Fish Market at the Center of the World*. Berkeley: University of California Press.

Bruce, Donald, and Ann Bruce (eds.) (2000). *Engineering Genesis: The Ethics of Genetic Engineering in Non-human Species*. London: Earthscan Publications.

Carney, Megan (2015). *The Unending Hunger: Tracing Women and Food Insecurity across Borders*. Oakland: University of California Press.

Estabrook, B. (2012). *Tomatoland: How Modern Industrial Agriculture Destroyed Our Most Alluring Fruit*. Kansas, MO: Andrews McMeel.

McMillan, T. (2012). *The American Way of Eating: Undercover at Walmart, Applebee's, Farm Fields and the Dinner Table*. New York: Scribner.

Millstone, Erik, and Tim Lang (2013). *The Atlas of Food: Who Eats What, Where and Why*. Berkeley: University of California Press.

Ruse, Michael, and David Castle (eds.) (2002). *Genetically Modified Foods: Debating Biotechnology*. Amherst: Prometheus Books.

Watson, James L. (ed.) (1997). *Golden Arches East: McDonald's in East Asia*. Stanford: Stanford University Press.

Weber, Devra (1994). *Dark Sweat, White Gold: California Farm Workers, Cotton, and the New Deal*. Berkeley: University of California Press.

Epilogue

Food Studies: A Hands-On Guide serves as a broad-ranging interdisciplinary and multidisciplinary introduction to the field of Food Studies. It is not meant to be an exhaustive, encyclopedic volume on everything Food Studies, but it is meant to introduce you to several key ideas and theories behind the field and to show how Food Studies permeates into our understandings of the world around us.

In this epilogue, I also want to encourage you to think about *the future* and your next steps. Perhaps it means taking more classes on food or finding a job in a food-related industry. Maybe you'd like to cook more to have a more intimate relationship with your dinner. Some of you may choose to start gardening or buying food from local sources. Whatever your next steps, remember to involve food in some way—whether in formal, organized ways (taking more classes) to informal acts (sharing a cookie with a friend and realizing that it is an act of commensality).

The final message is that Food Studies is not "finished" but, as the chapters have shown, there is still much work to be done. Food has been, remains, and will continue to be an ongoing concern for humans. Whether it is exploring the gastronomic side of food, investigating how food defines us as individuals and the societies around us, or the ever-present concern of how to feed everyone on the planet, food is an issue here to stay. Below are some final activities to tie the key themes of this book together.

E.1 Activity: Writing for change

This activity will vary depending on where in the world you live, but one of the most powerful ways to communicate your newfound knowledge and awareness of Food Studies issues is to speak with those in power. Advocate for changes large and small. Perhaps it is advocating for better quality food in your campus dining hall. Maybe you would like to see the campus participate in recycling and waste reduction efforts. It could be something you would like to see on a national or international level—perhaps more aid directed toward food relief programs in conflict zones. Whatever it is you care about, you have the ability to ask for change. It may not be granted, but you have the right to ask and express your concerns.

As a student, you have spent countless hours writing papers for classes. You may have been taught a certain way to write, which may include a thesis statement, citations, and a list of references and at-length argumentation. Writing takes on a different tone and style when done to convince someone in a position of power. When taking on a position, you will have to "un-learn" what you have adopted in class. Your argument must be made quickly, concisely, and eloquently within a short space, normally within the span of one typed page.

Directions

1. Think about one issue or topic that is of importance to you. The issue does not have to be big (e.g., changing nutritional standards in American school lunches). Instead, a single, highly targeted issue is easier to focus on.
2. Think about two or three key points related to your topic. Think of statistics, facts, data, or other information that would support your position.
3. Pull these ideas together into a letter.
4. A letter should be formatted in the following manner:

   a. Beginning with an opening, including the date, address, and salutation.
   b. Explanation of the purpose for your letter.
   c. Summary of the issue or decision being considered.
   d. Explanation of your position on the issue, with facts, data, and other evidence as support.
   e. Discussion of what the decision would mean to you and its impact on your life/community.
   f. Description of the action you hope the letter recipient will take.
   g. Ending with a closing, including your signature and contact details for follow up.

Instructor's note

This activity is highly successful among American college students. Very few will have contacted their elected officials. This activity encourages them to take on civic responsibility and see themselves as part of a broader civil society. It also allows them to see that Food Studies issues are political issues. Students have reached out to me long after the end of class to tell me how they were thrilled that their elected officials responded to their concerns.

Further resources

The League of Women Voters has a resource that allows US-based residents to look up their elected officials. https://salsa.wiredforchange.com/o/5950/getLocal4.jsp.

E.2 Activity: Recipe for commensality

Sometimes the easiest way to apply Food Studies is to practice what you preach. Commensality, the sharing of food with other people, can be done in many ways, from the humble act of sharing a cookie with a friend to participating in elaborate holiday feasts and traditions. This activity encourages students to share their experiences of Food Studies with those outside the Food Studies community.

Directions

1. Write a recipe that explains your approach to food or the field of Food Studies. This recipe can be literal (e.g., a recipe for your grandmother's spaghetti and meatballs) or figurative (e.g., your recipe for a better food system). Be sure to consider the key concepts and themes from this textbook.
2. After you have completed your recipe, write a brief paragraph to explain the recipe and what you hope to share with others through this recipe. How might this recipe nourish or enrich others?
3. Print out copies of your recipe and share with classmates, loved ones, and friends.

Instructor's note

This activity lends itself well to a large class group. If doing this as a class project, collect all recipes together as a cookbook. The cookbook can be published online or in print—or both. Digital publishing allows a multimedia approach, such as the inclusion of video, sound recordings, interviews,

and photos. This can become an ongoing class project repeated over many
semesters.

E.3 From food waste to art

Food is often used as a medium for art. Food is successful as an artistic
media because it allows viewers to sensually engage with the subject
and to create an emotional relationship.

Many famous works of art, past and present, have used food. Futurist
artists of the 1930s used food to predict about the future. F. T. Marinetti
rewrote the rules of eating in *The Futurist Cookbook* (Marinetti 2014),
arguing that dietary change laid the groundwork for social change. More
recently, Kara Walker's sculpture *A Subtlety or the Marvelous Sugar
Baby: An Homage to the Unpaid and Overworked Artisans Who Have
Refined Our Sweet tastes from the Cane Fields to the Kitchens of the New
World on the Occasion of the Demolition of the Domino Sugar Refining
Plant* (2014) sparked conversations about sugar, the Caribbean slave trade,
and exploitation. Made entirely of white refined cane sugar and housed in
a former Domino Sugar factory, her sphinxlike sculpture of a black woman
drew viewers into the topic of discussion.

Using food waste—food otherwise destined for compost bins and
garbage cans—can also be used as a statement to help others consider
what is beautiful, useful, practical, and relevant in the field of Food Studies.

One easy way to get inspired is to look at the paintings of Renaissance
artist Giuseppe Archimboldo (1526 or 1527–1593). His portraits of faces
made of vegetables reflect seasons as well as personalities. While fruits
and vegetables are the obvious choice, also consider shells (clams, oysters,
mussels), animal and fish bones, and also pits and seeds.

Materials

Food waste—food headed for the compost bin, food scraps, even food
    packaging
Cutting board
Knife
A large plate or tray to serve as a canvas

Directions

1. Using your food waste, fashion a portrait or piece of art to your liking. Consider what you would like your audience to see or the discussions you would like your audience to engage in upon viewing your art.
2. When completed, take photos to share. Or if this is done in a classroom setting, host a class art show.
3. Invite others to comment and discuss.

Discussion questions

1. Describe how you chose to transform "ugly" food into "beautiful" art.
2. How might this activity feel different if you had used "good" food as opposed to food waste?
3. Consider the types of responses from your viewers. What did they have to say?

Glossary

Affine Relatives derived via marriage such as parents-in-law.

Band Small communities composed of roughly 100 people, all related through kinship, who live, acquire food, cook, and eat together. This is the primary form of social organization among foragers.

Biological determinism A theory that biological differences between males and females lead to fundamentally different capacities, preferences, and gendered behaviors. This theory has shaped popular discussions about gender, and perpetuates the notion that gender roles are rooted in biology as opposed to cultural expectations.

Broad spectrum diet A term used to describe the diets of foragers, which were based on a variety of food sources ranging from insects and rodents to plants and large animals.

Canning Invented by Nicolas Appert in the nineteenth century, canning is a method of food preservation that processes and seals food in an airtight container, which prohibits bacteria growth.

Carrying capacity The maximum population size of a species that can be sustained given the natural resources available, including food, water, and land, without destroying the ecological system. The carrying capacity for a given area is not fixed and can change based on human interaction and interference.

Climate change Long-term change in global or regional climate patterns, including warmer or cooler weather temperatures and the more frequent occurrence of extreme weather events. Changes in the early twenty-first century are increasing at an unprecedented rate and are exacerbated by human activities.

Commensality The sharing of food with other people, which helps facilitate social interaction and bonding.

Commodity An economic good that can be bought and sold, often raw materials (like minerals) or primary agricultural products (such as coffee and tea).

Consanguine Relatives derived through ancestry or "blood."

Cuisine A way of preparing food that takes into account basic foods selected from the broader environment of available edibles, a distinctive manner of food preparation, a set of seasonings that serve as group identity markers, parameters surrounding etiquette and manners regarding acceptable consumption, and a food chain or infrastructure of how food moves from the place of origin to the place of consumption. Cuisine must be supported by a community—a group of people who produce, eat, share, and identify with it.

Cultural capital The knowledge, behaviors, and skills that one possesses, which show their cultural competence and standing in a society.

Cultural ontology A system of classification and evaluation used to tag differences between social groups. Examples include kinship, gender, race, and ethnicity.

Diffusion The spread of plant or animal species from their origin point to other parts of the world.

Fair trade A social movement intended to help producers in developing countries to achieve better economic trading conditions and to promote sustainable farming. This movement targets producers of export commodities and aims to help producers receive fair prices for their commodities.

Family A group of people related in some way, either by ancestry or by blood (*consanguine*) or by marriage (*affine*).

Fictive kin Individuals who claim no blood or marriage ties yet are important to a family unit. Examples include someone as close to you as a brother or sister.

Food chain The journey that food takes as it moves from its original production point to its final consumption point. This journey takes into account all the processes and actors involved, ranging from the food producers to the distributors and the consumers.

Food culture A field of study engaged in understanding the food habits and foodways of an area or of a group of people.

Food memories Memories of food represent the connection between food and emotion.

Food rules Cultural classification or folk taxonomies about what a group of people considers acceptable in terms of food consumption.

Food security The social, cultural, economic, biological, political, and ecological stability of a food system that allows for an adequate food supply that maintains livelihoods.

Food sovereignty The right of peoples to healthy and culturally appropriate food produced through sustainable methods, as well as their right to define their own food and cultural systems.

Food Studies An interdisciplinary and multidisciplinary academic field devoted to examining the relationships between human beings and food.

Food system All activities, infrastructure, social institutions, and cultural beliefs within a social group across the stages of production, processing, transport, and the consumption of food.

Food voice The way in which food serves as a dynamic, creative, symbolic, and highly individualized channel of communication. Food serves as a voice in communicating aspects of identity and culture.

Foodways The study of what we eat, as well as how and why and under what circumstances we eat. Foodways takes into account the beliefs and behaviors surrounding the production, distribution, and consumption of food.

Foraging Also known as *hunting and gathering*. This is a subsistence system that involves finding and harvesting wild plant and animal food resources from land and by water through hunting, fishing, gathering, and scavenging.

Gastronomy Derived from the ancient Greek words of *gastro* and *nomos*, meaning "the laws of the stomach," gastronomy deals with the art and science of good food. As an academic field, gastronomy is sometimes used as a synonym for Food Studies.

Genetically modified organism (GMO) An organism whose genome has been scientifically altered in a laboratory setting to favor certain physiological traits or the production of specific biological products.

Globalization The process of increasingly interconnected economic, political, social, and cultural interactions and exchanges across the planet.

Global North A term used to refer to the wealthy industrialized nations of the world, particularly those of Western Europe and North America.

Global South A term used to refer to the poorer nations of the world, many of which are dependent on primary production. Members of the Global South are generally located in the southern hemisphere and include the low-income countries of the African continent, Central and South America, and the Asian continent.

Glocalization The process of adapting a global good or object to local political, social, and economic systems, as well as to local tastes.

Heirloom An old or traditional seed or animal type not used in commercial agricultural production.

Horticulture A subsistence system that is a low-tech form of farming or gardening.

Hunting and gathering A synonym for *foraging*.

Hybrid The offspring of two plants or animals of different species or varieties.

Industrial Revolution A technological revolution from the late eighteenth to the mid-nineteenth century that led to the rise of industrial manufacturing and, ultimately, changes to our modern economic and political systems. This movement also led to the industrialization of the food supply and introduced mass-produced processed foods to human diets.

Intensive agriculture A subsistence system based on intensive farming that has extensive use of tools and machinery and tends to focus on yield and profit.

Kinship How family members define their affiliation with one another.

Malthusian crisis A situation in which the population in a given area is greater than its food supply and can no longer be sustained, eventually resulting in mass starvation and population decline over time.

Mise en place A French term meaning everything in its place.

Monocrop The reliance on a single plant species.

Narrative How a story or series of events is framed, discussed, recalled, and passed on.

Nuclear family The close immediate family members, often composed of parents and their offspring.

Nutritional science A field that emerged in the nineteenth century focused on quantifying and classifying calories and nutrients necessary for human growth and the prevention of diseases.

Omnivore An animal that can consume both plant and animal foods.

The omnivore's dilemma Omnivores can eat both plant- and animal-based foods yet may choose not to, based upon biological, geographical, or cultural values, beliefs, or barriers.

Pastoralism A subsistence system that centers on domesticated animals as food, fuel, transportation, wealth, and power. Also known as ranching or herding.

Primates Members of a zoological order with apes, monkeys, prosimians, and humans.

Sexual division of labor The separation of tasks and social roles based on biological sexual differences.

Staple foods Foods eaten in regular quantities that are the major sources of carbohydrates and serve as caloric staples in a diet. They include grains and cereals, legumes, tubers, or starchy fruits.

Subsistence system A set of practices, technologies, and techniques used by members of a society to acquire food.

Taboo That which is forbidden.

World system A complex web through which goods circulate through the globe.

References

Adler, T. A., 1981. "Making Pancakes on Sunday: The Male Cook in Family Tradition." *Western Folklore*, 40(1), pp. 45–54. Available at: http://www.jstor.org/stable/1499848.

Albala, K., 2013. *Food: A Cultural Culinary History* [DVD]. Chantilly: The Great Courses.

Allen, E., 2015. "Supper Club." *New Yorker*. Available at: http://www.newyorker.com/magazine/2015/10/26/supper-club.

Allen, J. S., 2012. *The Omnivorous Mind: Our Evolving Relationship with Food*. Cambridge, MA: Harvard University Press.

Allen, P., and C. Sachs, 2012. "Women and Food Chains: The Gendered Politics of Food." In P. W. Forson and C. Counihan, eds. *Taking Food Public: Redefining Foodways in a Changing World*. New York: Routledge, pp. 23–40.

Amanor, K., Walter de Boef, Kate Wellard, and Anthony Bebbington, 1993. "Introduction." In W. de Boef, K. Amanor, and K. Wellard, with A. Bebbington, eds. *Cultivating Knowledge: Genetic Diversity, Farmer Experimentation and Crop Research*. London: Intermediate Technology, pp. 1–13.

Anderson, H. A., 2013. *Breakfast: A History*. Lanham, MD: AltaMira Press.

Andrée, P., et al., 2014. *Globalization and Food Sovereignty: Global and Local Change in the New Politics of Food*. Toronto: University of Toronto Press. Available at: https://books.google.com/books?id=V6A9AwAAQBAJ.

Annear, C. M., 2004. "'GM or Death': Food and Choice in Zambia." *Gastronomica*, 4(2), pp. 16–23.

Anon, (n.d.) "Advice: Top Ten Table Manners." *The Emily Post Institute*. Available at: http://emilypost.com/advice/top-ten-table-manners/ [Accessed February 26, 2017].

Anon, 1939. "Menu For Picnic at Hyde Park." Available at: https://fdrlibrary.org/documents/356632/390886/royal_picnicmenu.pdf/018cd7fe-fb8b-47d5-a2bd-a8d8c9f18ddd.

Anon, 2014. *Eat: The Story of Food*, primary source document held in Franklin D. Roosevelt Presidential Library Archives, New York.

Appadurai, A., 1988. "How to Make a National Cuisine: Cookbooks in Contemporary India." *Comparative Studies in Society and History*, 30(1), pp. 3–24.

Ariel, A., 2012. "The Hummus Wars." *Gastronomica*, 12(1), p. 34.

Armelagos, G. J., 2010. "The Omnivore's Dilemma: The Evolution of the Brain and the Determinants of Food Choice." *Journal of Anthropological Research*, 66(2), pp. 161–186.

Avieli, N., 2016. "The Hummus Wars Revisited: Israeli-Arab Food Politics and Gastromediation." *Gastronomica: The Journal of Critical Food Studies*, 16(3), pp. 19–30.

BBDO Atlanta, 2013. *Millennials: Eating out of Both Sides of Their Mouth*, report published by BBDO Atlanta.

Babette's Feast, 1987. [Film]. Dir. Gabriel Axel. Denmark: Orion Classics.

Barnard, A., 1998. "The Foraging Spectrum: Diversity in Hunter-Gatherer Lifeways." *American Ethnologist*, 25(1), pp. 36–37.

Barr, A., and P. Levy, 1984. *The Official Foodie Handbook*, London: Ebury.

Barthes, R., 2008. "Toward a Psychosociology of Contemporary Food Consumption." In C. Counihan and P. Van Esterik, eds. *Food and Culture: A Reader*. London: Routledge, pp. 22–24.

Belair Jr., F., 1939. "King Tries Hot Dog and Asks for More: And He Drinks Beer with Them—Uses Own Camera to Snap Guests Photographing Him." *New York Times*. Available at: http://query.nytimes.com/gst/abstract.html?res= 9506E7D81430E53ABC4A52DFB0668382629EDE&legacy=true.

Belasco, W., 1989. *Appetite for Change: How the Counterculture Took on the Food Industry, 1966–1988*. New York: Pantheon Books.

Belasco, W., 1999. "Why Food Matters." *Culture, Agriculture, Food and Environment*, 21(1), pp. 27–34.

Belasco, W., 2008. *Food: The Key Concepts*. Oxford: Berg. Available at: https:// books.google.com/books?id=fPNc3uA3OmgC.

Belasco, W., 2008. "Why Food Matters." *Culture & Agriculture*, 21, pp. 27–34.

Bell, D., and G. Valentine, 1997. *Consuming Geographies: We Are Where We Eat*. London: Routledge.

Bentley, A., 2001. "Martha's Food: Whiteness of a Certain Kind." *American Studies*, 42(2), pp. 89–100.

Bentley, A., 2014. *Inventing Baby Food: Taste, Health, and the Industrialization of the American Diet*. Oakland: University of California Press.

Berchoux, J., 1801. *La gastronomie, ou L'homme des champs à table, pëme didactique en quatre chants, pour servir de suite à L'homme des champs par Joseph B***x, ... Delille*, Paris: Giguet et Michaud. Available at: https:// books.google.com/books?id=zbXKlcjwz2wC.

Berg, J., M. Nestle, and A. Bentley, 2003. "Food Studies." In S. H. Katz and W. W. Weaver, eds. *Encyclopedia of Food and Culture*, New York: Charles Scribner and Sons.

Bestor, T. C., 2004. *Tsukiji: The Fish Market at the Center of the World*. Berkeley: University of California Press.

Birkenholz, R. H., 1993. *Pilot Study of Agricultural Literacy*, Missouri University, Columbia, Department of Agricultural Education. Available at: http://files.eric. ed.gov/fulltext/ED369890.pdf.

Bittman, M., 2017. "The New Foodieism." *Grub Street*. Available at: http://www. grubstreet.com/2017/06/mark-bittman-on-the-new-foodieism.html [Accessed June 25, 2017].

Bjerga, A., et al., 2017. "If You Are What You Eat, America Tastes Like Chicken." *Bloomberg*. Available at: https://www.bloomberg.com/ graphics/2017-peak-food/?wpmm=1&wpisrc=nl_todayworld.

Black Gold, 2006. [Film]. Dir. Marc J. Francis and Nick Francis. United Kingdom: Speakit Films.

Blum-Kulka, S., 2012. *Dinner Talk: Cultural Patterns of Sociability and Socialization in Family Discourse*. New York: Routledge.

Boas, F., 1921. *Ethnology of the Kwakiutl.* Washington, DC: Government Printing Office.

Bobrow-Strain, A., 2012. *White Bread: A Social History of the Store-Bought Loaf.* Boston: Beacon Press.

Boesch, C., 1994. "Cooperative Hunting in Wild Chimpanzees." *Animal Behaviour*, 48(3), pp. 653–667.

Bourdain, A., 2000. *Kitchen Confidential: Adventures in the Culinary Underbelly*, 1st US edn. New York: Bloomsbury. Available at: http://www.loc.gov/catdir/description/hol053/2003267610.html.

Bove, C. F., and J. Sobal, 2006. "Foodwork in Newly Married Couples: Making Family Meals." *Food, Culture & Society*, 9(1), pp. 69–89.

Bove, C. F., J. Sobal, and B. S. Rauschenbach, 2003. "Food Choices among Newly Married Couples: Convergence, Conflict, Individualism, and Projects." *Appetite*, 40(1), pp. 25–41.

Bowles, S., 2011. "Cultivation of Cereals by the First Farmers Was Not More Productive than Foraging." *Proceedings of the National Academy of Sciences*, 108(12), pp. 4760–4765.

Braudel, F., 1992. *Civilization and Capitalism, 15th–18th Century: The Structure of Everyday Life.* Berkeley and Los Angeles: University of California Press.

Braun, J. von, 1992. *Improving Food Security of the Poor: Concept, Policy, and Programs.* Washington, DC: International Food Policy Research Institute.

Brembeck, H., 2005. "Home to McDonald's." *Food, Culture & Society*, 8(2), pp. 215–226. Available at: http://www.tandfonline.com/doi/abs/10.2752/155280105778055308.

Brillat-Savarin, J. A., 2009. *The Physiology of Taste; Or, Transcendental Gastronomy: Illustrated by Anecdotes of Distinguished Artists And Statesmen of Both Continents.* Berkeley and Los Angeles: Merchant Books.

Brush, S. B., H. J. Carney, and Z. Humán, 1981. "Dynamics of Andean Potato Agriculture." *Economic Botany*, 35(1), pp. 70–88.

Bunn, H. T., 1981. "Archaeological Evidence for Meat-Eating by Plio-Pleistocene Hominids from Koobi Fora and Olduvai Gorge." *Nature*, 291(5816), pp. 574–577.

Bureau of Labor Statistics, 2015. *Census of Fatal Occupational Injuries Summary.* Washington, DC. Available at: https://www.bls.gov/news.release/cfoi.nr0.htm.

Butler, J., 1990. *Gender Trouble: Feminism and the Subversion of Identity.* New York: Routledge.

Cafeteria Man, 2011. [Film] Dir. Richard Chisolm, USA: The Video Project.

Capatti, A., and M. Montanari, 2003. *Italian Cuisine: A Cultural History.* New York: Columbia University Press.

Carrington, C., 2008. "Feeding Lesbigay Families." In C. Counihan and P. Van Esterik, eds. *Food and Culture: A Reader.* New York: Routledge, pp. 259–286.

Carroll, A., 2013. *Three Squares: The Invention of the American Meal.* New York: Basic Books (AZ).

Ceccarini, R., 2011. *Pizza and Pizza Chefs in Japan: A Case of Culinary Globalization.* Leiden: Brill. Available at: https://books.google.com/books?id=MhSQEz1GkuwC.

Charles, N., and M. Kerr, 1988. *Women, Food and Families.* Manchester: Manchester University Press.

Chocano, C., 2014. "The Chef at 15." *New York Times Magazine*. Available at: https://www.nytimes.com/2014/03/30/magazine/the-chef-at-15.html?_r=0.

Chow, K., 2014. "Why Chipotle Is Accused of Contributing to a Culture of Invisibility." *NPR*.

Cinotto, S., 2013. *The Italian American Table: Food, Family, and Community in New York City*. Urbana: University of Illinois Press.

Cohen, M. N., 2003. Origins of Agriculture. In S. H. Katz and W. W. Weaver, eds. *Encyclopedia of Food and Culture*. New York: Scribner, pp. 49–53.

Commission on Sustainable Development, 1997. *Comprehensive Assessment of the Freshwater Resources of the World*, New York.

Cook, R., 2001. "Robin Cook's Chicken Tikka Masala Speech: Extracts from a Speech by the Foreign Secretary to the Social Market Foundation in London." *The Guardian*, April 19.

Cooked, 2016. [TV program]. Dir. Peter Bull, Alex Gibney, Ryan Miller, and Caroline Suh. USA: Netflix.

A Cook's Tour, 2000–2003. [TV program]. USA: Food Network.

Cope, S., 2014. *Small Batch: Pickles, Cheese, Chocolate, Spirits, and the Return of Artisanal Foods*. Lanham, MD: Rowman & Littlefield.

Cosgrove, E., 2015. "The Rise of Food-Studies Programs." *The Atlantic*. Available at: https://www.theatlantic.com/education/archive/2015/06/the-rise-of-food-studies-programs/394538/.

Counihan, C., 1999. *The Anthropology of Food and Body: Gender, Meaning, and Power*, New York: Routledge. Available at: https://books.google.com/books?id=f3UKRcaDifQC.

Counihan, C. M., 1984. "Bread as World: Food Habits and Social Relations in Modernizing Sardinia." *Anthropological Quarterly*, 57(2), pp. 47–59. Available at: http://www.jstor.org/stable/3317579.

Coveney, J., 2006. *Food, Morals and Meaning: The Pleasure and Anxiety of Eating*. New York: Routledge.

Cowan, R. S., 1983. *More Work for Mother: The Ironies of Household from the Open Hearth to the Microwave*. New York: Basic Books.

David, L., and K. Uhrenholdt, 2010. *The Family Dinner: Great Ways to Connect with Your Kids, One Meal at a Time*. New York: Grand Central Life & Style.

Deresiewicz, W., 2012. "A Matter of Taste?" *New York Times*. Available at: http://www.nytimes.com/2012/10/28/opinion/sunday/how-food-replaced-art-as-high-culture.html.

de Garine, I., 2001. "Views about Food Prejudice and Stereotypes." *Social Science Information*, 40(3), pp. 487–507. Available at: https://doi.org/10.1177/053901801040003006.

de Magistris, T., and A. Gracia, 2008. "The Decision to Buy Organic Food Products in Southern Italy." *British Food Journal*, 110(9), pp. 929–947. Available at: https://doi.org/10.1108/00070700810900620.

De Silva, C., ed., 1996. *In Memory's Kitchen: A Legacy From the Women of Terezin*. Northvale, NJ: Jason Aronson.

Deur, D., and N. J. Turner, 2005. *Keeping It Living: Traditions of Plant Use and Cultivation on the Northwest Coast of North America*. Seattle: University of Washington Press.

Deutsch, J., 2005. "'Please Pass the Chicken Tits': Rethinking Men and Cooking at an Urban Firehouse." *Food and Foodways*, 13(1–2), pp. 91–114.

Deutsch, J., and N. Murakhver, 2012. *They Eat That? A Cultural Encyclopedia of Weird and Exotic Food from Around the World.* Santa Barbara, CA: ABC-CLIO.

DeVault, M. L., 1991. *Feeding the Family: The Social Organization of Caring as Gendered Work.* Chicago; London: University of Chicago Press.

DeWalt, K., 1991. "Integrating Nutritional Concerns into Adaptive Small Farm Research Programs." In D. E. McMillan, ed. *Anthropology and Food Policy: Human Dimensions of Food Policy in Africa and Latin America.* Athens; London: University of Georgia Press, pp. 126–144.

Dewey, J., 1981. *John Dewey: The Later Works, 1925–1953. Volume 1: 1925.* Carbondale: Southern Illinois University Press.

DeWitt, D., 2010. *The Founding Foodies: How Washington, Jefferson, and Franklin Revolutionized American Cuisine.* Naperville, IL: Sourcebooks.

Diamond, J. 1997. *Guns, Germs, and Steel: The Fates of Human Societies.* New York: W. W. Norton.

Douglas, M., 1966. *Purity and Danger: An Analysis of Concepts of Pollution and Taboo.* London: Routledge & Kegan Paul.

Douglas, M., 1972. "Deciphering a Meal." *Myth, Symbol, and Culture*, 101(1), pp. 61–81.

Dufour, D. L., A. H. Goodman, and G. H. Pelto, eds., 2012. *Nutritional Anthropology*, 2nd edn. Oxford: Oxford University Press.

Duram, L., and M. Cawley, 2012. "Irish Chefs and Restaurants in the Geography of 'Local' Food Value Chains." *Open Geography Journal*, 5(1), pp. 16–25.

Durkheim, E., 1976. *The Elementary Forms of the Religious Life.* London: Allen & Unwin.

Eaton, S. B., S. B. Eaton III, and M. J. Konner, 1997. "Paleolithic Nutrition Revisited: A Twelve-Year Retrospective on Its Nature and Implications." *European Journal of Clinical Nutrition*, 51(4), pp. 207–216.

Edge, J. T., 2007. "Foodways." In J. T. Edge, ed. *The New Encyclopedia of Southern Culture.* Chapel Hill: University of North Carolina Press.

Edge, J. T., E. S. D. Engelhardt, and T. Ownby, 2013. *The Larder: Food Studies Methods from the American South.* Athens: University of Georgia Press. Available at: https://books.google.com/books?id=sWn-AAAAQBAJ.

El Bulli: Cooking in Progress, 2010. [Film]. Dir. Gereon Wetzel. Germany: GoDigital.

Elias, N., 1978. *The Civilizing Process: The History of Manners.* Oxford: Blackwell.

Endrijonas, E., 2001. "Processed Foods from Scratch: Cooking for a Family in the 1950s." In *Kitchen Culture in America: Popular Representations of Food, Gender, and Race.* Philadelphia: University of Pennsylvania Press, pp. 157–174.

Engelhaupt, E., 2008. "Do Food Miles Matter?" *Environmental Science & Technology*, 42(10), p. 3482.

Errington, F., T. Fujikura, and D. Gewertz, 2013. *The Noodle Narratives: The Global Rise of an Industrial Food into the Twenty-First Century.* Berkeley; Los Angeles: University of California Press.

Estabrook, B., 2012. *Tomatoland: How Modern Industrial Agriculture Destroyed Our Most Alluring Fruit.* Kansas City, MO: Andrews McMeel.

Fairhead, J., 1993. "Representing Knowledge: The 'New Farmer' in Research Fashions." In J. Pottier, ed. *Practising Development: Social Science Perspectives.* London; New York: Routledge, pp. 187–204.

Felder, R. M., H. Celanese, and R. Brent, 2009. "Active Learning: An
    Introduction." *ASQ Higher Education Brief*, 2(4), pp. 1–5.
Ferguson, P. P., 2004. *Accounting for Taste: The Triumph of French Cuisine*.
    Chicago: University of Chicago Press.
Fight Club, 1999. [Film]. Dir. David Fincher. USA: 20th Century Fox.
Flannery, K. V., 1969. "Origins and Ecological Effects of Early Domestication
    in Iran and the Near East." In P. J. Ucko and G. W. Dimbleby, eds. *The
    Domestication and Exploitation of Plants and Animals*. Chicago: Aldine.
Fonte, M., 2008. "Knowledge, Food and Place: A Way of Producing, a Way of
    Knowing." *Sociologia Ruralis*, 48(3), pp. 200–222. Available at: http://dx.doi.
    org/10.1111/j.1467-9523.2008.00462.x.
Food and Agriculture Organization, 2013. *Edible Insects: Future Prospects
    for Food and Feed Security*. FAO: Rome. Available at: http://www.fao.org/
    docrep/018/i3253e/i3253e00.htm.
Food, Inc., 2008. [Film]. Dir. Robert Kenner, USA: Netflix Original.
Foodies: The Culinary Jet Set, 2014. [Film]. Dir. Thomas Jackson, Charlotte
    Landelius, and Henrik Stockare Sweden: B-Reel.
Forks over Knives, 2011. [Film]. Dir. Lee Fulkerson. USA: Monica Beach Media.
Fox, K., 2014. *Watching the English, Second Edition: The Hidden Rules of English
    Behavior Revised and Updated*. Boston: Nicholas Brealey. Available at: https://
    books.google.com/books?id=RcPGAwAAQBAJ.
Frequently Asked Questions, United States Department of Agriculture,
    Washington, DC. Available at: https://www.usda.gov/oce/foodwaste/faqs.
Friedl, E., 1975. *Women and Men: An Anthropologist's View*. New York:
    Waveland Press.
Friedl, E., 1978. "Society and Sex Roles." *Human Nature*, 1(4), pp. 68–75.
The Fruit Hunters, 2012. [Film] Dir. Yung Chang, Canada: National Film Board of
    Canada and EyeSteelFilm.
Fulkerson, J. A., M. Story, A. Mellin, N. Leffert, D. Neumark-Sztainer, and
    S. A. French, 2006. "Family Dinner Meal Frequency and Adolescent
    Development: Relationships with Developmental Assets and High-Risk
    Behaviors." *Journal of Adolescent Health*, 39(3), pp. 337–345.
Furrow, D., 2016. *American Foodie: Taste, Art, and the Cultural Revolution*.
    London: Rowman & Littlefield. Available at: https://books.google.com/
    books?id=c-Y8CwAAQBAJ.
Gdula, S., 2008. *The Warmest Room in the House: How the Kitchen Became the
    Heart of the Twentieth-Century American Home*. Oxford: Berg.
Gibbons, A., 2007. "Food for Thought." *Science*, 316(5831), p. 1558 LP-1560.
    Available at: http://science.sciencemag.org/content/316/5831/1558.abstract.
Gillman, M. W., S. L. Rifas-Shiman, A. L. Frazier, H. R. Rockett, C. A. Camargo Jr.,
    A. E. Field, C. S. Berkey, G. A. Colditz, 2000. "Family Dinner and Diet Quality
    among Older Children and Adolescents." *Archives of Family Medicine*, 9(3),
    p. 235.
Goody, J., 1982. *Cooking, Cuisine and Class: A Study in Comparative Sociology*.
    Cambridge: Cambridge University Press.
Gordinier, J., 2010. "Waiter, There's Soup in My Bug." *New York Times*. Available
    at: http://www.nytimes.com/2010/09/22/dining/22bug.html.
Gordinier, J., 2016. "Massimo Bottura, the Chef Behind the World's Best
    Restaurant." *New York Times Style Magazine*. Available at: https://www.

nytimes.com/2016/10/17/t-magazine/massimo-bottura-chef-osteria-francescana.html?_r=0.

Goren-Inbar, N., N. Alperson, M. E. Kislev, O. Simchoni, Y. Melamed, A. Ben-Nun, and E. Werker, 2004. "Evidence of Hominin Control of Fire at Gesher Benot Yaaqov, Israel." *Science*, 304(5671), pp. 725–727.

Gray, M., 2013. *Labor and the Locavore: The Making of a Comprehensive Food Ethic.* Berkeley; Los Angeles: University of California Press. Available at: https://books.google.com/books?id=PXhAAQAAQBAJ.

Green, V. H., 1949. *The Negro Motorist Green Book.* New York: Victor H. Green.

Grieshaber, S., 1997. "Mealtime Rituals: Power and Resistance in the Construction of Mealtime Rules." *British Journal of Sociology*, 48(4), pp. 649–666.

Gurven, M., M. Gurven, and K. Hill, 2009. "Why Do Men Hunt? A Reevaluation of 'Man the Hunter' and the Sexual Division of Labor." *Current Anthropology*, 50(1), pp. 51–74.

Haber, B., 2005. "Follow the Food." In A. V. Avakian, ed. *Through the Kitchen Window: Women Explore the Intimate Meanings of Food and Cooking.* Oxford: Berg, pp. 65–74.

Hall, C. M., 2013. "Why Forage When You Don't Have To? Personal and Cultural Meaning in Recreational Foraging: A New Zealand Study." *Journal of Heritage Tourism*, 8(2–3), pp. 224–233. Available at: http://dx.doi.org/10.1080/1743873X.2013.767809.

Hammons, A. J., and B. H. Fiese, 2011. "Is Frequency of Shared Family Meals Related to the Nutritional Health of Children and Adolescents?" *Pediatrics*, June, 127(6), pp. e1565–1574.

Hansen, M. H., and T. E. Woronov, 2013. "Demanding and Resisting Vocational Education: A Comparative Study of Schools in Rural and Urban China." *Comparative Education*, 49(2), pp. 242–259.

Harris, M., 1998. *Good to Eat: Riddles of Food and Culture.* Long Grove, IL: Waveland Press.

Hauck-Lawson, A., 1992. "Hearing the Food Voice: An Epiphany for a Researcher." *Digest—An Interdisciplinary Study of Food and Foodways*, 12(1–2), pp. 6–7.

Hayden, B., 1981. "Subsistence and Ecological Adaptations of Modern Hunter/Gatherers." In S. O. Harding and G. Teleki, eds. *Omnivorous Primates: Gathering and Hunting in Human Evolution.* New York: Columbia University Press, pp. 344–421.

Heldke, L. M., 1992. "Foodmaking as a Thoughtful Practice." In D. W. Curtin and L. M. Heldke, eds. *Cooking, Eating, Thinking: Transformative Philosophies of Food.* Bloomington: Indiana University Press, pp. 203–229.

Helstosky, C., 2004. *Garlic & Oil: Food and Politics in Italy.* Oxford: Berg.

Henry, C. J. K., 1997. "New Food Processing Technologies: From Foraging to Farming to Food Technology." *Proceedings of the Nutrition Society*, 56(3), pp. 855–863.

Hertz, R., 2006. "Talking about 'Doing' Family." *Journal of Marriage and Family*, 68(4), pp. 796–799.

Hess, A. J., and C. J. Trexler, 2011. "A Qualitative Study of Agricultural Literacy in Urban Youth: What Do Elementary Students Understand about the Agri-Food System?" *Journal of Agricultural Education*, 52(4), pp. 1–12.

Hesterman, O. B., 2011. *Fair Food: Growing a Healthy, Sustainable Food System for All.* New York: PublicAffairs. Available at: https://books.google.com/books?id=JEFAPXaVJrgC.

Holden, T. J. M., 2005. "The Overcooked and Underdone: Masculinities in Japanese Food Programming." *Food and Foodways*, 13(1–2), pp. 39–65.

Hollows, J., and S. Jones, 2010. "'At Least He's Doing Something': Moral Entrepreneurship and Individual Responsibility in Jamie's Ministry of Food." *European Journal of Cultural Studies*, 13(3), pp. 307–322.

Holmberg, A. R., 1977. "Cooking and Eating among the Siriono of Bolivia." In J. Kuper, ed. *The Anthropologists' Cookbook.* New York: Universe Books, pp. 156–160.

Hsu, E. L. K., and V. Y. N. Hsu, 1977. "Modern China: North." In K. C. Chang, ed. *Food in Chinese Culture: Anthropological and Historical Perspectives.* New Haven, CT: Yale University Press.

Jackson, P., S. Olive, and G. Smith, 2009. "Myths of the Family Meal: Re-reading Edwardian Life Histories BT—Changing Families, Changing Food." In P. Jackson, ed. *Changing Families, Changing Food.* London: Palgrave Macmillan UK, pp. 131–145. Available at: https://doi.org/10.1057/9780230244795_8.

Jayaraman, S., 2013. *Behind the Kitchen Door.* Ithaca, NY: Cornell University Press.

Johnson, D., and S. P. Jacobs, 2015. "The State of Obama's Plate." *Time Magazine*, January 20. Available at: http://time.com/obama-plate/.

Johnston, J., and S. Baumann, 2010. *Foodies: Democracy and Distinction in the Gourmet Foodscape.* New York: Routledge.

Julier, A., and L. Lindenfeld, 2005. "Mapping Men onto the Menu: Masculinities and Food." *Food and Foodways*, 13(1–2), pp. 1–16.

Kaplan, A. R., 1984. "Ethnic Foodways in Everyday Life: Creativity and Change Among Contemporary Minnesotans," PhD diss., University of Pennsylvania. Available at: http://repository.upenn.edu/dissertations/AAI8422919/.

Kellogg, J. H., 1888. *Plain Facts for Old and Young: Embracing the Natural History and Hygiene of Organic Life,* rev. edn. Burlington, IA: I. F. Segner. Available at: https://archive.org/details/plainfactsforol00kell.

Kendall, S., 2008. "The Balancing Act: Framing Gendered Parental Identities at Dinnertime." *Language in Society*, 37(4), pp. 539–568.

King Corn, 2007. [Film]. Dir. Aaron Woolf. USA: Balcony Releasing.

Kiple, K. F., 2007. *A Movable Feast: Ten Millennia of Food Globalization.* Cambridge: Cambridge University Press.

Kitchen Stories, 2003. [Film]. Dir. Bent Hamer. Norway and Sweden: MGM Home Entertainment.

Konner, M., and S. B. Eaton, 2010. "Paleolithic Nutrition: Twenty-Five Years Later." *Nutrition in Clinical Practice*, 25(6), pp. 594–602.

Kranzberg, M., 1986. "Technology and History: Kranzberg's Laws." *Technology and Culture*, 27(3), pp. 544–560.

Kranzberg, M., 1991. "Science-Technology-Society: It's as Simple as XYZ!" *Theory into Practice*, 30(4), pp. 234–241.

Kwon, T. W., J. H. Hong, G. S. Moon, Y. S. Song, J. I. Kim, J. C. Kim, M. J. Kim, 2004. "Food Technology: Challenge for Health Promotion." *Biofactors*, 22(1–4), pp. 279–287.

Laudan, R., 2001. "A Plea for Culinary Modernism: Why We Should Love New, Fast, Processed Food." *Gastronomica*, 1(1), pp. 36–44.

Leach, H. M., 1999. "Food Processing Technology: Its Role in Inhibiting or Promoting Change in Staple Foods." In C. Gosden and J. Hather, eds. *The Prehistory of Food: Appetites for Change*. New York: Routledge, pp. 129–138.

Lee, R. B., 1988. "What Hunters Do for a Living, or, How to Make Out on Scarce Resources." In J. M. Gowdy, ed. *Limited Wants, Unlimited Means: A Reader on Hunter-Gatherer Economics and the Environment*. Washington, DC: Island Press, pp. 43–64.

Lee, R. B., 2003. *The Dobe Ju/'Hoansi*. Stamford, CT: Cengage Learning.

Lee, R. B., and R. H. Daly, 1999. *The Cambridge Encyclopedia of Hunters and Gatherers*. Cambridge: Cambridge University Press.

Leidner, R., 1993. *Fast Food, Fast Talk: Service Work and the Routinization of Everyday Life*. Berkeley; Los Angeles: University of California Press.

Leitch, A., 2003. "Slow Food and the Politics of Pork Fat: Italian Food and European Identity." *Ethnos*, 68(4), pp. 437–462.

Levenstein, H., 1980. "The New England Kitchen and the Origins of Modern American Eating Habits." *American Quarterly*, 32(4), pp. 369–386.

Levenstein, H., 1988. *New Reformers and New Immigrants*. New York; Oxford: Oxford University Press.

Levenstein, H., 1993. *Paradox of Plenty: A Social History of Eating in Modern America*. Oxford: Oxford University Press. Available at: https://books.google.com/books?id=9zd3-WI5S6QC.

Lévi-Strauss, C., 1969. *The Raw and the Cooked: Introduction to a Science of Mythology*. London: Pimlico.

Make Hummus Not War, 2012. [Film]. Dir. Trevor Graham. Australia: Yarra Bank Films.

Marinetti, F. T., 2014. *The Futurist Cookbook*. New York: Penguin.

Matejowsky, T., 2007. "SPAM and Fast-Food 'Glocalization' in the Philippines." *Food, Culture and Society: An International Journal of Multidisciplinary Research*, 10(1), pp. 23–41.

Matsuzawa, T., 1994. "Field Experiments on Use of Stone Tools in the Wild." In R. W. Wrangham, W. C. McGrew, F. B. M. de Waal, and P. G. Heltne, eds. *Chimpanzee Cultures*. Cambridge, MA: Harvard University Press in cooperation with the Chicago Academy of Sciences, pp. 351–370.

Matthews, G., 1987. *"Just a Housewife": The Rise and Fall of Domesticity in America*. Oxford: Oxford University Press.

McDonald's, 2017. "Artisan Grilled Chicken Sandwich." Available at: https://www.mcdonalds.com/us/en-us/product/artisan-grilled-chicken-sandwich.html [Accessed January 15, 2017].

McGee, H., 2007. *On Food and Cooking: The Science and Lore of the Kitchen*. New York: Scribner. Available at: https://books.google.com/books?id=bKVCtH4AjwgC.

McGrew, W. C., 1987. "Tools to Get Food: The Subsistants of Tasmanian Aborigines and Tanzanian Chimpanzees Compared." *Journal of Anthropological Research*, 43(3), pp. 247–258.

McIntosh, P., 1988. "White Privilege: Unpacking the Invisible Knapsack." *Peace and Freedom Magazine*, July/August, pp. 10–12.

McIntosh, W. A., and M. Zey, 1998. "Women as Gatekeepers." In C. Counihan and S. L. Kaplan, eds. *Food and Gender: Identity and Power*. Amsterdam: Harwood Academic.

Meneley, A., 2004. "Extra Virgin Olive Oil and Slow Food." *Anthropologica*, pp. 165–176.

Mennell, S., 1985. *All Manners of Food: Eating and Taste in England and France from the Middle Ages to the Present*. Oxford: Basil Blackwell.

Miller, D., 1998. "Coca-Cola: A Black Sweet Drink from Trinidad." In D. Miller, ed. *Material Cultures: Why Some Things Matter*. London: UCL Press, pp. 169–187.

Miller, H., 1952. *Remember to Remember*. London: Grey Walls Press.

Miller, J., and J. Deutsch, 2009. *Food Studies: An Introduction to Research Methods*. Oxford; New York: Berg.

Mintz, S., 1996. *Tasting Food, Tasting Freedom: Excursions into Eating, Culture and the Past*. Boston: Beacon Press.

Mintz, S. W., 2007. "Asia's Contributions to World Cuisine: A Beginning Inquiry." In S. Cheung and C.-B. Tan, eds. *Food and Foodways in Asia: Resource, Tradition and Cooking*. London; New York: Routledge, pp. 201–210.

Mitani, J. C., and D. P. Watts, 2001. "Why Do Chimpanzees Hunt and Share Meat?" *Animal Behaviour*, 61(5), pp. 915–924.

Mitchell, J., 2015. "A Younger Generation Sees Greener Pastures in Agriculture." *National Public Radio*. Available at: http://www.npr.org/2015/01/03/374629580/a-young-generation-sees-greener-pastures-in-agriculture.

Montagné, P., 2001. *Larousse Gastronomique: The World's Greatest Culinary Encyclopedia*. New York: Clarkson Potter. Available at: https://books.google.com/books?id=IBO0QgAACAAJ.

Moore, H. L., 1994. *A Passion for Difference: Essays in Anthropology and Gender*. Bloomington; Indianapolis: Indiana University Press.

Moore, J. A., 1985. "Forager/Farmer Interactions: Information, Social Organization, and the Frontier." In S. W. Green and S. M. Perlman, eds. *The Archaeology of Frontiers and Boundaries*. Orlando, FL: Academic Press, pp. 93–112.

Murcott, A., 1997. "Family Meals—a Thing of the Past?" In P. Caplan, ed. *Food, Health and Identity*. New York: Routledge, pp. 32–49.

Murdock, G. P., and C. Provost, 1973. "Factors in the Division of Labor by Sex: A Cross-Cultural Analysis." *Ethnology*, 12(2), pp. 203–225.

Myers, B. R., 2011. "The Moral Crusade against Foodies." *The Atlantic*, March 15.

Naccarato, P., and K. Lebesco, 2013. *Culinary Capital*. London: Bloomsbury. Available at: https://books.google.com/books?id=70upAgAAQBAJ.

National Dairy Council, 2017. *Survey: Some Americans Actually Think Chocolate Milk Comes From Brown Cows*. Available at: https://dairygood.org/content/2017/survey-some-americans-think-chocolate-milk-comes-from-brown-cows?ref=www.nationaldairycouncil.org.

Neimark, J., 2017. "Why Pu'er, a Complex Tea, Draws Rapt Fans and Big Dollars." *NPR The Salt*. Available at: http://www.npr.org/sections/thesalt/2017/03/14/518792925/why-puer-a-complex-tea-draws-rapt-fans-and-big-dollars [Accessed January 10, 2017].

Nelson, M. K., 2006. "Single Mothers 'Do' Family." *Journal of Marriage and Family*, 68(4), pp. 781–795.

Nestle, M., 2008. *Pet Food Politics: The Chihuahua in the Coal Mine*. Berkeley; Los Angeles: University of California Press.

Nestle, M., 2013. *Food Politics: How the Food Industry Influences Nutrition and Health*. Berkeley; Los Angeles: University of California Press.

Nestle, M., 2010. "Writing the Food Studies Movement." *Food, Culture and Society*, 13(2), pp. 159–179.

Neumark-Sztainer, D., M. Wall, M. Story, and J. A. Fulkerson, 2004. "Are Family Meal Patterns Associated with Disordered Eating Behaviors among Adolescents?" *Journal of Adolescent Health*, 35(5), pp. 350–359. Available at: http://www.sciencedirect.com/science/article/pii/S1054139X04000503.

Ochs, E., C. Pontecorvo, and A. Fasulo, 1996. "Socializing Taste." *Ethnos*, 61(1–2), pp. 7–46.

Ochs, E., and M. Shohet, 2006. "The Cultural Structuring of Mealtime Socialization." *New Directions for Child and Adolescent Development*, 2006(111), pp. 35–49.

O'Keefe, J. H., and L. Cordain, 2004. "Cardiovascular Disease Resulting from a Diet and Lifestyle at Odds with Our Paleolithic Genome: How to Become a 21st-Century Hunter-Gatherer." *Mayo Clinic Proceedings*, January, 79(1), pp. 101–108.

Omi, M., and H. Winant, 1986. *Racial Formation in the United States: From the 1960s to the 1980s*, New York: Routledge & Kegan Paul.

Outram, A. K., 2007. "Hunter-Gatherers and the First Farmers: The Evolution of Taste in Prehistory." *Food: The History of Taste*, 21, pp. 34–61.

Ouzounian, R., 2014. "Ferran Adrià, Father of 'Molecular Gastronomy,' in Toronto." *Toronto Star*. Available at: https://www.thestar.com/entertainment/stage/2014/03/07/ferran_adri_father_of_molecular_gastronomy_in_toronto.html.

Parasecoli, F., 2005. "Feeding Hard Bodies: Food and Masculinities in Men's Fitness Magazines." *Food and Foodways*, 13(1–2), pp. 17–37.

Parasecoli, F., 2016. "Food Studies in Trump's United States." *Huffington Post*. Available at: http://www.huffingtonpost.com/fabio-parasecoli/food-studies-in-trumps-un_b_12954292.html [Accessed November 15, 2016].

Patel, R., 2007. *Stuffed and Starved: Markets, Power and the Hidden Battle for the World Food System*. London: Portobello Books. Available at: https://books.google.com/books?id=HO8TAQAAIAAJ.

Paxson, H., 2012. *The Life of Cheese: Crafting Food and Value in America*. Berkeley; Los Angeles: University of California Press.

Pearlman, A., 2013. *Smart Casual: The Transformation of Gourmet Restaurant Style in America*. Chicago: University of Chicago Press.

Pennisi, E., 1999. "Did Cooked Tubers Spur the Evolution of Big Brains?" *Science*, 283(5410), pp. 2004–2005. Available at: http://science.sciencemag.org/content/283/5410/2004.abstract.

Pew Research Center, 2014. *The Rising Cost of Not Going to College*. Washington, DC. Available at: http://www.pewsocialtrends.org/2014/02/11/the-rising-cost-of-not-going-to-college/.

Pilcher, J., 2008. "The Globalization of Mexican Cuisine." *History Compass*, 6(2), pp. 529–551.

Pilcher, J., 2012. *Planet Taco: A Global History of Mexican Food*. New York: Oxford University Press.

Ploeg, J. D. van der, 1990. *Labor, Markets and Agricultural Production*. Boulder, CO: Westview Press.

Pollan, M., 2006. *The Omnivore's Dilemma: A Natural History of Four Meals*. New York: Penguin.

Pollan, M., 2008. *In Defense of Food: An Eater's Manifesto*, New York: Penguin.

Pollan, M., 2009. *Food Rules: An Eater's Manual*. New York: Penguin.

Pottier, J., 1999. *Anthropology of Food: The Social Dynamics of Food Security*. Oxford: Blackwell Publishers.

Proust, M., 1934. *Remembrance of Things Past*, Vol. 2, trans. C. K. Scott Moncrieff and Frederick A. Blossom. New York: Random House.

Ray, K., 2004. *The Migrants Table: Meals And Memories in Bengali-American Households*. Philadelphia: Temple University Press.

Reducing Food Waste for Business, 2014. Environmental Protection Agency, Washington, DC.

Reiter, E., 1996. *Making Fast Food: From the Frying Pan into the Fryer*. Kingston, Ontario: McGill-Queen's University Press.

Richards, A. I., 1932. "Hunger and Work in a Savage Tribe: A Functional Study of Nutrition among the Southern Bantu." *Nature*, 130(3293), p. 867.

Rockwell, N., 1943. "Freedom from Want." *Saturday Evening Post*, March 6, p. 6.

Roebroeks, W., and P. Villa, 2011. "On the Earliest Evidence for Habitual Use of Fire in Europe." *Proceedings of the National Academy of Sciences*, 108(13), pp. 5209–5214. Available at: http://www.pnas.org/content/108/13/5209.abstract.

Rosaldo, M. Z., 1974. "Woman, Culture, and Society: A Theoretical Overview." In M. Z. Rosaldo and L. Lamphere, eds. *Woman, Culture, and Society*. Stanford, CA: Stanford University Press, pp. 17–42.

Rose, L., and F. Marshall, 1996. "Meat Eating, Hominid Sociality, and Home Bases Revisited." *Current Anthropology*, 37(2), pp. 307–338.

Rosenstrach, J., 2012. *Dinner: A Love Story: It All Begins at the Family Table*. New York: Harper Collins.

Rosenstrach, J. 2014. *Dinner: The Playbook: A 30-Day Plan for Mastering the Art of the Family Meal*. New York: Ballantine Books Trade Paperbacks.

Roth, L. K., 2005. "'Beef. It's What's for Dinner' Vegetarians, Meat-Eaters and the Negotiation of Familial Relationships." *Food, Culture & Society*, 8(2), pp. 181–200.

Rozin, P., 1997. "Why We Eat What We Eat, and Why We Worry about It." *Bulletin of the American Academy of Arts and Sciences*, 50(5), pp. 26–48.

Rozin, P., 1999. "Food Is Fundamental, Fun, Frightening, and Far-Reaching." *Social Research*, 66(1), pp. 9–30.

Sahlins, M., 1972. "The Original Affluent Society." In *Stone Age Economics*. London: Tavistock, pp. 1–39.

Sahlins, M., 1988. "The Original Affluent Society." In J. M. Gowdy, ed. *Limited Wants, Unlimited Means: A Reader on Hunter-Gatherer Economics and the Environment*. Washington, DC: Island Press, pp. 5–42.

Salinas, B., 2014. "'Columbusing': The Art of Discovering Something That Is Not New." *NPR*. Available at: http://www.npr.org/sections/ codeswitch/2014/07/06/328466757/columbusing-the-art-of-discovering-something-that-is-not-new.

Schlosser, E., 2001. *Fast Food Nation*. New York: Houghton Mifflin.

Scrinis, G., 2013. *Nutritionism: The Science and Politics of Dietary Advice*. New York: Columbia University Press.

Shapiro, L., 1986. *Perfection Salad: Women and Cooking at the Turn of the Century*. New York: Farrar, Straus and Giroux. Available at: https://books.google.com/books?id=5EW9QgAACAAJ.

Shapiro, L., 2009. *Perfection Salad: Women and Cooking at the Turn of the Century*, new edn. Berkeley, CA; London: University of California Press.

Shipman, P., 2009. "Cooking Debate Goes off the Boil." *Nature*, 459(7250), pp. 1059–1060. Available at: http://dx.doi.org/10.1038/4591059a.

Shiva, V., 1992. "The Seed and the Earth: Biotechnology and the Colonisation of Regeneration." *Developmental Dialogue*, 1/2, pp. 151–168.

Short, F., 2006. *Kitchen Secrets: The Meaning of Cooking in Everyday Life*. Oxford; New York: Berg.

Slow Food International, 2015. "About Us." Available at: https://www.slowfood.com/about-us/ [Accessed November 17, 2016].

Smil, V., 2000. *Feeding the World: A Challenge for the Twenty-first Century*. Cambridge, MA: MIT Press.

Smith, D. E., 1993. "The Standard North American Family: SNAF as an Ideological Code." *Journal of Family Issues*, 14(1), pp. 50–65.

Sobal, J., 2005. "Men, Meat, and Marriage: Models of Masculinity." *Food and Foodways*, 13(1–2), pp. 135–158.

Soul Food, 1997. [Film] Dir. George Tillman Jr. USA: Fox.

Soul Food Junkies, 2012. [Film]. Dir. Byron Hurt. USA: ITVS.

Stack, C. B., 1975. *All Our Kin: Strategies for Survival in a Black Community*. New York: Basic Books.

Stanford, C. B., 1999. *The Hunting Apes: Meat Eating and the Origins of Human Behavior*. Princeton, NJ: Princeton University Press.

Stanford, C. B., and H. T. Bunn, eds., 2001. *Meat-Eating and Human Evolution*. New York: Oxford University Press.

Stearns, P. N., 2002. *Fat History: Bodies and Beauty in the Modern West*. New York: New York University Press. Available at: https://books.google.com/books?id=JAQXp5vbqcgC.

Sterponi, L., 2009. "Accountability in Family Discourse: Socialization into Norms and Standards and Negotiation of Responsibility in Italian Dinner Conversations." *Childhood*, 16(4), pp. 441–459.

Stevenson, S., 2009. "The Most Interesting Man in the World." Slate.com. Available at: http://www.slate.com/articles/business/ad_report_card/2009/05/the_most_interesting_man_in_the_world.html.

Stoller, P., and C. Olkes, 1986. "Bad Sauce, Good Ethnography." *Cultural Anthropology*, 1(3), pp. 336–352. Available at: http://www.jstor.org/stable/656197.

Super Size Me, 2004. [Film]. Dir. Morgan Spurlock. USA: Samuel Goldwyn Films; Roadside Attractions.

Sutter, J. W., 1987. "Cattle and Inequality: Herd Size Differences and Pastoral Production among the Fulani of Northeastern Senegal." *Africa*, 57(2), pp.1 96–218.

Sutton, D. E., 2001. *Remembrance of Repasts: An Anthropology of Food and Memory*. Oxford: Berg.

Tampopo, 1985. [Film]. Dir. Juzo Itami, Japan: Toho.

Tattersall, I., 1999. *Becoming Human: Evolution and Human Uniqueness.* New York: Harcourt Brace.

Taveras, E. M., S. L. Rifas-Shiman, C. S. Berkey, H. R. Rockett, A. E. Field, A. L. Frazier, G. A. Colditz, M. W. Gillman, 2005. "Family Dinner and Adolescent Overweight." *Obesity*, 13(5), pp. 900–906.

Tennie, C., I. C. Gilby, and R. Mundry, 2009. "The Meat-Scrap Hypothesis: Small Quantities of Meat May Promote Cooperative Hunting in Wild Chimpanzees (Pan Troglodytes)." *Behavioral Ecology and Sociobiology*, 63(3), pp. 421–431.

Thach, L., 2012a. "Male and Female Wine Drinkers—Are They Really That Different?" *Wine Business Monthly*. Available at: https://www.winebusiness.com/news/?go=getArticle&dataid=108156 [Accessed January 17, 2017].

Thach, L., 2012b. "Time for Wine? Identifying Differences in Wine-Drinking Occasions for Male and Female Wine Consumers." *Journal of Wine Research*, 23(2), pp. 134–154. Available at: http://dx.doi.org/10.1080/09571264.2012.676542.

Therien, J.-P., 1999. "Beyond the North-South Divide: The Two Tales of World Poverty." *Third World Quarterly*, 20(4), pp. 723–742.

Tortilla Soup, 2001. [Film]. Dir. Maria Ripoll, USA: Samuel Goldwyn Films.

Trubek, A. B., 2000. *Haute Cuisine: How the French Invented the Culinary Profession*. Philadelphia: University of Pennsylvania Press.

Trubek, A. B., 2009. *The Taste of Place: A Cultural Journey into Terroir*. Berkeley, CA; London: University of California Press.

Ueda, Makoto, 1992. *Basho and His Interpreters: Selected Hokku with Commentary*. Stanford, CA: Stanford University Press.

United Nations, 1975. *Report of the World Food Conference*, New York.

Vásquez, C., and A. Chik, 2015. "'I Am Not a Foodie . . .': Culinary Capital in Online Reviews of Michelin Restaurants." *Food and Foodways*, 23(4), pp. 231–250. Available at: http://dx.doi.org/10.1080/07409710.2015.1102483.

Velikova, N., T. H. Dodd, and J. B. Wilcox, 2013. "Meat Is Male; Champagne Is Female; Cheese Is Unisex: An Examination of Perceived Gender Images of Wine." Presented at the *7th International Conference of the Academy of Wine Business Research, St. Catharines, Canada*.

Visser, M., 2015. *The Rituals of Dinner: The Origins, Evolution, Eccentricities, and Meaning of Table Manners*. New York: Open Road Media.

Walraven, B., 2002. "Warm Mushroom Sushi? An Afterward." In K. Ciwertka and B. Walraven, eds. *Asian Food: The Global and the Local*. Richmond, UK: Curzon, pp. 167–173.

Warde, A., and L. Martens, 2000. *Eating Out: Social Differentiation, Consumption, and Pleasure*. Cambridge: Cambridge University Press.

Warin, M., 2011. "Foucault's Progeny: Jamie Oliver and the Art of Governing Obesity." *Social Theory & Health*, 9(1), pp. 24–40.

Washburn, S., and C. Lancaster, 1968. "The Evolution of Hunting." In R. B. Lee and I. DeVore, eds. *Man the Hunter*. Chicago: Aldine, pp. 293–303.

Weber, C. L., and H. S. Matthews, 2008. "Food-Miles and the Relative Climate Impacts of Food Choices in the United States." *Environmental Science & Technology*, May 15, 42(10), pp. 3508–3513.

West, C., and D. H. Zimmerman, 1987. "Doing Gender." *Gender & Society*, 1(2), pp. 125–151.

What's Cooking?, 2000. [Film] Dir. Gurinder Chadha. USA and UK: Trimark Pictures.

White, I., 1997. "The Natives Live Well." *Anthropologist's Cookbook*, 16(2), pp. 215–228.

White, M. I., 2001. "Ladies Who Lunch: Young Women and the Domestic Fallacy in Japan." In K. J. Cwiertka and B. Walraven, eds. *Asian Food: The Global and the Local*. Honolulu: University of Hawai'i Press.

Wilk, R., 2006. *Fast Food/Slow Food: The Cultural Economy of the Global Food System*. Lanham, MD: Rowman Altamira.

Wilson, B., 2012. *Consider the Fork: A History of How We Cook and Eat*. New York: Basic Books (AZ).

Wrangham, R. W., 2009. *Catching Fire: How Cooking Made Us Human*. London: Profile Books.

Zeanah, D. W., 2004. "Sexual Division of Labor and Central Place Foraging: A Model for the Carson Desert of Western Nevada." *Journal of Anthropological Archaeology*, 23(1), pp. 1–32.

Zeleny, J., 2007. "Obama's Down on the Farm." *New York Times*. Available at: https://thecaucus.blogs.nytimes.com/2007/07/27/obamas-down-on-the-farm/ [Accessed June 25, 2017].

Zink, K. D., and D. E. Lieberman, 2016. "Impact of Meat and Lower Palaeolithic Food Processing Techniques on Chewing in Humans." *Nature*, 531(7595), pp. 500–503. Available at: http://dx.doi.org/10.1038/nature16990.

Index